THOSE
TWENTIETH CENTURY
BLUES

By the same author

MOVING INTO AQUARIUS
MUSIC OF THE ANGELS

MICHAEL TIPPETT

Those Twentieth Century Blues

AN AUTOBIOGRAPHY

Michael Tippett

HUTCHINSON

London Sydney Auckland Johannesburg

© Sir Michael Tippett 1991

The right of Michael Tippett to be
identified as Author of this work has been asserted
by Michael Tippett in accordance with the
Copyright, Designs and Patents Act, 1988

This edition first published in 1991 by
Hutchinson

Random Century Group Ltd
20 Vauxhall Bridge Road, London SW1V 2SA

Random Century Australia (Pty) Ltd
20 Alfred Street, Milsons Point, Sydney, NSW 2061, Australia

Random Century New Zealand Ltd
PO Box 40–086, Glenfield, Auckland 10, New Zealand

Random Century South Africa (Pty) Ltd
PO Box 337, Bergvlei, 2012, South Africa

British Library Cataloguing-in-Publication Data

Tippett, Sir Michael
Those twentieth century blues.
I. Title
780.92

ISBN 0–09–175307–4

Set in Bembo by Speedset Ltd, Ellesmere Port
Printed and bound in Great Britain by
Clays Ltd, St Ives PLC

CONTENTS

for Tony & Agneta

From the series
Gates of Paradise
by William Blake, 1793

TEXT ACKNOWLEDGEMENTS

Grateful acknowledgement is made to the following for permission to reprint previously published material:

George Sassoon for the poem *Everyone Sang* from *Collected Works* by Siegfried Sassoon published by Faber and Faber.

BBC Television for an excerpt from *The Flip Side of Dominick Hyde*.

The Publishers have made every attempt to clear copyright, but in some cases this has not been possible. We would like to apologise in advance for any inconvenience this might cause.

AUTHOR'S ACKNOWLEDGEMENTS

I should first like to congratulate Random Century Ltd on making this book happen so quickly. I am particularly grateful to Kate Mosse, my publisher, who took the project on at such short notice, to the editors, Beth Humphries and Karen Holden, and to the support staff, especially Neil Bradford, all of whom worked so hard. The invaluable assistance of the staff of the Tippett Office, in particular of Nicholas Wright (who looked after the contractual negotiations and read the book in typescript), Peter Owens, who undertook some of the drudgery of reproducing material for the text, and occasionally helped as translator from German, and Alan Morrison, deserves acknowledgement.

Finally, my thanks also to David Ayerst and Michael Tillet whose recollections and advice were immensely helpful.

ILLUSTRATION ACKNOWLEDGEMENTS

Frontispiece: Reproduced by courtesy of the trustees of the British Museum

Plate Section

Page 1:	Top	From *Michael Tippett: An Introductory Study* by David Matthews published by Faber & Faber
	Middle	Tippett Archive, Schott & Co
	Bottom	Tippett Archive, Schott & Co
Page 2:	Top	© Rev Woodbridge/Tippett Archive, Schott & Co
	Middle	© Alan Bush
	Bottom	© Alan Bush/Tippett Archive, Schott & Co
Page 3:	Top	© The Portraits Dept. The Royal College of Music
	Bottom	© Daily Telegraph
Page 4:		© Stella Maude/Tippett Archive, Schott & Co
Page 5:		© Picture Post
Page 6:	Top	Courtesy British Library/Tippett Archive, Schott & Co
	Bottom	© News Chronicle 1955
Page 7:	Top	Photo by Michael Wickam © Condé Nast Publications Ltd
	Middle	Auerbach © The Hulton-Deutsch Collection
	Bottom	Auerbach © The Hulton-Deutsch Collection
Page 8:		© Michael Ward
Page 9:	Top	Courtesy the Aldeburgh foundation
	Bottom	Auerbach © The Hulton-Deutsch Collection
Page 10:	Top	© Zoë Dominic
	Bottom	© Mike Evans
Page 11:	Top	© Zoë Dominic
	Bottom	© Donald Southern
Page 12:	Top Left	© Anna Bush-Cruise
	Top Right	© John Rogers
	Bottom	© Meirion Bowen
Page 13:	Top	© Malcolm Crowthers
Page 14:	Top	© Mike Evans
	Bottom	© The Press Association Ltd
Page 15:	Top	© BBC Television
	Bottom	© Graham Parrish
Page 16:	Top	© Meirion Bowen
	Bottom	© Caroline Ayerst

INTIMATIONS OF
MORTALITY

I have long resisted the idea of writing an autobiography. Whenever the invitation to do so arrived, I was always up to my eyes in compositional work and had committed myself to further large-scale pieces which had to take priority. Moreover, others such as Ian Kemp were doing the proper, meticulous research needed to arrive at an authoritative account of my life. The current volume is not of that ilk: had I attempted anything of that sort, I would have quickly become bored.

Over the years, I have read a fair number of autobiographies and have noted the different techniques that can be used. One of the earliest to attract my attention was Goethe's *Dichtung und Wahrheit*, which chronicled his life only up as far as his appointment to the Court of Weimar, but appealed to me because of the intermingling (implied by its title) of Poetry and Truth (or more literally, Fiction and Fact). While it contained fascinating accounts of historical events, a fantasy element was also there. Yeats's *Autobiographies* I also found intriguing. Yeats deals with brief periods in his life under various poetic headings, such as *The Trembling of the Veil*. If I had been first and foremost a literary artist, that is the kind of autobiography I should like to have attempted.

Reading Michel Tournier's intellectual autobiography, *The Wind Spirit*, I came across a quotation from Nietzsche: 'One must have a chaos inside oneself to give birth to a dancing star.' That's me: it's also this maverick book – an account of my struggles to understand the chaotic inner world of dreams in such a way that I could create music of all kinds. The most crucial section of the book is thus Chapter 6, 'The Dreams Take Over'. The childhood dream recounted at the start is matched by an old man's dream at the close. As in Goethe, fantasy and actuality interweave to some extent throughout the narrative; and so the dreams of Chapter 6 are balanced by the wartime realities of Chapter 7.

Those Twentieth Century Blues is not a book of essays, like *Moving into Aquarius* or *Music of the Angels*: rather, it's a collection of stories revealing, I dare say, sides to myself that are not widely known. As will be evident, I appreciate being able to live now in a society more open about the intricacies of personal psychology and behaviour than that into which I was born: and I would oppose any attempt to turn the clock back. Some of my stories will (I hope) be found amusing, even bizarre; others reflect the epoch in which I've lived – a century, almost, deeply scarred by wars, revolution and other turmoil, in the course of which I've tried to communicate through music some alternative humane values. The plan of the book is vaguely chronological, but often I have looked forwards or backwards, or glanced sideways, as individual episodes seemed to dictate. The book is also part documentary, drawing upon letters written to and received from those people most crucial to my life.

Oddly enough, around the time I agreed to write this book, I had suddenly to undergo a major operation for colonic cancer: the operation was successful, but it was my first real intimation of mortality. For having lived to 83, remaining by and large healthy, enjoying a seemingly endless creativity (I was then in the middle of writing Act 2 of *New Year*), it was tempting to think that I might go on for ever. Genetically, the Tippetts have enjoyed longevity: both my parents lived into their late eighties, and my sailor-brother is still around, a lively old salt. But the operation gave me pause for thought. My advisers suggested that I could now happily cut down on all the interviews, university forums etc. which have proliferated over the years and become a bit wearing. They suggested that I should instead share my experiences through the medium of the written word.

The snag was that I have poor eyesight and could undertake relatively little of the actual writing alone. Much of the material was therefore recorded first, in the form of interviews with Meirion Bowen, who then transcribed it all into a prearranged chapter format. I myself modified, corrected and added to the various drafts of the text that he submitted to me. Meirion Bowen also helped in the research, compilation and transcription of relevant letters, dream-sequences and so on. As my closest, multi-purpose assistant of the last fifteen years or so, he will know how grateful I am to him for having made my task almost painless and sometimes quite enjoyable and amusing.

I'm glad *Those Twentieth Century Blues* is now written, for I dislike focusing endlessly on what is past and gone. The future matters more and my real hope is to see in the new millenium. With luck, I might get there.

CHAPTER ONE

THE PRE-WAR IDYLL

My first dream of any significance concerned the Biting Lady.

Soon after I was born, on 2 January 1905, my parents decided to take my brother, Peter (born the year before), and myself from Eastcote, Middlesex, to live in the little village of Wetherden in Suffolk. The cottage they had bought there was L-shaped: but in my dream, it seemed to be square. I slept in a cot in my parents' bedroom, where they lay separately in twin beds; I think I can remember them snoring. In my dream, I woke up and heard the Biting Lady arrive. I never saw her. She came to the front door and wanted to get in. I was terrified. I could hear her come round the house and back to the front door. She knocked and knocked, shouting very loudly, 'Front Door!': then I woke up.

This nightmare recurred often in my childhood. I later interpreted it in various ways. Maybe it was an omen of the difficulties I was to encounter later in relation to my mother – difficulties that persisted almost to the end of her days. Or, possibly, it was anterior to the horrors of a second circumcision – a quite dramatic affair, which certainly left an emotional scar. It was my father's decision that both Peter and I should be circumcised. This had nothing to do with religion. In his own first sexual encounter, in adult life, with a woman, he had experienced the common problems associated with a tight foreskin and decided he should himself undergo circumcision. Subsequently, he felt that Peter and I should be spared such problems; in addition, it might possibly be worthwhile for reasons of morality or cleanliness (a notion that later became prevalent in post-war America).

Unfortunately my operation proved unsatisfactory, and a second was needed. The doctor decided that I, aged 5, should not have an anaesthetic this time, but should be lulled into sleep by other means, while sitting on the basin in anticipation. When the cut occurred, I woke immediately and let out a piercing shriek. There was blood

1

everywhere. The Biting Lady had broken through. The little house (or my unconscious) was no longer safe and secure.

In a wider, yet related sense, the dream meant that one day I would have to grow up, cope with the turbulence within myself. The little house has, at any rate, remained an icon for the state of my psychological health. In countless subsequent dreams, I have returned to the childhood home; and the Biting Lady has been replaced by other symbolic threats, some more disturbing.

It was not out of revenge or conscious resentment that I decided later that I should like to knock a nail into my father's bald head: in my innocence, I simply found it fascinating. My father used to sit after lunch in an armchair reading the paper. One day I procured a hammer and nail and moved a chair into position behind him. Fortunately, as I tried to climb up to knock in the nail, the chair fell over.

I loved my father. He was a card, full of little quips and jokes that appealed to us children. He had quite a large library and, having had elocution lessons in his youth, greatly enjoyed reading out aloud to Peter and myself. He read us a great mixture of things, from history (in which he was steeped) and historical romances such as Ford Madox Ford's *Lady with Bright Eyes* to Tennyson's *Idylls of the King*, and Edgar Wallace's stories of African colonial and tribal life, in *Sanders of the River*. I am certainly indebted to my father for the argumentative and philosophical side of my nature. One of the books he read to us was called *The Legacy of Greece*, which gave me a passion for the ancient Greeks.

Soon, as a precocious child, I began reading everything for myself. One of my father's books was a little volume called *Ambidexterity and Mental Culture*, by H. Macnaughton-Jones. It dealt with the relationships between the different centres of the brain and our various intellectual and emotional capacities. One of the things it advocated was ambidexterity in writing and I determined I would cultivate this for myself. I practised writing with both hands, though I never succeeded, as I was naturally right-handed. But I did teach myself to dig with a spade left-handed; and if I was cutting bread at table, I would use my left or right hand according to which side the bread was turned.

My mother was a very different character and I can't say that I ever loved her in the same way that I did my father. She was strongly moralistic, with a deep sense of social obligation. After visiting an abattoir, which horrified her, she became a vegetarian. In those days it was very constricting to be vegetarian, for the variety of non-meat or non-fish dishes that are nowadays available hardly existed. But my mother remained committed to this to the end of life. She never tried to convert her husband and children to vegetarianism and cooked meat dishes for us without a qualm. There were times when I teased her, telling her, for instance, that the lettuces were quaking with fear and apprehension as she came down the garden path, at which she was justifiably outraged.

My mother believed in nature's remedies and would not take pills, in contrast with my father, who liked to try pills of every size, shape and colour. Their views on medication notwithstanding, both parents lived until their late eighties. While I myself have never been a vegetarian, as far as pills are concerned I take after my mother. On the other hand, my parents had a typical late Victorian obsession with constipation, and until I had my own home I suffered from it to a severe degree. At one stage they took me to a specialist who produced pills that I would have to take to the end of my life; once I left home, though, I soon gave them up. Some time later, when I suffered from haemorrhoids, my doctor prescribed a mouthwash to get rid of them, but I decided to buy a good bottle of red wine instead.

My father (who had been born in the last year of the Crimean War, 1859, and married late) had by now retired from his legal work and occupied himself during the day with his financial affairs. Meanwhile, my mother was involved in social work, campaigning for women's rights and helping to bring succour to the poor and needy. During my childhood I was taken to the East End of London by my mother, to help her serve soup to the hungry people there. My mother was daring enough to join the Labour Party and often as a Suffragette she held meetings with like-minded ladies at home. Once I went with her to London for one of the meetings of the Women's Freedom League, which had been founded by her cousin, Charlotte Despard, whom we knew as Cousin Lotte. I crawled under the table and found myself staring at these women's legs in their long skirts.

In 1911, the Liberal Government of Asquith reached the point of passing a women's suffrage bill in the House of Commons. But it was thrown out by the House of Lords and, as a result, all the suffragette organisations held a monster demonstration in Trafalgar Square. To do so within a mile of the Houses of Parliament, while MPs were sitting, was illegal and my mother, who was participating, was arrested and sent briefly to prison. When she returned home she told with pride how she had bought a set of dinner-bells from a large store nearby, where my father had an account: these were rung around the square at different intervals to outwit the police, who were trying to curb the protest at the points where it had erupted.

In general terms, my early childhood was a comfortable middle-class existence made possible by my father's business investments, most notably the income he derived from a hotel in Cannes, which he had bought and rented out to a manager. The home domestic work was done by two young girls from the village, whom my mother had trained, and a gardener, who also drove us around in a pony and trap. Our parents encouraged Peter and myself to treat kindly the uneducated village children, from whom we were generally kept somewhat apart. Once, though, we behaved rather nastily, rushing around the village with axes, shouting, 'We're better than you are.' My mother later told us of the social strictness of her own early life amongst the landed gentry. Her father, when a widower, would after breakfast ring the bell for the butler and, when he came, give the order, 'Tell Smith to saddle Miss Janet.' By contrast, our servants were known by their Christian names.

Travel away from home was mainly undertaken by pony and trap, which my father could drive. When my mother went four miles to the market town of Stowmarket, to do her weekly shopping, the gardener drove her there. Once we went along with her, and while she was in a shop, the pony broke free from the lamp-post to which it was tethered and dashed down the market-place, with ourselves in the trap screaming with fright. Fortunately, in that period, people knew how to cope with a runaway horse and it was soon halted and brought under control. When Peter and I had to visit the dentist in Bury St Edmunds, we travelled by train. To do this we walked two miles by ourselves along the lane to Elmswell station. Bury was two stations away, and I discovered many years later that the station-master at the intervening station, Thurston, was the father of the future stage-director, Peter Hall. As a child I was frightened by the steam train – I thought the engine might blow up – but I was intrigued by it all the same: I liked to measure myself against its large wheel. On the return journey you had to cross over the rails in front of the train. Needless to say, I was afraid it would start up before we reached the other side. On our birthdays, Peter and I could ask for a cake of some sort. My dream was always for a 'railway bun', obtainable at the station café.

Cars were a far more unusual phenomenon: in fact, there were none in the village. My father was able to buy a French car, a famous make called De Dion Bouton. This one was ultimately requisitioned for the First World War. It always seemed to be breaking down, and you could hear it a mile off because of its characteristic ringing sound. Towards the end of 1912 my father had bought a rather sleek open Humber. Everyone wound themselves up in scarves to travel about in it. This car he used to drive himself to Newmarket or sometimes to London.

We saw our relatives to a limited extent. There were numerous cousins on both my parents' sides. The one who eventually figured most prominently in my life was Phyllis Kemp, one of two girl cousins who came and stayed in the summer holidays or sometimes at Christmas. One of the cousins was regarded as 'belonging' to Peter, and eventually became his first wife. The other, Phyl, who was considered intellectual and maverick, was always thought of as 'belonging' to me and the association took root.

The first time I became at all close to her was in about 1912–13, when there was a diphtheria scare and my mother took Peter and myself out of Suffolk. We went off on a great train journey to Bedford, where Phyl and her younger sister lived with their divorced mother who was a lovely person. When the train reached Bedford and we climbed out, I was at once violently sick. They took me in a cab to the house and a doctor was called. I was diagnosed as having a heart murmur and it was some time before I recovered: as a result, I was left there with Phyl when my mother returned home with Peter. 10-year-old Phyl already impressed me as a lively character and our relationship deepened during my student days and thereafter.

The one thing missing in my childhood home was music, or at least contact with professional music-making. We were remote from the London concert scene, though I was once taken by an aunt to hear a recital by the great Russian bass, Chaliapin, who had been brought to London by Beecham. The only music that existed locally was amateur. We had a piano and my mother sang songs and ballads by Quilter etc. Nevertheless, I had some piano lessons with local teachers, and at one stage took to improvising crazily on the piano, which I called 'composing', though I only had the vaguest notion of what that meant.

What I recall most vividly were two tunes I heard in 1911, sung by one of our maids – one was 'Alexander's Ragtime Band', the other went 'Everybody's doing it, doing it, doing it . . .' – I had no idea at the time what it was all about; nor did I guess that it belonged to a world of popular music from which I would eventually draw so much inspiration.

CHAPTER TWO

THE CRACK-UP

More lasting than any other trauma in my childhood was the break-up of the family home at the end of the First World War. This was presaged by the disintegration of my family circumstances at the start of the war. Mother woke us one morning and said we were all going to take part in the housework from now on. The two parlour-maids were sent home. They left in tears, but my parents consoled them as much as they could. We boys were taken to the garden and set to dig what seemed to us an immense hole, which was to be used for rubbish. We were not pleased to be doing this, though we enjoyed other assignments, such as looking after hens (mine was called Henrietta and we 'sold' the eggs to our parents). My other tasks included laying the fire in the morning and cooking.

In 1913 my brother was sent to Brookfield Preparatory School in Dorset, and I followed a year later: I arrived, indeed, in September 1914, just at the outbreak of the war. Leaving home like this was in itself frightening, but I was determined to succeed. I became good at Greek and Latin, and even better at French. I continued piano lessons until they were stopped: like all other 'inessential' subjects, such as horse-riding, music was dropped from the curriculum as 'unpatriotic' during wartime. Having veered previously towards religious belief, I had by now determined that God did not exist, and I arrived at school bearing an essay which set out in logical terms why this must be so.

Many of my prep school teachers were called up to fight in the war and replacements had to be found. One such was a woman French teacher from the town. Her influence in matters of behaviour was notable. Most of us children had a crush on the headmaster, who was an intriguing figure – an amateur entomologist, with drawers and drawers of lepidoptera. The headmaster had established a custom whereby, at mealtimes, he and his wife, the French teacher and one other male teacher were joined by the schoolchildren, who sat at the corners of the two tables beside the adults. It was everyone's ambition to sit next to the headmaster and the choice was decided each week by lot or some other system. On one occasion the lot fell against me, and I was very upset to find that in the coming week I would have to sit next to the French teacher instead. I deliberately turned my back on her. She commented, 'I don't think that's very nice of you' – and by some curious instinct I took in what she was saying at once: it was my first serious lesson in good manners and I realised its importance. I grew to admire and love her very much: she was a marvellous teacher.

By the time I was 14, my parents' financial difficulties caused them to sell the cottage in Wetherden and go to live in France. Unable to bring the rental money for the Hôtel Beau-Site back to England, my father decided they would live abroad until conditions improved. At Christmas, in 1919, we all went to stay with them at the hotel, at the invitation of the manager. Thereafter my parents lived in a succession of small hotels and rented apartments around the continent. I realise now this meant the permanent break-up of the family. My mother told me to send a postcard if I were unhappy and they would come immediately. But it was never as straightforward as it sounded and I soon had to learn to fend for myself. My brother wanted to go into the Navy and was sent to a naval school. I won a classics scholarship to Fettes College in Edinburgh. Whenever Peter and I went to visit our parents in the holidays, they sent us money and expected us to travel alone across the continent to find them.

Fettes had its strong points. I was able to pursue my love of classics, and my piano lessons were resumed. But there were many disagreeable aspects of traditional public school life. I hated the system whereby the boys in each year bullied those in the year below, so I decided to persuade my fellow pupils not to observe this ritual – and succeeded. I hated wearing a kilt, which was necessary for the cadet corps. It was a typically Scottish spartan existence in general, which I found demanding.

Most alarming was the sexual side of things. My naive confessions on the subject in a letter to my mother brought my parents immediately over from France: they threatened to publicise the goings-on unless the headmaster was removed. A new headmaster arrived, who persuaded my parents I should stay on. I was then pressurised by my housemaster into standing before the entire school and accounting for the sexual behaviour of every boy I knew. This was particularly difficult as I was myself 'involved' with a boy. I

couldn't remain at Fettes much longer and decided the only way out
was to reveal all to my parents. I geared myself up to face my mother
to tell her I was no longer a virgin. It was the first time I stood up
openly to her, and it resulted in my being taken away from Fettes –
which indeed I desperately wanted. For decades afterwards I had such
amnesia about the whole experience that I hardly acknowledged the
existence of Fettes in any account of my early life.

Since I had been on a scholarship to Fettes, my education there had
been free. My father now searched for a cheap, affordable alternative
and finally arranged for me to study at Stamford Grammar School in
Lincolnshire, which was in many ways more congenial. The Fettes
trauma caused me to abandon Greek and Latin and go into the
sciences, which meant sitting as a lanky boy of 15 amidst the small
boys of the junior school. By dint of cleverness and enterprise, I got
through it all at great speed.

At Stamford, the rebel in me soon took over. Although I played for
the hymn singing at morning assemblies, eventually atheism reared its
head, and I refused to play any more. That made me a loner, but I
stuck to it. I divided the prefects – four or six of us – in our study,
putting up a curtain between ourselves and the 'wicked' ones on the
other side. This was partly an argument over cadet corps, which I
refused to join, causing a lot of trouble; I was also separating off the
'hearties' who went in for rough sports.

I found I could do all the required studies with the greatest facility, if
I so chose, but I stopped doing anything: in my last year at Stamford I
refused virtually to work at all, especially when it came to taking a
scholarship to university, which upset the school authorities considerably, as they had ambitions to go private (these they later realised). To
annoy them further, I arranged with my parents one Christmas that I
should remain in England. Secretly I went to London, stayed with
Phyl's family, and took external examinations for the London
Matriculation Board. At the start of the school term I then informed
the headmaster that I had passed in about six or seven subjects,
including Italian, which I had taught myself. He was furious. All I had
wanted to show was that I could surmount any of the academic
hurdles if I so wished, but felt negative about the school itself.

My closest friend at school was a doctor's son, called Bob Woolrich,
whose family lived on the Lincolnshire coast; he was a boarder like
myself (there were about fifty altogether). For some reason he was
known as 'Peggy', and he had a very nice sister who was a boarder in

9

the grammar school for girls in another part of Stamford. One year I spent a large part of my summer holidays with him and my parents in Cornwall. It was a good thing he was around, for my parents were at that time in grave marital difficulties – they nearly separated, in fact. My mother was going through the menopause. Meanwhile, my father had just had a prostate operation, and when he came back from hospital, she had found pictures of nice-looking nurses in his luggage. She was not amused: after all, she herself had been a nice-looking nurse when my father met and married her. I kept out of the way. 'Peggy' arrived on a two-stroke motorbike which he had ridden all the way down from Lincolnshire. We spent our time riding around Cornwall together, until the bike gave out. Later on, I bought a bicycle and cycled up the Great North Road across the fens into Lincolnshire and stayed with him and his parents.

If I was inclined to be negative about Stamford School generally, I did at the time make a positive decision to go into music. There was a piano teacher in the town, Mrs Tinkler, who had previously taught Malcolm Sargent (also an ex-pupil of Stamford School): she took me through some of Bach's 48 preludes and fugues, some Beethoven sonatas, Schubert and Chopin, and I used to practise every morning while the rest of the school did PT. She was wonderfully encouraging.

So was an English master at the school, Henry Waldo Acomb. He invited friends from Cambridge for musical weekends and sometimes took us to concerts: I recall hearing Pouishnov give a piano recital in this way, and most important, an orchestral concert in Leicester with Sargent as conductor. The programme included Ravel's *Mother Goose* Suite – on hearing which I made up my mind that I would become a composer. I had little idea what this meant; but then, my brother had previously developed a passion for the Navy, even though he had hardly seen the sea. My parents understood the matter of composing even less and were quite disconcerted: since I had the 'gift of the gab' (I was sometimes nicknamed 'the non-stop' on account of my endless chatter), they thought I should go into Law and restore the family fortunes. My housemaster did not help matters when he opined that I would not earn enough from music to afford a boiled egg let alone a boiled shirt!

My rebelliousness eventually came to a head when I boycotted house prayers for a fortnight. The headmaster summoned my parents and asked them to take me away. I continued to live in lodgings in Stamford (which the headmaster placed out of bounds to Stamford

School boys, though I still managed to see them), while for the time being I trained as a pianist with Mrs Tinkler. I decided that if one could buy books on how to make furniture or do plumbing, one ought to be able to buy one on how to compose. So I went to a bookshop in the town, where in their catalogues they found the title, *Musical Composition*, by Charles Stanford. This was ordered, and when it arrived I began my compositional studies. My artistic life has been full of accidents of this sort; for Stanford's book led me straight away into the world of contrapuntal music – and that became the basis of all my compositional efforts for decades to come. Through Mrs Tinkler I met the organist of St Mary's Church, who agreed that if I sang tenor in his choir, he would give me counterpoint lessons.

My father, meanwhile, had a chance meeting with a Doctor of Music on a train. He told my parents of the existence of the Royal College of Music in London, of which they were entirely ignorant. On condition that I too would become a Doctor of Music, they agreed to support me at college. My interview with Sir Hugh Allen, the principal, revealed only the extent of my ignorance. Nevertheless, I was accepted as a student and I moved to London in time for the summer term of 1923.

CHAPTER THREE

SPRING AWAKENING

BOULT'S DARLING

At the end of my first term at the Royal College of Music, I was asked by the Registrar to play in the annual cricket match between the College and the Royal Academy of Music. I agreed, reluctantly – hockey was much more to my liking – and turned up on the appropriate day, dressed in cricket flannels. Waiting with the rest of the team in the College foyer was an attractive young man called Herbert Sumsion (he was known to his friends as John) and I contrived to sit next to him on the tram journey to the playing fields in Camberwell. My contribution to the game that day was negligible: I think that, when batting, I was given out first ball. Nevertheless, afterwards I continued my conversation with John back at his rooms: in the end, it was too late for me to try and go to my lodgings, so I stayed with him.

As far as music was concerned, John seemed to me to know everything: he had been an articled pupil under Herbert Brewer at Gloucester Cathedral and was destined to succeed him as organist there, playing an important part also in the Three Choirs' Festival. Three days after our first encounter I had to leave for Italy to visit my parents at a little hotel on Lake Garda, and John came to Victoria Station to see me off. On the train to Dover, not really aware of what was happening to me, I wrote him a love-letter. Once I had reached my parents, I wrote him letters almost daily. Without knowing it, my feelings were moving beyond public-schoolboy sex towards love and tenderness. But John found this intensity all too much: after a while, he asked me not to see him any more – love and heartbreak within a few months! When I came back from Italy, I went to stay with him and his brother in Cornwall: and it was John who drew my attention to the Henry Wood Promenade Concerts, which were to provide the most revelatory musical experiences of my early life as a music student. On returning to London I found I had missed the first week of the Proms, but I attended all the rest of the concerts that season, standing throughout, of course, in the arena. Thus began the springtime of my life, as a human being and as a musician.

In those days, Henry Wood did all the conducting, except for the last items in the second half of each concert, which were always instrumental solos, vocal ballads etc. plus a final orchestral item conducted by the leader: and on successive Fridays he presented all the Beethoven symphonies, in order from 1 to 9. These I followed with the scores John had lent me. Their impact was devastating: Beethoven became my musical god and has remained so ever since. I also encountered for the first time many other standard or recent repertoire pieces: Wood conducted a lot of Elgar, for instance, and I was very taken by the *Enigma Variations* and *Introduction and Allegro*, not so enthralled by the two symphonies which, I subsequently declared, were lacking in technique; only over the last few decades have I realised what nonsense that was.

At the RCM, composition was my first study: everything else was subordinate. I was assigned to Charles Wood, who was then, as I subsequently discovered, dying from cancer and had often to absent himself because of ill-health. Wood admired Beethoven as much as I did; especially the string quartets and piano sonatas. In the two-year period he taught me, I learnt a tremendous amount about classic techniques of musical construction. After his death, in order to fulfil the promise I had made to my parents to become a fully certified Doctor of Music, I arranged for composition lessons with the most pedantic of all the RCM staff, Dr C.H. Kitson. Although I was enthusiastic and intelligent enough, I found it difficult to reconcile his harmony-based teaching with my obsession with counterpoint. We were often at loggerheads. Kitson gave me past London University examination papers to work on, and once I foolishly commented, 'What a silly question.' 'I set it,' he retorted.

At the examinations I was hopelessly at sea, in reality because I could not hear in my head the notes I was writing 'by calculation' on the manuscript paper. I was already struck by the absurdity of having to write even pastiche music away from the actual sounds of instruments or voices, let alone do composition like that. The tradition at the RCM was that one never used a piano for such work. I quickly realised that this was impossible for me. Beethoven may have been deaf, but that didn't mean everyone else had to be. I have worked

13

with the piano ever since, keeping in direct contact with actual sounds all the time. Most ironic, perhaps, was my response to the exam question, 'Discuss the importance of Orlando Gibbons in English music': not having heard any Gibbons, I said he was completely unimportant – I never foresaw the significance this composer's anthems and fantasies would have for me later!

I decided I could at least pursue my interest in contrapuntal music by finding out which sixteenth-century motet or mass would be sung in services at Westminster Cathedral, copying out the score in the RCM library and taking it along to follow in performance. This was much more illuminating than doing theoretical exercises in so-called 'species' counterpoint. I studied piano-playing with Aubin Raymar, who was a good teacher and keen on new music. He tried to teach me to play recently published works like Ravel's *Sonatine* and Bartók's *Allegro Barbaro*. Sadly, I didn't practise enough. I acquired just enough piano technique to play in a peculiar way for myself as a composer.

Singing and conducting were probably more useful to me. I sang in the RCM choir; everybody had to – that was a tradition which Hugh Allen maintained. He himself conducted and the choir sang some interesting pieces: the two most adventurous ones that stick in my mind were Holst's *Hymn of Jesus* and *Ode to Death*, both recent works and very tricky to perform. Allen had a reputation for being difficult with everyone, like most choirmasters: he made people stand up and sing their parts alone. But he never persecuted the tenors in this way, as we were few in number and he needed us!

I learnt most about conducting from Adrian Boult and Malcolm Sargent, who conducted the First and Second Orchestras respectively. They were opposite personalities in every way. While Dr Boult would arrive by bus, the flamboyant Dr Sargent would sail in by taxi. Boult once chided him about this, but Sargent responded, 'All the more room for you, Adrian, on the bus'. During Boult's First Orchestra rehearsals, many students would sit and do their 'exercises' – harmonising Bach chorales etc. I myself asked Boult if I could stand by his rostrum to observe and listen more carefully to what was going on. He agreed and I turned up regularly. I stood by his side like this every Friday afternoon for three years; soon he asked me to come inside the rostrum, so that I could follow the score as well. On account of this I was nicknamed 'Boult's darling'. Boult conducted the First Orchestra in recent Delius compositions (e.g. the Double Concerto with the Harrison sisters, May on violin and Beatrice on cello) and Elgar's

Enigma Variations. The major operatic projects included Wagner's *Parsifal*, in German, Debussy's *Pelléas et Mélisande* and Charpentier's *Louise* in French. Boult provided musical education at a high level.

Matters were rather different with Sargent, who had been trained as an organ scholar in Peterborough Cathedral and was fluent in every conceivable way. Right from the start he expressed the view that we were all hopeless and the most useful thing we should learn would be how to conduct amateurs. He sent a student to the library to obtain a vocal score of a Handel oratorio. Opening at a page of recitative, he then asked, 'Which one of you can sing at sight?' No one responded. 'Which one of you can play at sight?' Silence. 'Right. I will play and sing and you will take it in turns to conduct.' In this way, we all learnt how to cope with singers who sang freely. To the end of his days, Sargent half-retained a master–pupil relationship with me. Once, in the 1960s, we met in a lift at the BBC. 'Ah, Michael,' he said, 'every time I see you, I think I'm about to give you another lesson!'

My conducting was not of a high order. With the second orchestra, I did struggle through a few pieces – Beethoven's Overture, 'Leonora No. 3,' Brahms's *Tragic Overture* etc. But it was through conducting that I had a tiny encounter with Gustav Holst. Sargent asked each of us to conduct one movement of Holst's *St Paul's Suite* for strings, with the other students playing (then as now, students didn't particularly like being conducted by other students). I forget which movement I did: it caused me great anxiety at performance, I don't know why. Holst attended. After it was all over, we lined up and he came and solemnly shook hands with each of us. Holst's eyes were a deep, penetrating blue: I was taken aback, as I was to be later in an equally brief encounter with Bartók at a BBC concert. Holst seemed to look right inside me with an acute spiritual vision. Through the performances we did of Holst's music, he made a much stronger impression on me than did Vaughan Williams. The latter I came to know when we gave the first performance of his opera, *Hugh the Drover*, at the RCM. But I felt that his pupils simply wrote feeble, watered down V.W., so I avoided study with him.

From my earliest schooldays and on into adolescence, I had nurtured a genuine curiosity about ideas and intellectual things. I bought cheap editions in the World's Classics and Everyman series and lots of second-hand books. I had read the Greek classical authors in translation and studied the tradition of philosophy from Plato and Aristotle onwards. I became entangled at times in wayward, hermetic, semi-mystical philosophy and read about the Egyptians and the Gnostics; and the thrill of opening Kant's *Critique of Pure Reason* I have never forgotten. In all this I found food for my creative imagination. But at the RCM and subsequently, in English musical life in general, I found an anti-intellectualism which disturbed and irritated me. The Vaughan Williams school was a part of this, which is another reason I did not wish to study with him. For myself, I found it perfectly right to accept the example of Shaw and Butler, and deploy the intellect as part of one's creativity. There was also a view that if you composed, you didn't write – which seemed to me nonsense, when there were so many composers who were also fine writers, e.g. Berlioz, Schumann, Debussy – and this reluctance to accept the notion of the composer as thinker later dogged my reputation considerably. Looking back, the drive to make musical and theatrical artefacts was always strong, but absorbed into it was an intellectuality which I could never refuse.

Outside of college, I saw relatively little of my student contemporaries, though I observed what was happening to some of them. Constant Lambert was generally considered the whizz-kid, and he eventually received a commission to write for the Diaghilev Ballet, which many regarded as the gateway to success. Of the others, I particularly enjoyed talking to Imogen Holst and Elizabeth Maconchy. But most of my social and cultural life was away from college – either reading and talking with non-music students at my lodgings, or going to concerts, opera or theatre. On rare occasions, I participated in some outside musical function: for instance, the British Women's Symphony Orchestra had to draft into their concerts some music-college students to play percussion (there being no female percussionists around) and I found myself wielding a pair of cymbals in Berlioz's *Roman Carnaval* Overture under Sargent. In the performance at the old Queen's Hall, the task of clashing the cymbals on the last quaver of fast ⁶⁄₈ bars quite terrified me; Sargent glowered ominously.

During term time, the only member of my family I met at all often was cousin Phyl, who was at that time studying Slavonic languages at London University. She was clever and lively and I enjoyed seeing her. I can remember talking with her on the doorstep of her mother's flat about her intended future and her interest in languages. I said, 'You'll be a kind of linguist like George Borrow.' Phyl replied, 'No, not at all.' I realised what she meant was that this wasn't the real thing for a professional academic. She took a job teaching languages and subsequently went to study folk-culture in Yugoslavia: the outcome was a book on the peasant healing rituals of the Southern Slavs. After that, her life took a political course which (in my view) stopped her intellectual development. Quite early on, she declared her love for me, but I could not respond to her on that level. It was always a difficult issue between us and she envied my friendships with other women. Ironically, it was through her that I met one of two women most crucial to my life for the next twenty years – a young musician called Francesca Allinson. Phyl was staying in Fresca's family house in Christchurch Avenue, just after Fresca's father had died. I recall arriving there one day and descending to the basement kitchen to find Phyl: there was Fresca with that large goitre on her neck, from which she suffered so badly and for so long. Something happened between us. Phyl was very disturbed: especially so, a few years later, when I went off to Germany with Fresca. She put it very sharply: 'If I hear you're going to do anything, I'll come and rip your balls off.' Her jealousy ran deep indeed.

Student life naturally introduced me to a number of new friends. My first accommodation was in a little two-storey house in Chiswick, where four of us occupied a small room. I shared my bed with an Australian who had returned from the war, having lost an arm; he was completing his studies at the RCM. There was also an older man, who had an affair with the landlady and was virtually living with her. On Saturdays I went off to play hockey at a club near Harrow. Often at weekends a number of us left London on bicycles. There were huge crowds of people at Waterloo and Victoria stations taking advantage of the cheap tickets available to bring a bicycle on the train and spend the day in the countryside. I explored the South Downs, Guildford etc. in this way. I enjoyed cycling, partly because it was good exercise. In London it could be hazardous, especially if you allowed your attention to be diverted. One day I was cycling along Prince Consort Road away from the RCM, deep in thought on some musical matter. I rode straight into a stationary car and landed on the bonnet. Cycling also ended my short flirtation with pipe-smoking, for I tried to smoke while cycling and turned green with sickness; never again have I smoked.

Although not well-off, I was able to afford the cheaper tickets for some Queen's Hall concerts and entry to the gods or upper gallery at Covent Garden. In order to attend Melba's farewell performance of *La*

Bohème at Covent Garden, I queued all day. It was well worth it: I can still recall her purity of tone when she first sang off-stage – a young voice, still, quite contradicted by the figure of the older woman as she eventually appeared on stage. I also went to nearly all the performances there of the Diaghilev Ballet Company – *Petrushka*, *Les Biches*, *Jeux* etc. etc. Ravel came to conduct – a tiny man who stood bolt upright and conducted with what looked to me like a pencil. Stravinsky came to play his *Capriccio* for piano and orchestra, returning somewhat later to conduct his Violin Concerto and to give recitals with Samuel Dushkin: his hard-edged, percussive piano-playing in the *Petrushka* excerpts made a particularly strong impact on me. From an older tradition of pianism there was Vladimir de Pachmann, who used to turn to the audience in mid-trill and say, 'Nobody trills like Pachmann'! Quite contrasting, but on a notably high level, were the first concerts given in England after the First World War by the Vienna Philharmonic Orchestra, conducted by Weingartner and the Berlin Philharmonic Orchestra, conducted by Furtwängler in succession. But then a few years later Beecham came along with his newly formed London Philharmonic Orchestra and the results were just as stunning: I still remember the knockout impression made by the opening piece, the *Roman Carnaval* Overture. Beecham constantly caused a stir with his concerts and opera seasons. Some time later, in 1929, I attended his Delius Festival in London and well recollect the blind composer being lifted up to receive an ovation after *The Mass of Life*.

During my first visits to the Proms, I struck up a friendship with Aubrey Russ, a theatre enthusiast who had not long lost his job as a schoolteacher for interfering with the boys and now worked in his father's firm of solicitors. He was somewhat older than I was and attracted to me, and though I never reciprocated physically, our friendship endured for several years. He often took me to the theatre, especially to the Sunday night performances in theatre clubs which managed to avoid censorship. Thus I had my first encounters with Ibsen, Toller's *Masse und Mensch*, and unexpurgated Restoration comedies. Occasionally I cycled out to stay with Aubrey at his parents' house in Forest Hill, partly so that I could visit the Horniman Museum nearby. At Christmas, in 1925, I was invited to join Aubrey, his sister and parents for a week in Brighton, where we all stayed in a cheap boarding-house. It was my first chance to see the pier there and look through a 'What the Butler Saw' machine!

Aubrey could afford to buy books and records, and he lent or gave me many of them. Thus I acquired his discs of the Beethoven string quartets played by the Lener Quartet. These I played so obsessively that I had to stop, as I was memorising the music in terms of the changes of side for each disc. I still possess the complete edition of Frazer's *The Golden Bough* which Aubrey gave me at that time, and which opened my eyes to the ritualistic origins of theatre, affecting considerably the way I was later to conceive of opera.

After a year in Chiswick, a friend persuaded me to move to a public school mission, Hazelbury House, in Stepney Green. This didn't last more than about a term. Everyone stayed up so late at night that I wasn't able to work and I felt I couldn't continue. My previous landlady let me come back to Chiswick for a while. Then two other students and myself decided to share a flat in Redcliffe Gardens close to the RCM. One of the students was Ralph Downes, subsequently the organist at Brompton Oratory; I recall we had long arguments over the Catholic attitude to homosexuality.

This flat-share arrangement remained until I met Roy Langford, a young theatre manager responsible for the two theatres in Hammer-smith and Wimbledon. Roy was gay, slightly older than me and attractive, and we got on extremely well. It was his belief that he had been the illegitimate son of one of the Russian grand-dukes (Michael), which was why he was called 'Roy'; he certainly looked like a Romanoff. It was fun being with him, most of all because I could gain admittance to theatre rehearsals and performances. He tried eventually to arrange a job for me conducting a little theatre orchestra. I had gone to visit my parents in Yugoslavia at the time and received a telegram from him suggesting that an appointment of this kind was imminent, so I returned after only three days. Sadly, nothing came of it. The owner of the theatres – a lady called Mulholland – wanted Roy to be her gigolo: he refused, whereupon she dismissed him from his job.

After his dismissal, Roy and I moved into a quite spacious flat in West Hampstead, off West End Lane, thinking that we would survive by taking in lodgers. My parents had let me have some furniture and the piano from the Wetherden cottage while they were abroad, so we were able to live fairly comfortably, if on a low level. We stayed together like this until after my student days; and for a while, Aubrey lived there also as one of the lodgers, to get away from his parents. We provided the lodgers with breakfast, but not much else. Every

Saturday night we went to a street market in Maida Vale where they sold off everything cheaply; I used to buy six pairs of kippers at twopence each: I also acquired my first pair of tails from a shop that had discarded theatre costumes – no doubt someone had previously danced the can-can in them! Living with Roy was my first experience of cohabiting with anyone. In actuality, I was less concerned with sex than with the amount of sleep I would get and the compositional work I might accomplish.

During this period I first met David Ayerst, who has remained to this day my oldest friend. Curiously, this came about through my interest in Samuel Butler, which was first stimulated by Waldo Acomb, the English master at Stamford School. Acomb had studied at Cambridge, where he belonged to a group of Handel lovers around Edward J. Dent and his gifted student, Boris Ord. Butler's passionate love of Handel drew this group towards Butler's biographer and lifelong friend, Henry Festing Jones, known to his intimates as Enrico. When I came to London, Acomb introduced me to Enrico, and I often went to tea with him to talk about Butler and Handel. He told me once of Butler's meeting with Bernard Shaw. All went well until Shaw mentioned *his* love of Wagner. That was the end: Butler loathed Wagner.

During Christmas of 1926 Aubrey went to Oxford to dine at his old college, Oriel. Also dining at High Table was David Ayerst, recently graduated in history and deputising for two terms as a history tutor at Oriel. Aubrey, in conversation with David, discovered that he was a great admirer of Butler and suggested that some time he should come and meet me, as I knew Festing Jones. This was arranged. We saw each other intermittently from then onward, until left-wing political activity brought us closer together in the 1930s.

FINDING A LIFE-STYLE

At the end of my RCM days, I broke away from this partnership with Roy because I wanted to leave London. I realised that maturing as a composer would be a long process and could only take place away from the whirl of London life. My specific needs were simply time, peace and quiet. I was prepared to live on next to nothing and I knew this was more feasible away from the distractions of the city.

I had managed to obtain a job conducting a small choir in Oxted, Surrey and this had gone extremely well – both for them and for me.

They liked working with me; for my part, I had the opportunity to try out more of the contrapuntal repertoire that I regarded as my main musical focus – Elizabethan madrigals in particular. Through this choir, and the Oxted and Limpsfield Players, I became friendly with a number of young married couples in Oxted, many of them city commuters and their wives: they were generous in their hospitality and sympathetic to my aims and ambitions. Amongst them was Evelyn Maude, who (like Francesca Allinson) loomed large in my life during the next twenty years: she was the husband of John Maude (later Sir John Maude, the Permanent Secretary in the Ministry of Health), an amateur cellist in the Oxted Players. Evelyn discovered that there was a little cottage at the Hazelwood Preparatory School in Oxted, which was so rarely used for its main purpose as a sanatorium that it was available to be let out. It had a downstairs dining-room and little kitchen and, on the upper level, a single bedroom and a big bedroom with a balcony. When I moved there in 1929 I quickly got to know many of the school staff and pupils. I was persuaded to do some French teaching and play the organ for services, from which I earned about £80 a year. Irving, the headmaster, and his assistant were straightforward enough to deal with, so for the most part I had the conditions I needed in order to do my composition.

My employment there was minimal. I preferred to teach French rather than music, and then under a special part-time arrangement that included having lunch for free. As a French teacher I was quite assiduous, going to the trouble of visiting the Institut Français in London to find out the best and most up-to-date methods of teaching. Almost all the time I tried to use very little English with the children, so that they became accustomed to spoken French. I was less successful as an organist, for I never played the pedals properly. But again I used the opportunity to experiment, writing descants for the children's choir to sing with the congregational hymns. The hymn-book they had was a Welsh one called *Hymns of the Kingdom*, containing marvellous tunes from many countries, and I often surprised the parents who came to Sunday services by selecting unfamiliar hymn-tunes, such as 'Hills of the North rejoice'.

Through the Maudes, whose son I taught at Hazelwood, I met Christopher Fry. He was teaching English at the school; his real name was Arthur Hammond Harris but for some reason he wanted to be known as Fry, and I suggested he should be called Christopher. He was already living in what used to be the matron's room at the cottage.

21

Over the three-year period I lived there we became very involved on an artistic level. During my first Christmas in Oxted, we went off to Bonn – I wanted to see the birthplace of Beethoven – and to Cologne, where we saw Max Reinhardt's production, *The Miracle*, which bowled us over completely.

In order to afford the tenancy of the cottage, I had agreed that Aubrey, who wanted to get away from his parents, should come and share my rooms. Aubrey would take the train each morning to work in his father's London firm, so our scheme for sharing worked quite well – until the time when Christopher returned early from a Cornwall holiday. It was high summer and I had suggested that Christopher should sleep on the balcony outside my room. During the night he was woken by a commotion in the main bedroom: Aubrey had brought back a male prostitute, who was now trying to blackmail him. Christopher sharply disapproved of all this and reported the situation to the headmaster. Aubrey had to leave: he took lodgings close to Hurst Green Halt railway station. I thought that I too would be forced to leave, but three of the local families whose children I taught said that if I were sacked, they would withdraw their children. Christopher was the one who left. I continued to see Aubrey: subsequently, his family firm having done rather badly, he returned to teaching, taking a classics post at St George's Choir School, Windsor. While still at Oxted, he acquired a new boyfriend from his legal circles, Neville New, who eventually went to work in Nigeria and became a judge. Neville was a fine and distinguished man: and when Aubrey later became senile and had to live in a special home for the incapacitated, Neville provided the necessary finance.

I made a number of friends locally in Oxted. One such was a Mrs Henderson, sister of one of the lodgers at the West Hampstead apartment I had shared with Roy: she lived in a tiny flat by the railway station, was very much the blue stocking and had formed an attachment with another woman who taught the violin. At that time I thought it a good idea if I were to learn to play a stringed instrument, and took lessons from the latter: but I soon changed to the viola, which entailed simpler parts! I enjoyed many long conversations with Mrs Henderson: she was of the same generation as Ethel Smyth, had known Brahms and been in Dresden before the First World War.

Lacking a family of my own, I was invariably drawn into the local ones. Amongst the closest were the Shaxsons – Eric and Dorothy – whose four sons I taught at Hazelwood School. Eric worked in his father's stockbroker firm but, foreseeing the 1929 Wall Street Crash, had persuaded his father to let him leave and go into farming instead. Later on, I was often invited to stay at the farm in the summer. Some of the sons' girl-friends were temporary teachers in a riding school and while they were out riding, I composed at the Shaxsons' piano. Eric himself was a good tenor and undertook solo parts in some of the performances I conducted. The sons, after the Second World War, all went to work on the farm, except the second of them, Bruce, who got fed up with his parents and decided instead to marry a Welsh harpist and emigrate to Australia: it fell to me to announce this decision to his parents. I lost touch with Bruce and Lydia after they left, until the late 1970s, when their two children – who were now studying at the Royal Academy of Music – visited me at my current home. Then, in 1978, during my first visit to Australia, I had a fond reunion with Bruce and Lydia in Adelaide. Lydia had been one of the first professional harpists in modern Australia and her harp now sat nobly in the front parlour; she still had a strong Welsh accent; and indeed they have now retired back to Wales.

In 1932 I was able to move into a cottage on another local farm in Limpsfield, owned by Sidney and Mabel Parvin, who were also amateur musicians. It was really one half of a workman's double cottage. It gave me the isolation and quiet I craved in order to compose, yet I was within twenty minutes of the railway station whenever I needed to go to London. About six years later my father lent me enough money to buy the double cottage and some land around it and I rented out the other half to a Welsh coal-miner and his wife, Ben and Miriam Lewis; Ben had left Wales when unemployed during the Depression and was now working as a council road-worker. Living with them were their daughter Bronwen and son-in-law Jack. Ben was active in the local Labour Party – such as there was in well-heeled Oxted – and came to be known as Bolshie Ben. My political contacts there also included the local signalman, Fred Turnbull, who lived with his wife in a nearby cottage. He was a Labour Party man and I used to visit him in his signal-box for long talks both about the Revolution (I tried to convert him to Trotskyism) and about his other great interest, romantic novels such as *All Passion Spent*.

In this period, I began a lasting friendship with a Hungarian mathematician, Paul Dienes and his second wife, Sari. Paul had played a part in the brief and abortive Communist Government that took over in Budapest after the First World War: he acted as Commissar for Education. This government had not lasted long: a counter-revolution soon followed. Paul found himself on the list of those to be arrested, so he fled, leaving behind his first wife and two sons. Looked after by Sari, he arrived in Vienna and then went to Paris, where he studied with the mathematician Poincaré. He came to Britain, taught maths at University College, Cardiff and then became Professor of Mathematics at Birkbeck College in London. Sari, with her flaming red hair, was a mixture of Polish and Greek: she was a painter who had been taught by Léger; and when, at the outbreak of the Second World War, Léger emigrated to the USA, Sari followed him there.

Paul had a particular enthusiasm for Bartók and through him, later, I became very much drawn to the Bartók string quartets. Naturally I had long discussions with him on the politics of revolution. He introduced me to the writings of the anarchists Kropotkin, Bakunin and so on, whom I read avidly. For Paul anarchism was the next step after the Communist Revolution.

Quite near me in Limpsfield lived the wonderfully eccentric Harrison sisters, May and Beatrice. I used to visit them from time to time and inspect their pet alligator. It was particularly well known that when Beatrice played her cello to the nightingales in her garden in the summer, the birds sang to her. This the BBC broadcast live on a few occasions, though once they invited far too many guests, and the nightingales, put off by the number of people and the coaches, refused to sing. Beatrice, upset, withdrew inside to the company of her alligator, until the birds once more burst into song.

In 1935 May and Beatrice went off to bring back to England the body of Delius, who had died the previous year at Grez-sur-Loing. In fulfilment of his wishes, they arranged for him to be buried in his native country, choosing a spot near their own mother's grave at Limpsfield Parish Church. I myself attended the funeral: Beecham presided, bringing a section of his London Philharmonic Orchestra to play some Delius pieces and afterwards leading the procession to the grave, where he made an oration.

Teaching, music-making with amateurs and socialising all, nevertheless, took second place in my life to composition. I had now made for myself a kind of life-style which gave composition pride of place. It was frugal. My meals were basic. Someone had given me a review copy of *Minnie, Lady Hindlip's Cook Book* from which I learned to do some very elementary cooking, with the cheapest ingredients. I took to making my own porridge with fresh oatmeal, letting it cook slowly overnight. I simplified Minnie's recipe for marmalade – merely using bitter Seville oranges, sugar and water - and have favoured this ever since. In the course of my early visits to France, I had discovered *café au lait* (coffee with hot milk) and made this a habit for breakfast, grinding my own coffee by hand; it is still my preferred early-morning beverage. At lunch I went up the lane to a cottage, where I joined a married couple for a cooked lunch, for which I was asked to pay sixpence, though I gave them a shilling. (The wife was a lovely woman whose job it was to lay out and dress corpses; I once lent her my white cricket socks for the purpose.) In the evening I contented myself with simple cheese, egg or other dishes, using vegetables from the garden. Beer I never liked, and wine and other alcoholic drinks were too expensive. Whereas I was happy to see friends and colleagues at the weekend, I enjoyed nothing more than to be free and on my own, so that I could compose; if, during the winter, the snow was so deep that no one could reach me, and I could be excused from attendance elsewhere, that was an added bonus. What was already vital, since I was living alone, was to have a telephone, not to make extravagant calls, but to keep in touch with everyone: this has been essential ever since.

By 1930 I had enough works written, and enough confidence, to organise the first ever concert of my own music, which took place on 5 April that year. The performers were a mixture of Oxted singers (included Eric Shaxson) and some professional soloists and orchestra (paid for by Evelyn Maude). Believing it essential to have a practical and efficient conductor, I invited David Moule-Evans, who had been a fellow student at the RCM and had beaten me to one of the main composition prizes, the Mendelssohn Scholarship. There were rehearsal problems, all the same, not least the nuisance of finding that the local amateur double-bass player, Mr Strange (of Strange Electrics Ltd), was out on the golf course and would have to be brought back. Taking responsibility for designing the programme, I absent-mindedly omitted my own name as composer! Sir Hugh Allen accepted an invitation to attend and apparently commented, 'Immature, but very interesting'. A critic from *The Daily Telegraph* reviewed the concert and, while enthusiastic, suggested that 'Michael Tippett will probably prefer to put all behind him and go on to fresh ideas'. He was correct. What the concert revealed to me was my lack of an individual voice. True, there were hints of what was to be characteristic of my later work: I already had a passion for the magical, evocative sound of horns – what Tennyson called 'the horns of Elfland faintly blowing' – and used four of them in one work (a concerto for string quartet, string orchestra, four horns and two oboes). But I knew I had a lot to learn and decided I needed further tuition.

I now remembered that on one of the occasions when Charles Wood had been absent from the RCM through illness, I was taught by R.O. Morris, one of the leading authorities on sixteenth-century contrapuntal music. In my headstrong way, I had declared that only Beethoven's string quartets mattered, and that there was little of interest in Mozart's. Morris took out a score of a Mozart quartet and gave me a lesson there and then on the subtleties of texture etc. in these masterworks, and I was lost in admiration. It was to Morris that I now went. I couldn't afford to pay him, so he very kindly arranged for me to enrol again at the RCM, receive a grant and simply come to him for lessons. For four whole terms, he concentrated my mind on fugue after the manner of Bach, extolling the virtues of stylistic consistency and formal discipline: and only after that did I return to original composition.

CHAPTER FOUR

THE WANDERING YEARS

KENNST DU DAS LAND . . .

When my parents sold the Wetherden cottage and went to live abroad, their first brief sojourn was at the Hôtel Beau-Site, near Cannes: at the invitation of the manager, who had bought the hotel from my father, they stayed there for a couple of weeks. Peter and I went with them there for our first Christmas vacation abroad in 1919. In the 1890s, at the time when my father had actually run the hotel himself, Beau-Site had become known for its *haute cuisine* and hard tennis courts and, indeed, its reputation as a tennis venue still remained when I went there. Peter and I liked tennis, so we were active as ballboys and I was able to act as an umpire in some of the early heats of the championships. The renowned tennis champions Suzanne Lenglen and Jean Borotra were staying there at the time: Lenglen was the first woman to figure seriously in tennis. Dinner in the evenings was followed by a dance, and Lenglen's father would let her do one dance only: I recall the impact she made in an exhibition tango, with either a Spanish boyfriend or Borotra himself as her partner.

My parents now lived in a succession of small hotels and apartments, and Peter and I were expected to visit them wherever they happened to be. They firmly believed that their children should learn to fend for themselves and simply sent us money to buy second-class rail tickets, leaving us to find our own way across a continent recently ravaged by war.

At first I found this frightening and exhausting. On the first occasion, Peter and I took the night crossing from Newhaven to Dieppe and then had to stand all the way on the train to Paris. Arriving at the Gare du Nord, I fainted on the platform and Peter had to take care of me; we nevertheless crossed Paris with our trunks to the Gare de Lyon and took another night train down to the Riviera. Gradually I became used to it all, and quickly realised I could see more of the continent if I travelled third class instead. Trains then began to intrigue me a lot. I got hold of a continental Bradshaw and studied all the possible routes, to work out ways of reaching my parents later than intended.

Already when we went to preparatory school, we had our own bank accounts. Our parents sent us money direct – £10 per year – the only obligation being to buy our own clothes. I steadfastly saved my money for other things, which infuriated the matrons at both this school and Fettes: they were accustomed to taking charge of the boys' finances and seeing that they wore the right clothes. My mother was very angry, especially at the state of my underwear, but kept to the agreement that had been made with me.

My first unaccompanied expedition across the continent was in the summer of 1919 to see my parents in Corsica: they were staying in a small hotel up in the mountains at Vizzavona, reached by a slow train from Ajaccio. I travelled down from Fettes and stopped off in London to stay with an aunt. To my annoyance, she insisted that I buy a bowler hat, cane and gloves. I continued on my journey and reached Marseilles, only to find that the weekly boat to Ajaccio had already left. Off I went off to the local branch of Thomas Cook Ltd, raised my bowler hat and said, 'My name is Tippett. I have missed the boat to Ajaccio. Would you please find me a moderately priced hotel?' I sent a telegram to my parents informing them of what had happened and then settled down to do what I liked most, exploring the local tram routes. Sitting at the top of a tram, I found that the extreme heat of Marseilles had caused the glue in my bowler hat to melt, so I threw it – along with the cane and gloves – into the sea. Peter and I had been told by my father to say, rudely, 'Fichez-moi la paix!' if anyone bothered us, and I put this to good use, notably when I was pestered by a man trying to sell me a gold ring.

I discovered that there was an overnight boat leaving three days later for Calvi and that it was possible to go from there by train to Vizzavona. I sat up on deck all night and at 4 a.m. was woken by a blast from the steamer. Before me was the outline of a great black mountain and tiny points of light in the distance. A little later we reached the harbour and I went on the famous narrow-gauge railway up into the mountains to Vizzavona, to be greeted with a telling-off from my parents for having arrived late: in future I would not be allowed to travel without my brother.

Peter, meanwhile, was due to arrive from naval school and I could hardly conceal my glee when a telegram arrived from him, saying he too had missed the weekly boat from Marseilles, and would travel later via Calvi. Like me he had been to the local branch of Thomas Cook Ltd, had raised his hat and said, 'My name is Tippett, I have missed the boat to Ajaccio, please find me a moderately priced hotel'; and he received the expected reprimand from our parents on his arrival.

The hotel was a small pension, with no English or French people staying there – just Algerians (known as *les colonnes*); it was all just as described by Prosper Mérimée in his novel, *Colomba*, which my father gave me to read while I was there. At my mother's instigation, we taught the Algerians to play kicky-cog, a game popular amongst miners in Yorkshire, really an elaborate version of hide-and-seek, with a tin can ('cog' in Yorkshire dialect) which has to be protected. In the *maquis* (or scrubland) there were bandits, who rode about on little ponies: and one morning, tipped off by the hotel management, we all watched one of these bandits having breakfast outside on the terrace. We were once allowed to join the hotel guests on a nocturnal climb up Monte Doro. We left at supper, reaching a *bergerie* (with goats) around 10 p.m. Everyone then was given a bowl of *café au lait*, after which we built ourselves a fire and curled up to sleep. At 4 a.m. we were woken and led by a guide to the peak: and at sunrise, everywhere was blanketed in white mist. Unexpectedly, like a grand operatic transformation, the mist lifted and the whole island was suddenly visible, almost across to the coast of Italy. I loved Corsica, but never managed to return there until 1988, nearly seventy years later. When I descended from the plane at midnight in Ajaccio, the first thing I smelt again and recognised instantly was the *maquis*.

My parents continued to move around. In 1923 they lived at a pension in Florence and socialised with the expatriate community there, of whom the most interesting were the novelist Norman Douglas and his friend, known as Mr Gee. Also amongst them were a number of White Russian refugees, including a Prince who lived in a single room with his religious relics. He suggested to my mother that he should take me to a Russian Orthodox Church service and there for the first time I heard those wonderful deep bass voices. We also went to Midnight Mass in the Duomo where, under the cupola, the choir was singing from enormous manuscripts written, it seemed to me, in mediaeval notation.

The elation I felt as I passed through one of the big railway tunnels into Italy in those days has never left me. Goethe expressed it for all time – that sensation of going into the warmth of the south, into the land of flowering lemon, the radiance of Mediterranean culture:

Kennst du das Land, wo die Zitronen blühn,
Im dunkeln Laub die Gold-Orangen glühn,
Ein sanfter Wind vom blauen Himmel weht,
Die Myrte still und hoch der Lorbeer steht?
Kennst du es wohl?
Dahin! Dahin
Möcht ich mit dir, o mein Geliebter, ziehn.

Do you know the land where the lemons
    blossom?
Where golden oranges glow among the dark
    leaves,
a soft breeze blows from the blue sky,
and the still myrtle and the tall laurels grow?
Do you know it?
There, there
I long to go with you, my love

GERMANY – ROMANTICISM AND FORMALITY

When I arrived at the Royal College of Music, I was already fluent in French and had reasonably good Italian. I decided that it would be useful to learn German – for musical purposes, and also so that I could read the literature. Over breakfast each morning in my lodgings, I pored over Hugo's *Basic German Grammar*, and gradually then started reading German books. It was a laborious business: I had a flair for the Romance languages, but learning all the different German inflexions took a long time. What I was learning, however, was *hoch-deutsch*, the High German of Goethe's writings; thus, when I first visited Germany – Bavaria, in the summer of 1924 – I was often in difficulties, because everyone spoke local dialect (*schwäbisch*).

I went there with a cellist friend, Gethin, ostensibly on a walking-tour – which was an odd notion, since he was rather lame – the main aim being to see the Bavarian castles, built by Ludwig II, and end up in Munich where we would be able to attend performances of Wagner's *Ring*. The only guidebook we had was an old pre-war Baedeker lent to me by David Ayerst. Unfortunately, during the war the mountain paths had become overgrown and we often had to cut our way through. Another problem was that we were wandering near disputed frontiers between Germany and Italy. Once, to get away from the hordes of horseflies that descended upon us, we ran across a frontier and were hauled back by some soldiers, who took a sceptical view of our reasons for trespass, though we were obviously innocent enough.

Most memorable from that trip was visiting Mittenwald Garmisch-partenkirchen to see the violins being made there. We had to go through Oberammergau (the Passion Play was not on), travelling in turn by train, by bus or on foot. We also reached the castles at Neuschwanstein (by the mountain path at the back) and Linderhof – romantic experiences which were a kind of preparation for *The Ring* soon to follow. In Munich I was able to buy second-hand a complete set of study scores of *The Ring*, and I still have them. I had also studied a concordance to the *leitmotiven*, so I quickly assimilated this tumultuous music (which was performed there under the baton of the young Hans Knappertsbusch).

We stayed in Munich in a family boarding-house, where there was an old lady who taught deportment to young girls. It was all incredibly formal: when we came down to breakfast, we bowed and clicked our heels and made polite conversation. Germany was not, in fact, a dreamlike experience for me. True, when I first saw the German *Wälder*, I was pulled very deeply – maybe because Celts like myself came from the Bavarian forest. But it was also the Germany that has since been tellingly evoked by Michel Tournier in his novel, *The Erl King*. The protagonist of this novel is a French prisoner of the Second World War who is taken into the old, untouched East Prussia of little villages and historic towns, with everyone living in their uniforms. He contrasts this with the French disdain of uniform and position: 'A French postman always liked to remind people, by a certain unbuttoned look to his uniform, that he was also a father, a voter, and a bowling enthusiast. Whereas the German postman, bundled up in his smart uniform, exactly coincided with his role.'

I never went to north-east Germany until much later. But I realised that it was a different world – as described by Tournier, a country of peat-bogs and marshes, a winter world of masses of migrating birds. A book came out called *Die Versändungen Europe* (The Sanding Up of Europe), which suggested that the migration of Eastern Slavs would bring with it a metaphorical sanding up of the European continent.

A year later I briefly visited Germany again, *en route* to see my parents in Biarritz; this time I was accompanied by Aubrey Russ and we went to Heidelberg and Rothenburg. Leaving Heidelberg I took a night train to Strasbourg, then another over the Massif Central to Bordeaux, arriving in the early afternoon. I decided to walk down the main street to see if I could reach the port: observing me with my rucksack, the local people mistook me for a German, and some hissed, 'Sale boche!'; the war had left its scars indeed.

THE CHILDREN OF OUR TIME

One of my summer holidays – in 1923 – was spent with my parents on Lake Garda. Garda had been German and was now Italian, but its townspeople still spoke German. I got to know two boys there, aged about 10 and 12, who had been left by their parents in a hotel on their own. Their mother was German, their father American. They were pupils at a famous school, Odenwaldschule, run by the children themselves under the guidance of a Jewish man, called Geheeb. They were taught in French, German and English. This so intrigued me that when I undertook a further, extended trip to Germany in 1930, I thought I would explore what went on in the field of children's education.

I decided to stay at a children's home (*Kinderheim*) in Bavaria, which had been started by a young couple, cousins of Fresca on her Berlin Jewish mother's side. Their aim was to do something for some of the waifs abandoned in the streets in Berlin, after the Allies had continued their blockade of Germany after the war; a sickening business, which was eventually broken by the efforts of the Swiss and the Swedes in setting up the Save the Children Fund. The children at the *Kinderheim* had no parents, no nationality, but formed a family of their own with their foster parents. Being with them affected me deeply.

One of my notions was that I would do some composing there, and I did indeed begin a string quartet (one of the unpublished ones); but it wasn't very satisfactory – I have only really been able to compose in my home environment with my piano. I was at the *Kinderheim* for about six weeks and at first became curiously homesick, writing many letters about it to Evelyn Maude; but I soon grew out of this. One day I borrowed a bicycle from one of the kids and cycled 10–12 kilometres to Lake Constance down to the little town of Markdorf and took a steamer which went all round the lake, calling in, effectively, on Switzerland, Italy and Austria. It took the whole day. When I returned in the evening, tired and worn out, all the children were waiting to meet me; I suddenly realised that home could be anywhere and my homesickness disappeared.

On the way back to England, I decided to visit the Odenwald school itself, near Michelstadt. I took a room in a tiny inn in the town and went into the school classes and wandered about without question or hindrance. I had meals with the children and even played hockey with them. The eldest of the two boys I had met at Lake Constance had already left. The younger boy was still at the Odenwald school, however, and he looked after me. He once said, 'Look, the problem for us, if you want to know, is that we've never been children as such at this school, as we're too busy running it.' He taught me a lot about the difficulties children were then encountering. It was nonetheless fascinating to watch how the children themselves made the school rules by common agreement. When the Nazis came to power the school had to move to Switzerland, on account of Geheeb's Jewishness.

BEDS AND BEDBUGS IN BELGRADE

Undoubtedly the most bizarre holiday I had came at the end of my RCM days. I was staying in Oxted with Evelyn Maude, working on an adaptation of the music for a ballad opera I had discovered in an eighteenth-century edition at the RCM, *The Village Opera*. A postcard reached my London address (the flat in West Hampstead) from Phyl in Belgrade. It read, 'Come at once, I'm in trouble.' I told Evelyn I must go and I made arrangements to travel to Belgrade by the cheapest possible method – by train through Venice and Trieste, two nights and a day on hard seats. On the way I studied some basic Serbo-Croat, learnt the Cyrillic alphabet and enough vocabulary to get by. Dressed in what was commonly called a trench coat and carrying a rucksack, I arrived in Belgrade and was met by Phyl. She didn't explain in detail what the problem was, but I guessed. Phyl had 'gone native' as they say – had found herself a local married lover. She merely told me that tomorrow I must go out to the countryside, find him and bring him back. Inclined to be dramatic, she warned me that I should be careful in case the man's wife was there, and observe if there was blood above the kitchen door.

We walked from the station across Belgrade to a suburb, an unpaved, wet, muddy area, where she had a minute flat – a single room with one bed, a bathroom and a tiny kitchen with charcoal stove. Next morning she explained that the man's name was Milutin Ivanovich and I would just have to ask local peasants where he might be. There were two main railway lines out of Belgrade, one to the south-east and one to the south-west: after an hour or so down the main line, there was a small junction where they parted; but there was also a cross-line between them, with a linking train service. I was to take the south-east line, followed by the cross-line to a small local station; after that I would go on foot through the countryside. However, it didn't work out so simply: Phyl had sent me down the incorrect railway line, so I ended up in the wrong main-line station and had to walk.

I set off in my trench coat, striding down beside the railway line on a track road which was absolutely straight, leading across absolutely flat countryside; it was the first time I had encountered the great Danubian plain. I walked on and on, passing more railway stations. At one point, I decided I would like some lunch and went into an inn and asked for food. The innkeeper, speaking German, offered only bread and spring onions, which I gratefully accepted. He brought them and then said, 'Would you like me to read your passport?' I said, 'No, not particularly.' I then realised he must be the only person in the village who could read and was in fact offering a service.

Phyl had drawn me a map, from which I deduced that once I reached the proper local station, whose name I could read in Cyrillic, I should go north across the fields. I saw some peasant women working in the fields and enquired of them where Milutin Ivanovich might be and they pointed to a little cottage. I walked over and knocked at the door. A woman appeared and looked very suspicious when I asked to see Milutin Ivanovich. She simply said, 'Belgrade'. I asked for a glass of water and she refused: probably she didn't understand what I said. Anyway, I had no option but to return to the station: sooner or later a train would appear and take me back to the main line to Belgrade.

I entered the station café and asked for food. They said there wasn't any. I remarked that there seemed to be a quantity of soup already prepared, but this turned out to be reserved for some special customers. Once again I was offered bread and spring onions. The special customers arrived in due course and settled down to their soup. Then came two gypsy fiddlers and I was enthralled to hear authentic gypsy music for the first time. As night fell, the train appeared and took us all (including the gypsies) to the main-line station, where I could catch a night express going through at 4 a.m. to the city. Everybody hopped out and went into the large station café – the gypsies immediately joining forces with another gypsy band on a platform.

All I could afford was a cup of black coffee. I tried to sleep on a large table, but the music kept me awake and, exhausted, I asked a waitress, 'Can you find me a bed?' She went off and I thought that was the end of that: but she returned, carrying a candle, led me into a courtyard and knocked on a door. It was opened by a man dressed entirely in serge underclothes – he was sewn up like that for the winter, and he was quite angry at being woken. The waitress showed me to a room where there were four beds, and pointed to one. I asked to be called before 4 a.m. so that I could catch the train. Totally fatigued, I threw myself onto the bed, still in my trench coat. When I woke up, it dawned on me why the man was sewn up, for all the exposed parts of my arms and legs were eaten by bedbugs. The train arrived, full, but I found a seat up against the toilet in the continental wagons, put my head between my knees and went to sleep. On reaching Belgrade I was able quite easily to retrace my path across the city to Phyl's flat, where I found both Phyl and Milutin. I was very angry.

Meanwhile, Phyl had sent another postcard to England saying 'Come at once, am in trouble' to a Jewish friend of Francesca Allinson's called Kitty Zeidmann: Kitty had telegraphed back at once, indicating she would arrive next day. The sleeping arrangements were now becoming complex. I had managed to appropriate the mattress for myself on the floor, leaving Phyl and Milutin to sleep on the bedsprings. When Kitty arrived, she immediately declared her intention of sleeping with me, I said, 'No, I don't sleep with strange women on mattresses on the floor. I want another mattress.' Phyl recommended the cheapest available, made of hay, and we went off to buy one.

Belgrade itself I enjoyed: it was in a beautiful position and I went on an outing by boat across the Danube to a folk festival, where I danced the *kolo* with the local peasants. But there were limitations to our life-style, as no one except myself had any money (I had brought a small sum out of my recent savings). We lived mainly on cabbage soup, obtainable at a White Russian basement restaurant on the main street of Belgrade. Unable to continue financing everyone for much longer, however, I talked Kitty into returning to London. Then a real blow fell: Phyllis developed typhus. She was unwilling to go into a state hospital – and that I quite understood; she wanted instead to be taken to a convent hospital where she could be looked after by Slovenian nuns. I paid for her to do so and decided to send Milutin back to his wife, leaving me with the flat to myself. A further catastrophe followed. I woke up in the middle of the night to find bedbugs streaming down the walls and falling off the ceiling on to me. I went off to see Phyl and asked her what to do. She said the bugs could only be removed by poisonous gas and I would have to leave the flat while an official from the city de-bugging department undertook the operation. This I arranged: and by luck, I found alternative accommodation through the British Consulate, where a young man, who was gay, kindly offered to put me up.

I was now running out of money and told Phyl she would have to go into the state hospital. I talked to the nurses in French and arranged that she should be moved. An ambulance was sent for – but this turned out to be a four-wheel horse-drawn cab. As Phyl was wearing only a thin nightdress, I asked the nuns for a blanket. They refused, saying it would never be returned by the state hospital. I protested and eventually obtained one for her, taking full responsibility for returning it. It was a hell of a journey over cobblestones, and the ward in which Phyl was placed was in a dreadful, rusted condition: it was, in fact, a special ward for people with infectious diseases, and when I went to see her I had to wear protective clothing. I was determined to get her out: I made a rumpus, and ultimately talked to a Swiss-trained doctor, who recommended her transference to a new hospital recently built for special cases. Even so, in order to visit her I had to be innoculated against typhus – and of course, I became acutely sick from the innoculation.

I realised the only place where I could be properly looked after was an English-run children's hospital in Belgrade. So off I went there, announced that I was ill, and asked for a bed. They said, 'You are not a child, you can't stay here.' I refused to leave, so they suggested that since the matron was away for the weekend, I could temporarily use her bed. Unfortunately, they forgot to tell the matron and she returned to find a strange Englishman in her bed! When I explained, she agreed to place me in one of the children's wards, though it seemed to her that I was rather a large child. On my recovery I sent a telegram to Phyl's aunt, asking her to come and look after Phyl; I could do no more.

At this point, I received a telegram from my mother in Italy which read, 'Father bitten by tarantula. Come immediately.' This meant I would have to leave for Padua, and my ploy was to get a sleeping car on the Orient Express, by travelling in one of the cheap berths. The guard who saw me entering this grand train, with my rucksack, blinked his eyes in amazement. My father had not, as it turned out, been bitten by a tarantula, but by a wasp. What was really serious was the telegram that then arrived saying that Peter was dying because he had had to have his leg amputated after an accident. (Happily, he survived.) My parents determined to leave at once for England and entrusted me with bringing their luggage back for them. They packed their trunks and planned to leave on the Orient Express. I looked up the departure time for them, but got it wrong: fortunately, the train was two hours late. When it arrived, a guard opened a door and said that my parents couldn't travel on it, as they had no tickets. Defiantly, I shoved them on board and the train started up immediately.

Left on my own in an empty hotel in Abano, the spa near Padua where my parents had been taking mud baths, I decided to enjoy myself for the next three days (which was the longest I could stay without incurring my parents' wrath). I went off to Mantua to see the Giotto paintings. While I was there, I was propositioned by a young Italian in the street. Being relatively inexperienced at such exploits I ran away, but he followed and quickly overcame my fears. After all, he declared knowingly, no less a figure than the Prince of Wales was gay; the speculations of later biographers of the future Duke of Windsor may not, perhaps, have been without substance!

Finally I collected the luggage together and took a train to Milan. There were then two trains, standing side by side on the station, one which went through Paris to Boulogne or Calais, the other going over the St Gothard Pass, through Basle and Lille to Calais. My ticket was for the former route, but I thought it would be nicer to go the other way. I enquired of the engine driver what would happen if the luggage went on one route and I myself travelled by the other: would the luggage cross the Swiss and French customs on its own? The engine driver said it would be OK, so off I went, not having realised that the Italians will often simply tell you what you want to hear. Needless to say when I reached home and went to meet my mother, no luggage appeared: it had stopped at the frontier. My mother was furious and at first said I would have to go and retrieve it. Seeing my face light up, she changed her mind: the keys would be sent instead, the luggage would then be opened and inspected at the frontier, and pass through for delivery to England.

CHAPTER FIVE

THE WORLD'S STAGE

To work in the theatre was a persistent dream from my earliest days.

I had my first taste of active theatrical participation shortly after I left school, when I sang in the chorus in the Stamford Operatic Society's production of Planquette's *Les Cloches de Corneville*, which Sargent conducted. I also played the role of the King's Fool in Edward German's *Merrie England*. During the General Strike of 1926 students were invited to 'strike-break' by taking part as 'extras' at Covent Garden: these roles were usually taken by Grenadier guardsmen, but they had currently been called out on duty to police the strike. The opportunity was irresistible. About twenty or thirty of us took part in a production of Wagner's *Die Meistersinger*, with Bruno Walter conducting, and a cast that included Lotte Lehmann. We rehearsed with the stage-manager, coming on in a procession at the back of the stage and lifting our hats at a key moment. Some of the excitement for me lay in the sheer size of the stage; but my chief fascination was with the antics of the prompter in the prompt-box – and what I observed I stored up as a lesson for the future. Most crucial of all was the experience of working on *Parsifal* and *Pelléas* with Boult at the RCM, and then studying Wagner's writings on the musical theatre. I found a large book on the structure of Wagner's opera – Alfred Lorenz's *Das Geheimnis der Form bei Richard Wagner* – and became absorbed in the various methods of measuring out the lengths and proportions of scenes.

When I came to work in Oxted I took advantage of the little Barn Theatre there run by a Mrs Whitmore. She had built up a large collection of costumes, which she loaned out to other little theatres. It was through her that I was able to help arrange for the Oxted singers and players, in 1927, to do a staged performance of *Everyman*. I had first to choose suitable off-stage music and took advice from someone who suggested anthems by Orlando Gibbons – those wonderful pieces that I hadn't previously known, such as *Hosanna to the Son of David*. We also decided to pair *Everyman* with Vaughan Williams's *The Shepherds of the Delectable Mountains*, which the composer attended. Somebody pointed out how much the two works had in common. In the one, Everyman goes alone to his God, as does Christian in the other. After being looked after by the shepherds of the Delectable Mountains, Christian's last moment is to cross the great river: he sings, 'The waters go over my head'; the shepherds sing, 'And the trumpets shall sound for him on the other side.' It was real theatre. Years later, I referred back to it when I incorporated the spiritual 'Deep River' into *A Child of Our Time*.

The main problem in the Barn Theatre was that there was no pit. But by opening up the front of the stage it was possible for the orchestra to play underneath it, with myself sitting on the floor to conduct. Unfortunately, the players were then slightly under water, and had to come in wellingtons! More seriously, the singers (amongst them, Eric Shaxson) found it difficult to hear the orchestra, so we had to drill 'hear-holes' through the stage floor, and every so often the singers went to them and cupped their ears to listen.

I followed this with a ballad opera the next year. When I had first come to London I had seen a production at the Lyric Theatre, Hammersmith, of *The Beggar's Opera* and knew this piece had originally been followed by others of the same genre. So I began looking at eighteenth-century editions at the RCM and found one – *The Village Opera* – which was just right. I made quite an elaborate version of it, rewriting one act completely as a real opera, without ballads. I then tackled a fully-fledged opera – Stanford's *The Travelling Companion*, which was suggested to me by one of my room-mates from RCM days. I became fascinated with this 'Turandot' piece, which contained two enormous Wagnerian ensembles. I arranged the score for string quartet and harmonium (having learnt that a harmonium was the most effective way of simulating wind instruments). What I liked most about it was its setting of almost colloquial English: 'Holidays, holidays, hurrah, hurrah!' has always stuck in my mind.

The important thing about all this was that one worked in a specific place all the time with specific people, and even if they were amateurs, a lot could be achieved. One of my major projects was a complete performance (rare in those days) of Handel's *Messiah*, with the small orchestral forces for which he had written it. We spent a year rehearsing it. For me it was far more than just another concert. It was a lesson in the dramatic relationships between words and music. I was becoming clear in my mind about the distinction between what was theatrical on the stage and what was theatrical in an oratorio. I gleaned this partly from Albert Schweitzer's book on Bach, where early on he dealt with the various modes of word-setting. The great revelation of *Messiah* was simply looking at the libretto – just to discover what Handel's starting-point had been and how he proceeded from words to music.

Then there was the matter of performance and how the tempi related to the articulation of the words. When I'd heard the work sung under Sir Hugh Allen, I found the tempi wrong, because they were disrelated to the words; on the other hand, Beecham, for all his eccentricities, perceived exactly the right kind of tempi and delivery. I also observed that the various cut performances I'd heard using huge forces were out of scale with Handel's lithe and lucid music, subverting its impact. So at Oxted, although I had no real historical knowledge, and was ignorant of the traditions of playing the continuo part from a figured bass on the harpsichord (we used a piano), I decided simply to follow what was specified in the Chrysander edition. We presented the piece twice, giving the audience free copies of the libretto (purchased from the publishers at one penny each), and I myself gave a short talk before each part of the work, describing its structure and contents. All of this was crucial to me as a composer: it certainly shaped my thinking when, later, I came to write *A Child of Our Time*.

In the early 1930s I began to sense the importance of music-making and the theatre in communicating messages and ideas of significance, especially to the more deprived sections of the community. I gave up my work at Hazelwood School and started conducting amateur choirs – e.g. the Royal Arsenal Co-operative Society choir, and two others in south London, sponsored by the RACS, at Abbey Wood and New Malden. I also did some work as a choral adjudicator for the London Labour Choral Union competitions.

Through David Ayerst, I became involved in the Yorkshire work-camps at Cleveland and Boosbeck, which brought students and local people together in an effort to alleviate their poverty and unemployment. In the village of Boosbeck everyone was out of work, and there was no social security or 'dole' money to fill the gap. One of the main landowners in the region, Major Pennyman and his wife Ruth (who had left-wing sympathies), initiated a co-operative market garden scheme to help the ironstone miners, and these self-help projects were extended to include furniture-making, music and drama. The first of the camps led by Rolf Gardiner, Alan Collingridge and Georg Goetsch, attracted a number of German students from the Youth (or *Wandervogel*) Movement, whose main interests were folk-song and choral singing. Goetsch (who rang a school for such vocal music in Germany) was not available for the second camp in 1933 and David recommended me. This was approved by Gardiner and, in advance, I attended a course at Goetsch's Musikheim in Frankfurt an der Oder, so that I could carry on where he left off.

When I suggested to Fresca that she should join me for the course and then go on a walking holiday together, she readily agreed, thinking that it would draw us closer together. My German was not as good as Fresca's and I often became lost during choral recitation classes. Of considerable interest to Fresca was the remarkable puppeteer from Berlin, who taught on the course; it was partly because of her interest in puppets that we went on from Frankfurt to Prague.

We set off first by train to the foothills of Bavaria and then walked. In the mountain peasant world we were now down to basics, living rough and sleeping mostly in haybarns; Fresca, being the frailer of us, sometimes found this hard going; I was only too delighted to be breaking free of a conventional type of existence. On one occasion we reached a farm, and I caused some mirth when I inadvertently told the owners that we had been walking through *Der Mist* (meaning dung) when I really should have said *Der Nebel* (mist)! They were very kind and, instead of showing us to the haybarn, took us into the house and gave us their own large double-bed. In case we needed to pee in the night, they provided a bucket. Neither of us felt we could do so in the same room as each other so I decided to put the bucket in the next room along; in this way we were both able to relieve ourselves in the middle of the night. We were slightly disconcerted, however, the following morning, when we found out that this was the very room where our hosts had been sleeping!

We walked for four days over the Reisengebirge and then took a train into Prague, where we found accommodation in a student hostel. Over a period of four or five days, Fresca visited all the

Baroque churches in Prague (for which she had a passion) and studied puppetry, while I swam in the Moldau. Coming back we stayed the night in Dresden – then a city of great beauty – where we saw Rossini's *The Barber of Seville* at the Semper Opera House. Fresca stayed on with friends in Germany, while I returned; and we met up again in Boosbeck.

At the 1933 Boosbeck work-camp I joined in the digging of the land, living in a tent with the students. I thought ultimately the best means of bringing everyone together would be a theatrical performance and decided to create for them a version of *The Beggar's Opera*. The local milkman played Macheath, Polly was played by a miner's daughter and Fresca took the role of Lucy. The performance took place in the local welfare hall: entrance cost adults one penny each and children one halfpenny. The audience that appeared was so considerable that I was crushed up against the little orchestra I was conducting. One lady, arriving late, was turned away by the local policeman. She waved her umbrella threateningly and said, 'I'll beat yer bloodie brains in, yer buggers, if you don't let me in!' The following year I wrote a ballad opera of my own, *Robin Hood*, with a libretto 'by David Michael Penniless' (i.e. David Ayerst, myself and Ruth Pennyman). It enabled me to reinterpret the legend of the famous outlaw in terms of the class war then dividing English society:

> So God he made us outlaws
> To beat the devil's man;
> To rob the rich, to feed the poor
> By Robin's ten-year plan.

For the wedding procession I used the mediaeval tune 'Angelus ad virginem', and the local children had to return to school in the afternoons to learn Latin so that they could understand the words they were singing. I became even closer to the villagers this time, staying in Boosbeck with the family of an unemployed miner and his wife, Mr and Mrs Jack Bough.

One of David's friends, Alan Collingridge, who had participated in the work-camps from the start, suggested that I should form an orchestra in London from the many cinema musicians who had previously played for silent films and who now, with the arrival of talkies, lost their jobs. In addition, there were available a number of out-of-work theatre musicians and recently qualified music students who had not yet obtained jobs. Thus began the South London Orchestra, whose rehearsal base was Morley College. It was led by Fred May, who was later to suffer a term of imprisonment as a wartime pacifist. The orchestra rehearsed once a week from 1932 until 1940. We gave concerts in schools, hospitals, churches and parks, as well as at Morley College itself. The little income obtained thereby was shared equally amongst the players (I was paid by the London County Council): but on a couple of occasions I managed to have them paid official rates, when they played for a Coronation pageant in 1937 and later at a big outdoor 'Symphony of Youth' (a pageant which also involved about a thousand children). The repertoire was mainly popular classics and light music, but occasionally I was able to infiltrate pieces that I, as a composer, wanted to try out. One such was Stravinsky's Violin Concerto, not long given its première by Samuel Dushkin. I went to the publishers, Schott, and said that since they were unlikely to obtain many more performances of the work in the near future, I would like to borrow the parts for free, to do it with my impoverished orchestra. Schott agreed on condition that if the parts were needed, I would bring them back immediately. Thus I was able to present a performance of the piece, with a young girl soloist. The players found it a strange experience!

To help the players accrue a little income I succeeded in persuading some celebrated solo pianists of the time to come free of charge and perform concertos. Amongst them were Harriet Cohen, Myra Hess, Irene Scharrer, Cyril Smith and Solomon. The audiences were often unexpectedly large as a result. At one concert Myra Hess was due to play Beethoven's Fourth Piano Concerto. Not long before the start, the administrator of Morley College rushed backstage in great distress: the audience had filled the hall and was overflowing on to the stage and into the lobby. I explained the situation to Myra, who took it all calmly; I then went to speak to the audience to ensure they created no disturbance, otherwise the fire department would come and have us all removed and the concert cancelled. Myra's performance that evening, before an audience that loved and appreciated her deeply, was quite unforgettable.

Already in the late 1920s, I had come to know Alan Bush. I met him through Fresca: he was conductor of the London Labour Choral Union, to which her own choir, the Clarion Glee Club, was affiliated. He was five years my senior and I learnt much from him. His music at the time seemed so adventurous and vigorous. We discussed our respective compositions with each other and I can remember the excitement I felt when he outlined to me his plans for a major string quartet (only a part of which was later published, under the title, *Dialectic*); I recall also the fascinated incomprehension I felt when he first played the piece for cello and piano which he had written for Norina Semino. He was quite sharp, even prophetic when I played him my own compositions at that time, such as the slow movement of my First String Quartet. Much later I showed him the score of *A Child of Our Time* and sang (all the parts) and played it to him on the piano. He was quite moved, so he told me, by the immediacy of the piece and its simplicity. But by that stage our sensibilities had caused us to go our separate ways.

Alan became the figurehead in England for politically slanted music-making during the thirties and we joined forces for an immense Pageant of Labour at the Crystal Palace in 1934, to commemorate the centenary of the Tolpuddle Martyrs. Alan wrote the music, I provided the South London Orchestra and conducted one or two of the seven performances. The following year I went to sing tenor with his choir in the International Workers' Music Olympiad in Strasbourg – an effort to counter the rising tide of Fascism with a demonstration of working-class solidarity; and in 1936 I became a member of the executive committee of the newly formed Workers' Music Association.

It was not always easy to convince the amateur singers that they should be singing political songs: most often they wanted to do Gilbert and Sullivan or *Merrie England*. I sympathised: for some of the political repertory struck me too as uninteresting musically – for example Hanns Eisler came and sang his songs and thumped the piano, but left me unimpressed. I couldn't help being wryly amused later when Alan's Piano Concerto was given its première at a special BBC concert in the small Broadcasting House concert hall. This work (which Alan had told me he was modelling on Busoni's five-movement Piano Concerto) had a choral finale, with a strongly leftist text by Randall Swingler. Alan, as ever, was the splendid pianist, and Boult conducted. To counter the radical tendencies of the finale, however, Boult forced the applause to an end by unexpectedly performing the National Anthem!

I managed to arrange a further performance of *Robin Hood*, with the New Malden amateur choir: but more interesting was a collaboration with Christopher Fry on two non-political pieces, *Robert of Sicily* (adapted from a poem by Longfellow) and *Seven at One Stroke* (based on a Grimm fairytale). The various components were divided amongst five children's choirs and the performances took place in a small hall with a stage at the Peckham Co-op. In producing *Robert of Sicily*, we deliberately aped some of the methods used in Reinhardt's production, *The Miracle*, using actors in the auditorium. I was less happy with an Eisler-ish piece called *Miners*, for chorus and piano, to a text by Fresca's actress friend, Judy Wogan; and just as dissatisfied with a setting I did of Blake's 'Song of Liberty', whose marvellous opening line – 'The Eternal Female groan'd! it was heard over all the Earth' – is (I realise now) almost contemporaneous with Goethe's 'Eternal Feminine draws us upward' (*Das Ewig-Weibliche zieht uns hinan*).

My involvement in such grass-roots activity, with amateurs, the poor and unemployed, was not basically political in motivation, although I had certainly developed strong opinions during this period. Their cornerstone was the compassion I felt for the deprived and poor people – especially the children I had encountered both in this country and abroad – and for those maimed in war and other conflicts. My first intimation of what the First World War had really been occurred when I went to the RCM and encountered many mature students (like the one-armed Australian sharing my lodgings in Chiswick) who had lost limbs or were otherwise disabled.

It had all come home quite vividly to me when I went to see a Rudolph Valentino film, *The Four Horsemen of the Apocalypse*. The love story passed me by: I was riveted by the sight of the four horsemen flying across the screen at every moment of destruction, supported by the silent-film pianist playing Beethoven's *Coriolan* Overture; and then at the end, the first pictures I had ever seen of the Flanders graveyards – endless rows of little white crosses. I thought to myself, 'So this is what happened to all those young men I had heard in my teens going off singing cheerful songs like, "It's a long way to Tipperary".' This fratricidal war in the heartland of Christian Europe was difficult to comprehend: I knew that, as well as identifying with the victims, I must work with others towards ensuring a climate of opinion in which a repetition of such brutalities would never be acceptable.

Amongst my close friends was Jeffrey Mark, a mature student at the RCM, who had entered the Army in the First World War when very young, and was utterly traumatised by the experience: indeed, in order to try and deal with his manic-depressive illness, he had gone to the USA. Jeff was a Percy Grainger-ish person, who came from the North of England and had an intimate knowledge of the folk-songs and dances of the region. He himself composed orchestral strathspeys which he brought to show me later at my cottage: to my delight, even though he was a large-built man, he danced the strathspey for me. He was very anti-classicist, feeling that the music we were all writing was fundamentally based on German folk-song and we should try to get away from that. He influenced me quite a lot – hence the polyrhythms and Northumbrian elements in my subsequent Concerto for Double String Orchestra (which I dedicated to him). Jeff's great hero was Robert Burns, who combined sexual exploits with women with the writing of poetry. Jeff set the whole of 'Tam o'Shanter' to music; and if he had followed my example and written ballad operas, he would certainly have drawn upon Burns's life for his subject matter.

When he left the RCM, Jeff quite soon obtained a job in the London office of *Time/Life* magazine. He showed me something he had written on T.S. Eliot, about whom he felt dubious. Jeff was much more affected by the ideas of Ezra Pound, with whom he corresponded. I hadn't before encountered a political theory based on anti-Semitism and I was intrigued. The Jews figured as bankers, and Jeff observed that the banks always had the corner sites – the best sites in town. I found it all naive, but fascinating. It was mixed up with anti-Marxist ideas and 'dig-it-and-dung-it' notions (a term David Ayerst and I purloined from Evelyn Waugh's *Decline and Fall*). Talking to someone so different from myself, as Jeff was in every way, about my own ideas and artistic ambitions, provided a lot of stimulation.

In the mid-1930s I was persuaded by Phyl to read Marx, but found Trotsky's *History of the Russian Revolution* more in tune with my thinking. Another book, John Reed's *Ten Days that shook the World* – an eyewitness account of the October Revolution by an American, which Trotsky approved – drew me in the direction of Trotskyism. I found Stalin antipathetic, inherently a tyrant. When Phyl persuaded me to join the British Communist Party, which was slavishly Stalinist, I agreed, thinking I would set about converting them to Trotskyism. We both went to be cross-examined in a bed-sitter in Bloomsbury. Two others – a man known as Tank and his wife, Monica Felton (who later joined the Labour Party and became active in London County Council) – were also being questioned by Emil Burns, the party-worker Phyl regarded as a possible leader. Phyl, when asked what she had read, responded, 'The whole of Marx and Lenin in the original.' When my turn came, I nearly mentioned Trotsky but tactfully changed to Marx instead. Thus was I accepted as a card-carrying member of the British Communist Party, assigned to the Camden Town branch. But the inconvenience of journeying back and forth between Oxted and Camden Town, the preoccupation at meetings with matters of which I had no knowledge, and the fact that I had found more fellow-Trotskyists around led me to leave the party after a few months.

I had few regrets. The Stalinist purges and show trials, and the intimidation of Soviet artists and composers, following Stalin's attack on Shostakovich in 1936, were incompatible with my own humane beliefs. The fact of my being a Trot precipitated the break-up of my relationship with Phyl. It was quite dramatic. One morning she arrived at my cottage in Oxted, accompanied by a party official, and announced, 'There is blood between us. We shall never see each other again.' I appealed to her to preserve our friendship as two human beings, but she would not budge. I lost contact with her for many years; and (like Alan Bush) she remained a Stalinist to the end.

Stalinists like Alan were prepared to put political principles first: Alan even said that if the Party told him to stick a knife in my back, he would do it! The arrival in England of numerous Jewish communist refugees, like the musicologist E.H. Meyer, brought further provocation, for some took the view that all Germany was evil. I found this un-Marxist and very upsetting. Meyer, for all his knowledge of seventeenth-century music, I particularly disliked, for he exuded a bitterness and bile that I found intolerable. The Spanish Civil War forced many of my generation to take sides – notably, Auden and George Orwell. I was anti-Franco, but profoundly disillusioned when the communists on the Republican side betrayed the Trots and the anarchists.

My revolutionary zeal was for the time being channelled into work with the South London Orchestra and various choirs. Meanwhile, I had tried my hand at an agit-prop play, *War Ramp*, which was performed in various Labour Party premises in or near London during 1935. Jeff's views greatly affected this enterprise: sharing Ezra Pound's attraction to C.B. Douglas's theory of 'social credit', Jeff had written two books on the way the banking system was used, and some of his ideas helped shape the play. It was not at all a good piece of dramatic writing, but its exposure of the way wars have been built upon a 'ramp' of credit, which the ordinary people have ultimately to finance, still holds good. In creative terms, it quickly provided one of the negatives against which I could react, for I was not destined to be a 'political' artist in any strict sense. What I said in the Foreword to the play was prescient:

We have tried in this play to present the irreconcilable clash between payment for war in arms and legs, and payment for war in money. The sinister force of the money ramp, though satiric, is presented with a fair degree of accuracy. The figures are not far short of truth, and the whole process is simplified so as to be presentable on the stage, but not thereby misrepresented in principle.

To those who imagine that payment for purchases and trade is all a matter of currency, we need to point out that in every big capitalist country about 98 per cent of the existing purchasing power is really loans from the banks. About 2 per cent only is notes and coins issued by the state, money as we commonly understand it. The bankers hold a dominating position in advanced capitalist countries and their shareholders share out the 'rewards' of this colossal usury. One to ten per cent is paid in interest to them for these bank loans without which capitalist society could not go on. Bankers are no worse than other exploiters under capitalism, but they hold the key positions, and that more and more as they buy out the industrialists.

In a war the money ramp assumes unbelievable proportions. And the usury and the bonus share capital generated in a war (exactly as we show it in this play) is grimly compensated by the slaughter of men at the fronts, and the starvation of the women and children in the rear. And after the war is over, the men and women do not cash a farthing of the increased rent, profit and interest. On the contrary they must 'pay' for these till kingdom come, as taxes for the national (!) debt; suffer bad conditions and low wages in order that the industrialists can compete in an artificially dwindling world market, by undercutting the workers of a rival country. International 'patriotic' competition means international falling wages. Even within 'our' Empire, Lancashire unemployment and starvation wages have been accentuated by British prohibition of Indian Trades Unions. As capitalism becomes frantic in its efforts to survive, only the armaments industry flourishes.

Are we not fools to let ourselves be so misused?

The question we ask in this play is a serious one for us all.

If the murderous weapons of war are to be forced once again into our hands, what are we going to do with them; where is the real enemy?

When I saw the play on the stage, I found myself recoiling from the ending: two soldiers return from the First World War, wounded, unemployed and ignored; and one tells the other, 'But there's a job for me to do yet. I've got to get my gun back somehow.' The suggestion that a violent revolution was the answer was unacceptable.

At the same time, contemporary events in Europe indicated that this might be on the horizon. I now began to read the classical literature of pacifism and was drawn to Gandhi. I came across Ulia de Beausobre's book, *The Woman who could not die*, in 1938, and from this I learnt what was really happening in Stalinist Russia – torture and persecution, the suppression of dissidents, and the labour camps. I lost my earlier illusion that gradually in Russia a utopia was evolving. My instincts had irrevocably led me to pacifism.

During this period I was moving towards a major artistic statement of all that I felt about the state of the world. *War Ramp* was one attempt in this direction, but an unsatisfactory one. I had previously become entangled with the symbolism of Easter as a vehicle for such a statement. My cousin Charlotte Despard was now in her nineties, and a supporter of Sinn Fein, and it was she who suggested that I should write an opera on the Easter Rebellion of 1916. I pondered this a long time and discussed it with Jeff Mark. I read a great deal about the political history of the period. It all came to an end when I asked Jeff Mark about the crucial scene, a Dublin committee meeting: in emulating the Last Supper, I asked Jeff, what would they be eating and drinking – bread and wine? Jeff replied, 'No – whiskey!' Jeff brought me back from symbolism to actuality. I concluded the whole project was unmanageable.

Looking back at Handel's *Messiah* and the Bach Passions led me to realise that if I could not make my big statement work effectively in the actual theatre, I could do so in a dramatic piece for the concert hall. A whole succession of ideas and events impinged on the oratorio that I now began to formulate: most important of all was the shooting of a German diplomat in Paris by a 17-year-old Jewish boy, Herschel Grynspan, and the terrible pogrom against the Jews that followed. Grynspan seemed to me the protagonist of a modern Passion story – not of a man-god, but of a man as such. When Paul Dienes showed me a review in *The Times Literary Supplement* of Odon von Horvath's recently translated short novel, *Ein Kind unserer Zeit (A Child of Our Time)*, I knew that here I had a title that was absolutely right. I sent for it and discovered in it another of the many scapegoats I wished to commemorate – the unnamed, deranged soldier/murderer, who sleeps on a park bench in the snow, at the end, frozen to death like a snowman. The work began to come together with the sounds of the shot itself – prophetic of the imminent gunfire of the war – and the shattering of glass in the *Kristallnacht*.

For the five places in the oratorio where I would need songs equivalent in twentieth-century terms to the chorales in Bach's Lutheran Passions – hymn tunes known to the congregation and in which they could join – I thought at first of using Jewish tunes; but then I heard a black vocalist on the radio sing the Negro spiritual, 'Steal Away to Jesus'. At the phrase, 'The trumpet sounds within-a my soul' I was blessed with an intuition: that I was being moved by this phrase far beyond its obvious context. I sent to America for a book of American spirituals, and when it came I saw that there was one for every key situation in the oratorio. The rightness of my choice was confirmed when I saw *Green Pastures* – Marcus C. Connelly's marvellous film (made in 1936 with an all-black cast) – and heard the Hal Johnson Choir on the soundtrack singing spirituals in a free, bluesy manner. The scene in the film where Moses strikes dead Pharaoh's son and the succeeding spiritual, 'Go Down, Moses', accompanied on the screen by the sight of feet tramping away, moved me deeply: here was the same ideological self-righteousness that Wilfred Owen had discovered in the Old Testament story of Abraham and Isaac and given a modern ironic, twist:

> Then Abram bound the youth with belts and straps,
> And builded parapets and trenches there,
> And stretched forth the knife to slay his son.
> When lo! an angel called him out of heaven,
> Saying, Lay not thy hand upon the lad,
> Neither do anything to him. Behold,
> A ram, caught in a thicket by its horns:
> Offer the Ram of Pride instead of him.
> But the old man would not so, but slew his son, –
> *And half the seed of Europe, one by one.*

The evolution of major works using my own texts has always entailed consultation with sympathetic friends and colleagues, especially those outside the musical domain. By accident, at this time, I had met the most influential of them, T.S. Eliot. He was to become my spiritual and artistic mentor and his advice in the early stages of writing *A Child of Our Time* proved absolutely crucial. I met him through Francis Morley, an American colleague of his, who had been seconded from Harcourt Brace, the New York publisher, to Faber & Faber in London, where Eliot worked in the afternoons. Morley's younger son, Oliver, then about six, while musically very talented, was almost inarticulate verbally. He confined himself to a few remarks like, 'That dog barks in B flat.' Morley asked W.H. Auden for advice. I had met Auden through David Ayerst and he now recommended me as a trained musician with an interest in psychology and in the education of children. Morley thus stopped off at my Oxted cottage, on his way home to Crowhurst, and discussed the possibility of my teaching Oliver music, as a way of tempting him to speak. Meanwhile, mooching about on the grass outside I could see Eliot, wearing his famous clerical hat. My sessions with Oliver brought me some vicarious family life with the Morleys and with Eliot, who had rented rooms nearby (they were soon known as Uncle Tom's Cabin) and also turned up at the house (although I did not know at the time, he had lately left his first wife). This was the domestic Eliot, helping in the kitchen and studiously picking blackcurrants in the garden. We also played Monopoly, at which Eliot was quite good. Oliver always caused a scene if he lost, which Eliot bore with good humour.

Subsequently, he invited me to tea at his room at Faber & Faber, where we discussed extensively the nature of poetry and drama. When I needed a text for *A Child of Our Time*, I plucked up courage and asked him if he would like to write it. Eliot said he would consider the matter, as long as I provided him with a precise scheme of musical sections, and an exact indication of the numbers and kinds of words I felt were necessary at each stage. I did so immediately, returning to him with a 'Sketch for a Modern Oratorio', as I called it, which he took away for some weeks. He then surprised me by telling me it would be better to write the words myself, as any words he might write would be of such greater *poetic* quality, they would 'stick out a mile' and impede the music. This I did; and although thereafter I occasionally toyed with the notion of a collaboration with a writer or dramatist, ultimately, for good or ill, I have always written my own texts.

Although it was some years before *A Child of Our Time* attained performance and recognition, I knew even then it was the turning-point in my compositional output, both in terms of technique – I had learnt how to handle an extended dramatic form – and in subject matter: for now at last I had found my true role in singing those twentieth-century blues.

CHAPTER SIX

THE DREAMS TAKE OVER

Throughout the 1930s I had to wrestle not only with conflicts that arose between my social commitments and creative ambitions but with strong personal drives as well. Some reconciliation was ultimately necessary, if I were to continue to compose. Dealing with this inner turbulence brought me to the main climacteric of my personal and creative life.

As a child, I had read a volume from my father's library entitled *Marriage and the Sex War*, but had little perception as to what it was all about. At school I learnt about sex in the normal way, but I did not understand that there was a dupe element, because of the public school taboos on male tenderness. Then, in my youth, my homosexual side revealed itself. I accepted it without reservation, as something instinctive and therefore natural. The fact that such physical relations were illegal then even in private led me, like all others, to play various tricks.

As far as possible I tried to be open about it, particularly since so many women seemed to find me attractive. I was never a misogynist, I simply had to go my own individual way. Some years later, at a bun-fight with some of the Royal Arsenal Co-operative Society choirs in the garden of a large house in Woolwich, one of the female singers came and sat on my knee. I recall thinking how difficult it was to explain that if she went too far, it would all come to grief and she would be hurt. What I found hard to accept was my likely isolation from normal family life: being unable to enter into a biological relationship with a woman, it seemed that I was excluded from an understanding of half the human race. In a haphazard manner, I began to search for some way of coming to terms with this.

I talked a lot to Enrico (Festing Jones) about it. His view was that going with a boy or a woman amounted to much the same experience:

'a woman is more comfortable,' he said, 'but the boy is more interesting to talk to afterwards!' I wrote to Bernard Shaw to obtain his views on homosexuality, but his secretary replied with a postcard: 'Mr Shaw has asked me to say he has no knowledge of this matter, and that since it has nothing to do with the great march of evolution, it is irrelevant.' That grandiose statement for a while made me determined to prove him wrong: for perhaps even Shaw was afraid of it.

Through Christopher, I met various literary figures, notably the Welsh nature-poet, W.H. Davies, and Dorothy Edwards, author of *The Winter Sonata*, a fascinating collection of vignettes of life in rural Wales. When she came to visit two other Limpsfield writers, David Garnett (author of *Lady into Fox*) and his brother Richard, she stayed overnight at my cottage. The following day she threw herself under a train at Hurst Green station. It was the first time I had encountered someone who was to be broken by her emotional problems. Dorothy had strongly recommended Dostoevsky and Proust and I immediately read *The Brothers Karamazov*; I then borrowed Fresca's complete edition of Proust in French and became fascinated by his subtle strategies for dealing with homosexual relations. I wrote to Fresca:

> . . . I looked in *Sodom & Gomorrhe II* & was amused to see how much easier it is to read those sort of bits now when one is less & less wound up in the subjective peculiarity of such experiences oneself – & how much more general it all appears to my ear when written of in French, & with the same sort of nuances: 'désireux de retrouver quelqu'un à qui il devait tant de plaisir et de largesses . . .' though, as I get older, I realise more & more that while in Plato's time, the *general* myth was probably as he represented it, & it was neither offensive nor impossible to use that form to mean the other – so now the general myth is so forcibly 'boy meets girl', that individual experiences of all orders have to be subsumed under that heading – & one of the results is Albertine [a girl-friend in the novel; a boy-friend in actual life] – not nearly so much a lie as I would have felt, as an adolescent – the only other result comes out like the 'Well of Loneliness' [a novel banned in 1928 because of its lesbian content] which by its title has the anti-general flavour. I don't think that to be stupid, necessarily; it rather depends on what, artistically, one is about – a realistic description of the actual problems of queerness in a

world of such rigid conventional 'boy meets girl' order, is quite different from the myth-making of the eternal lover. Actually the 'boy meets girl' convention is, to my feeling, so rigid that I sense a break forming. But I can't guess what: & the masque [the earliest form of the opera *The Midsummer Marriage*] is technically within the convention even if I suspect the feelings & emotions are not truly *of* the convention – if you get me . . .

I was not able to tell everyone straight out, as I might now, about my sexual orientation. Some, like Jeff Mark, certainly guessed and he was sympathetic. He and I were opposites in many respects, but very drawn to each other. He had odd views on most things. He once decided that people should avoid washing their hands, other than after doing obviously dirty things, as it took away the body oils. I told Phyl about this and she opined that the genitals should at least be washed after sexual intercourse. But Jeff said he had put the matter to the test with women and they had not minded. Despite holding anti-Semitic views, Jeff later came to know two Jewish sisters (they may have been refugees), and his psychological imbalance showed when he told me, after the Munich crisis, 'If I don't marry one of them, war will break out. If I do, it'll be OK.' He did marry one of them and they spent their honeymoon in my Oxted cottage. I used to take them tea in bed in the morning. On one occasion, Jeff said, 'It's very interesting, we have discovered a method of sleeping naked in each other's arms all night without getting pins and needles.' One evening, we were walking up towards Waterloo station together and he said, 'You know, Michael, of all the people I know who drinks milk not beer, you're the only one I appreciate.'

Two years after T.E. Lawrence died in 1935 a collection of essays about him appeared in the *Atlantic Monthly*, all of them hagiographical except one by the artist, Eric Kennington. He revealed something of Lawrence's true character, telling how Lawrence had come to see him and his wife in Chiswick with a young soldier on the pillion of his motor-cycle. The soldier (Jock Bruce from Aberdeen) was Lawrence's unofficial batman, bodyguard and flagellant, and the sado-masochistic nature of their relationship was overt:

> This time – for the first time – [Lawrence] dropped all disguises. There was a world of pain between him and us . . . . Everything was

attacked. Life itself. Marriage, parenthood, work, morality and especially Hope . . . . [Angered,] the young man [who was more positive] banged his fist on the tea-table and threatened, 'Now, none of that. How often have I told you? Look me straight in the face.' Aside to my wife, the young man revealed his grief at T.E.'s suffering. I don't know who he was, but he had great courage and love for T.E.

I knew at once that Kennington had seen through Lawrence, and what he wrote reactivated my own internal struggles with the problems of masculinity: Fresca herself had recently commented that she did not like it when I appeared to be feminine in relation to another man.

I decided I should go to see Kennington and this was arranged through a woman friend of Evelyn Maude. I went by train to Reading, where Kennington met me and drove me to his farm in Ipsden, near Oxford. He had two children, one a gentle son called Christopher, the other a tough, energetic girl. At one stage that weekend I could not resist pointing out that he had a feminine son and a masculine daughter. He was intensely annoyed. Kennington thought I had come to pay homage to Lawrence and he took me to an upper room, brought out Lawrence's Arabic costume and told me to put it on – which I did. But then the real purpose of my visit dawned upon him – to discuss the problems of homosexuality – which annoyed him further. After preparing to depart, I went to find him: he was hard at work, chipping away at his statue of Lawrence. Meanwhile, as an oblique way of commenting upon my behaviour, he had taken a billboard and some newspaper cuttings and so arranged them that all that remained at the top was MIDDLESEX.

Kennington attained prominence later as a war artist, doing a large number of crayon drawings of young aircraftsmen. Fresca said they were marvellous examples of the heroic and the bedworthy: 'they are men exactly as women would have seen them', she said. It so happened I was in London on one occasion with a woman from one of my choirs (she had fallen for me and used to treat me to meals and visits to the theatre). We had come out of Charing Cross station and started down Villiers Street, when who should appear but Kennington. Rather rudely, I asked my lady-friend to leave us alone for a while, declaring I had important things to discuss with Kennington. He and I immediately erupted into an argument about the war. He told me, 'You may think it is OK to be a conscientious objector, but believe me, you will come to nothing unless you realise that rivers of blood will flow down this street.' I retorted with Fresca's comment about his pictures of airmen looking exactly as a woman would see them. On that acrimonious note, we parted.

With both Evelyn and Fresca, I could talk openly and frankly about my problems. Evelyn was ten years older than me and a very mature individual. She never wished me to pretend to respond to her love: my inability to develop a sexual relationship with her she accepted, though it often made me feel guilty. She had great integrity – sex for her belonged to deep, personal relationships, and the thought of one-night stands disgusted her; I learnt much from her profoundly considered attitudes. When later I went to prison, it was to Evelyn, rather than anyone else, that I wrote the permitted letters: they were almost public letters – like those Goethe wrote to Frau von Stein from Italy.

Early on in my relationship with Fresca, we discussed marriage and children, which I wanted as much as she did. We both of us appeared to have our turbulent homosexual sides, but our own relationship was one of great serenity. Once, walking with her in a London square, arm in arm, I said, 'You know, Fresca, we really belong to one another.' She responded, cryptically, 'You see that woman ahead of us. It's Virginia Woolf.' At one stage Fresca was intending to come on holiday with me in Spain. But at the last moment she decided to go to Switzerland to have her goitre removed, leaving then for New York, for one of what she called her 'rutting seasons', with men who had to be foreign or Jewish. She sent me a telegram from New York which read: 'If I have children with a man will you accept marriage and fake fatherhood?' I consulted Evelyn Maude and David Ayerst about this and finally wrote back saying, 'If there are to be children they would have to be mine as well as yours.' When she returned we began to discuss seriously the possibility of having children through artificial insemination by the husband. But my problems ran deeper and this all came to nothing.

For a while, Fresca went to live with a lesbian actress, but in the long term found this produced tension. Eventually she left saying that she was bringing into her life a turbulence which might have disturbed her life as an accepting lesbian and as an actress. I realised that for me it was the other way round: I accepted the turbulence as necessary for creative work.

Fresca's life centred on three main activities: firstly, her interest in puppets, which she had pursued during our holiday in Germany and Czechoslovakia; this was allied to her work as a choral conductor – e.g. she directed in Oxford a version of Orazio Vecchi's madrigal comedy, *L'Amfiparnasso*, with puppets; then she thought about becoming a writer (hence her identification with Virginia Woolf) and published an autobiographical volume, *A Childhood*; finally, she became absorbed in folk-song and helped me find the right tunes for *Robert of Sicily*. In her own research, she questioned Cecil Sharp's assertion of the racial purity of English folksong. She compared his tunes with those in the *Fitzwilliam Virginal Book*, in *The Beggar's Opera* and Chappell's collection, *Popular Music of the Olden Time*, coming to the conclusion that they were deeply influenced by Irish folk-music, due to the emigration of labourers during the Industrial Revolution. She wrote all this up and sent a copy to Vaughan Williams, asking if he would contribute a preface for publication. V.W. was outraged that his cherished English folk-songs should turn out to be impure! At her death, Fresca left her book to me, hoping I would arrange for its publication. But I was rather dilatory about it and in the end, presented it (perhaps ironically) to the Vaughan Williams Memorial Library.

In the spring of 1932 I went to stay with David Ayerst at his mother's home in Prestwick, Manchester. He had just returned from the first Boosbeck work-camps and came to meet me on the railway station platform. With him was a younger, shorter man, with coal-black hair and large brown eyes, dressed in a green shirt and green shorts. His name was Wilfred Franks and I immediately fell for him in a way that I had never previously known. Wilf was a London-born painter and craftsman, fresh from studies at the Bauhaus in Weimar and various wanderings through Germany and Italy. When Wilf went back to London I sought him out at his father's house near Archway, and suggested he might like to come and see me at my cottage in Oxted. He was suspicious of this and as I was not prepared to be candid at that stage, I let it ride.

Eventually he did appear, and I then got to know him well. At bedtime, I showed him the spare bedroom, but he wanted to share mine with me. Pyjamas he would not tolerate, and we slept naked together many nights – chastely, to the amazement of David – until the inevitable happened. Later Wilf said, 'I only do this for your sake.' All I had been taught by Evelyn Maude came back into my mind and I said, 'In that case you will go into the other room.' That physical division between us lasted for about a year. Meeting with Wilf was the deepest, most shattering experience of falling in love: and I am quite certain that it was a major factor underlying the discovery of my own individual musical 'voice' – something that couldn't be analysed purely in technical terms: all that love flowed out in the slow movement of my First String Quartet, an unbroken span of lyrical music in which all four instruments sing ardently from start to finish.

Right from schooldays I was trying to break free of my middle-class background. To some extent, when I met Wilf I romanticised working-class life. He accompanied me in my two years' involvement in the work-camps, and over the next five years we went on hiking holidays in the North of England, as well as to Spain in the company of David.

After the second work-camp at Boosbeck, Wilf and I decided to walk across the Pennines, which was only possible if we passed one night out on the Fells. We borrowed David's tiny Swedish tent, which was really meant for only one person and very simple to put up; we also carried rucksacks and blankets, and the minimum of clothing. We set off by train to Middleton in Teesdale . . . or so we thought: when we suddenly spotted Durham Cathedral it dawned on us that the train was going in the opposite direction, so we returned and continued along to Middleton, arriving around lunchtime. Sitting on the kerbside, we lunched on bread, cheese and apples. The apple cores we threw away were immediately seized by some small children nearby: these poor mites had sores on their faces and were obviously half-starved; coming from the well-fed South, I found it mortifying. The sight of these under privileged, malnourished northern children haunted me for years afterwards.

In the afternoon, we hiked up the valley track and at Cauldron Snout set out across the mountains, whereupon a thick mist enveloped us. A young couple returning the other way called out, 'Don't be silly, you can't see anything up there.' Wilf was undaunted. I was fearful about the cold night ahead of us. Suddenly I heard cowbells. I said, 'Wilf, where there are cows, there must be a croft.' I was correct. Soon we encountered a farmer and asked if we could put the tent up in his field. He sent us into the haybarn instead.

Next morning his wife provided us all with a wonderful breakfast, after which the farmer asked, 'Would you like to see my loot?' I thought he meant 'lute' – but then he produced a silver chalice which he had brought back from Belgium in the First World War. He gave Wilf instructions as to how to find Cairns, the last part of the Fells, and avoid the bog. Needless to say, we missed the Fells and got stuck in the bog. The view, nevertheless, was marvellous. Walking on down, we spent the next night in a tent beside a stream, hiking, the following day, further west to reach the lakes at the south-east edge of Ullswater, where we set up tent. Heavy rain fell in the night and Wilf sent me out to tighten the guy-ropes. Soon after daylight, I told Wilf the groundsheet was rising on water. We leapt out and found the bed and our possessions soaked through. Collecting together our belongings we caught a bus into Penrith, wondering how to dry our sodden clothes. I then had a brilliant idea – there must be a gasometer nearby and if we went there, the workmen would let us dry our laundry. This worked out as planned and we went off, meanwhile, to have fish and chips. When we returned, the bedding and clothes were scorched almost to a cinder!

Originally, I learnt to drive a car in the period when a test was not required: you could just buy a licence for five shillings. It all came about when I went on holiday to Spain, in 1933, with Wilf Franks and David Ayerst. Fresca was supposed to come, too, so that there would be two cars – Fresca's mini and David's new Morris Minor: but in the end Fresca decided to go to New York instead, and the three of us remaining could just about fit into David's car, along with a vast amount of camping equipment. David was then working for the *Guardian* in Manchester and could not leave in time to catch the morning ferry from Dover. So I went up to Manchester by train and collected his car, David following on the overnight sleeper train. He gave me a driving lesson in Manchester, but I never became terribly accomplished at it: I was not good at double-declutching and I took too many risks when overtaking other cars.

I drove down from Manchester – stopping at Oxford on the way for an orchestration lesson with Gordon Jacob – collected Wilf at the Oxted bungalow and continued on to Dover, where David duly met us. At Calais, David persuaded me to do the driving and I set off at great speed across the typical French *pavé* cobblestones. At one stage we were mockingly cheered on by the driver of a French lorry and his companions, and I decided to race them. I enjoyed this immensely, but David issued a stern warning that if the axle was broken I would be responsible for getting the car back. I think the lorry won.

When we stopped in a cathedral town, a lot of young French boys came to chat with us. Naturally, I did all the talking. They wanted to know what horsepower the car was and I gave what seemed to them a tremendous figure, not realising that the term was not the same in French. David had maps and navigated. We went down on the east side of the Rhône, avoiding Paris, and over the next two days, drove towards Spain. Just before the Spanish frontier we stopped by the coast for a picnic and a swim. The sea was warm and there was no one about, so we leapt in naked. Far across the bay someone with gimlet eyes (or a good pair of binoculars) alerted the police and soon a gendarme appeared on a bicycle and threatened us with all sorts of punishment before sending us on our way. We had our picnic in the shade of a grove of trees. A cowherd turned up with his herd and played the flute to them. I talked with him and found that he wandered backwards and forwards from France to Spain like this across the Pyrenees.

Further on, the road descended to the Spanish frontier. When we reached it we found the guards sitting in *chaises-longues* in the middle of the road, taking a siesta. They stopped us and told us our papers were invalid: there had just been a revolution – Spain was now a republic – and the documents for the car had been issued by the Royal Spanish Automobile Club. We remonstrated and eventually one of them said we must go back five miles over the mountains to the railway station at Port Bou and ask for his brother-in-law, M. Gaston, in the second- class buffet. On payment of 400 francs he would give us the correct document. I was furious and decided to take all the luggage out of the car and leave it in the middle of the road at the frontier, under Wilf's supervision, while David and I drove back to Port Bou railway station and obtained the appropriate document from M. Gaston at the second-class buffet. The official document turned out to be a page torn from an exercise book, rubber-stamped and signed (illegibly); and when we returned we found Wilf, true to character, stretched out in a *chaise-longue*, drinking and smoking large cigars with the guards.

We camped on the Costa Brava – then an untouched, unspoilt area of Spain – on a wooded part of the coast, where there was a well. I alone drank water from the well, which was not very sensible – I paid the price later. We had a tiny tent for two and one of us always slept outside. Only David had any money and when I eventually fell sick, I had to spend it on a hotel for the night. At David's behest we lived mainly on tinned sardines, which I hated.

In the few days we were there, we saw the remains of a classic Mediterranean colony, half Greek, half Roman – two cities side by side, my first encounter with anything of this sort. David pressured us into visiting a monastery high up in the Pyrenees. We left the car at the bottom of a steep hill and walked up. It got colder and colder and David was concerned that the car would be frozen when we returned. Needing extra clothes to keep warm, I borrowed Wilf's under-shorts. Our arrival in the monastery was greeted by a monk playing Bach fugues on the organ. We were given some kind of cot and some charcoal to cook our own meal, which Wilf set about doing with his usual skill. Next day we climbed in the sunshine to the very top and looked down at the spectacular views on either side. We were away about three weeks. In the end, I became tired of travelling by car and left the others to return, while I took a train, intending to meet them at Boulogne. David was not pleased, when we met up, to find that I had spent quite a bit of our pool of money on some Basque china, to which I had taken a fancy.

This was my last trip abroad until after the war.

Throughout this period, my relationship with Wilf was a tempestuous one. He was so sure that there was no such thing as being queer, though he certainly acted differently. We never talked about it fully. I simply kidded myself, as people often do, that if you desire someone strongly enough, then they will reciprocate. That is what it was partly about: I clung to this feeling that Wilf really would accept – but it would not work. He eventually found himself a girlfriend, Meg Masters, though he still found it difficult to practise sex with women. Wilf certainly wanted it but there were blockages caused by the age-old problem of to what extent gender, sex and love corresponded. I had these problems, too, perhaps more sharply.

The level of distress we reached was sometimes acute. I remember being in bed with Wilf and feeling that I did not know which of our personalities was his and which was mine.

At the time it occurred to me how close this was to the Blake picture of Job, when he was forsaken by his Creator and could no longer distinguish between the action of Satan and the action of God. I knew that it was not Wilf's fault: but felt it was emanating from Wilf. Obviously, too, it was causing him great difficulties: he was going the other way and would get married.

Wilf and I used to meet each week in a café, after one of my RACS choir rehearsals in London, before I caught the train back to Oxted. One evening in 1938, I reached the café ahead of him and sat with my head in my hands, brooding on the section I had reached in the slow movement of my Double Concerto. When Wilf arrived he said, 'I have decided to marry this girl.' I went completely cold. At the very moment he said that, I cut off relations absolutely. Wilf was deeply hurt. I returned to Oxted and had such violent dreams, it was as if a whole dam had opened. I had to do something about it.

I had often gone to talk with Paul and Sari Dienes about all these problems and they tried to help me round the corner. But Paul's main comment was that he would find it extraordinary if he were able to be for a short time homosexual: it would mean having a friendship with a woman that would not immediately lead to sex. I took his point. David Ayerst (who had not long met, fallen in love with and married Larema, sister of Stanley Fisher, another student on the same staircase at his Oxford college) was also kind and sympathetic, but wasn't able to suggest a way out.

Fresca, trying to sort out her own problems, had been to a professional Freudian psychoanalyst. I couldn't afford such treatment. Some time earlier, however, Evelyn Maude had given me Jung's *Psychology of the Unconscious*, and I had become fascinated by its ways of interpreting dreams. Then I read more and more Jung, even the hefty volume, *Psychological Types*, and I discussed with Wilf and others which types we all were. The 'introverted intuition' type seemed to suit me quite well. The type farthest from me would be the 'extraverted sensation' type, and I decided this applied to Wilf. Wilf constructed an actual object to represent the four main types – a three-sided pyramid and base – in such a way that it could be stood on any side as a new base; if stood against a table, three sides were visible, one unseen. We had endless arguments as to what colours were what types. Blue was the thinking type (association with heaven); red was obviously sensation; yellow, feeling; and green, intuition. This was all schematic. Nevertheless, I found that Jung had much to offer in

62

relation to my difficulties. For example, it was consoling to read that he felt that homosexual relations between men were valuable because they produced a tenderness between them that might not otherwise get expressed.

David had introduced me to a maverick Jungian analyst, John Layard, some time before, and I used to go and talk with him. I had no money to pay him, but he analysed one early dream:

I was descending the stairs at my childhood home. At the bottom I turned right into the kitchen. As I turned, an unknown girl slipped in front of me, and once inside she went off to the left and disappeared. Before the kitchen door was the old-fashioned cooking range and in front of this was washing hanging on a clothes line. Underneath the washing I could see a pair of legs which I knew were Wilf's; but I couldn't see the torso. I went forward and with both hands drew the washing back so that I could see the face. It was Wilf's, shining like the sun. I went to embrace him and then a moral inhibition entered my mind. I said to myself, 'But where is the girl?' I turned to the left, to find the girl: she fell dead into my arms.

According the Layard's analysis, the dream told me that if I didn't give up homosexuality, the anima would die. A few days later, I ventured an alternative interpretation: if you cannot accept love with the shining face, then the soul is dead. That ended my consulations with Layard.

By then I knew that Jung himself could not treat the considerable number of individuals who wanted to be his patients and he regarded self-analysis as an acceptable alternative. So, when the break with Wilf came, I decided to start writing down my own dreams and, independently of Layard, made my own analyses (italicised in the following excerpts) from a Jungian standpoint. I continued this dialogue with myself for nine months.

My emotional problems were at first the obvious contents of the dreams. The characters in them were, of course, a mixture of actual and 'invented' figures.

EXCERPTS FROM THE 1939 DREAM SEQUENCE

Monday night, 30 January

A. On hike. Rucksack full of wheat-grain. Reach a hill. Two companions (male) get ahead. Seat themselves, looking back over valley, near the top: I pass them and sit, similarly, above. But difficult to hold myself there on the sliding sand. Begin to slip down on my behind. Enjoy it. Pass the two. They warn me that I am in danger of returning to the bottom. I stop myself and climb back again, above them. Dig my feet in to keep myself in position. Difficult.

[Probability that I ought to be sitting on their level.]

B. Looking round what is to be my new rooms – very involved – lots of passages – difficult choice between two, at opposite ends of the 'flat' – the one I like best has a fireplace on the north, a long big French window on the east looking over the country. The window on the south is blocked to the sunlight rather, by a high bank of earth – like being in a basement. I think later on I could perhaps dig it down a bit. Every little bit will help. The west side has a door out in the corner and outside, right up against the room-hall is a shed that would do for a garage, if I ever wanted one. But the shed-entrance is on the end up against the house and a car could not be got into it without reversing the shed doors.

[North is intellect. Cold, but can be heated by internal fire. East is intuition – open to the rising potentialities and with a view. South is feeling and cannot be cleared to the midday, mid-life warmth without digging. West is a sensation, is blocked – contains the way out and a 'home' for the powerful vehicle, only the thing is turned inwards against itself.]

Wednesday night, 1 February

A. Crossing a long 'shed' with an egg in an egg-cup in my right hand and a piece of bread in my left. In the shed were John (Layard), his baby girl and wife Doris. The baby is playing on a piano, and John is dancing to it.

Wilf speaks in some unseen manner to the little girl and sings: 'You can make your daddy dance to any tune you like.' He is quite friendly. But John becomes shy and stops dancing. I go over to see what the child is doing, as she is playing in a remarkable way for her age. I find that she is on her hands and knees on a big keyboard and playing the music by an incredibly rapid movement of a single finger. I try to put down my egg and bread in order to go to show her how she could use all her hand. I am doubtful if she will consent to be taught or helped.

[Possibly the overstressing of the rational moral attitude again.]

[Later remarks: It is unconscious elements in me (John) who are dancing to the new-baby feminine function. It is probably quite right that the potential new king should make the old dance to any tune it wants. But the ego, by its moral, didactic attitude is too high and mighty to dance to a body, and so the drama and the possibilities remain unconscious and unassimilated.]

B. We have an appointment later in the day up North. We are waiting for my brother who is having an operation. Suddenly he is there, brought in by nurses, still under the anaesthetic. They lay him on a sort of bed, feet close to where I am sitting.

I notice they are very fleshy and discoloured by the anaesthetic. Peter comes to and looks up for a moment. I can't believe he can possibly get well enough to travel to the appointment the same day. A muddle anyhow ensues about trains and cars.

[Peter is probably the symbolical death and resurrection of the unacceptable half of me. The muddle ensues probably because of my fear for his condition. He has been made unconscious by gas!]

C. Again the question of new 'digs'. Mrs Lewis [my tenant] puts my food for me in the long narrow room, like two small rooms on end, with a small window one end. It is dark and narrow. Perhaps, I think, it would be nicer to use the room the other side of the passage which is squarer and lighter. It is a question of the cost of coal, to heat it in winter.

[The power of the anima mother image elongates the room out of the square. The return of this power might produce the energy needed to heat the square room. The oblong room was a light and a dark room on end. I only proposed to live in the light end. The anima, an eventual function of the unconscious, still has the power, and the light and dark portions are not able to be united yet in a square, airy room.]

D. I want to explain or tell [the pianist] Phyllis Sellick something of the previous dream adventures – especially this question of the appointment up North. Bryan Fisher [*Larema's brother*] is somewhere in the background and Phyllis and I are playing at the piano together before an immense printed sheet of music which at times looks exactly like railway timetables. We laugh heartily together over this.

[Later remarks: Peter may be the function of relation to the personal conscious world and is sick. Phyllis Sellick is the function of relation to the unconscious and is getting on well! This is as it should be.]

Thursday night, 2 February

A. Phyllis Kemp standing below me on a path in the old childhood's garden wants some money. I give her all in my pocket. She drops some through her fingers. I think it might get lost for good, but it is caught on the big leaves of a plant. She gathers it up. Several half-crowns and some pennies. She thinks it is all I've got, though I don't tell her I've just made £5. I walk off to make another £5. I come to a square-looking reservoir. I go in this to swim. I swim about. I am surprised how dirty the water is. Perhaps a lot of people use it illegally for swimming. I get out on the edge near the road. A man sees me. I feel he will warn 'authority'. True enough, there comes an old, weather-beaten man down the path towards me, gesticulating. Now for it! But before he reaches me he seems to totter as if ill. I begin to go instinctively to his assistance.

B. I get into a business train for a long journey. I choose a strange, unusual for me, saloon carriage, with sort of couches around. One of them is labelled 'reserved for Lady ? (some name)'. It is a question of a night journey. At the next station herds of businessmen flood into the saloon. I am on a couch-seat at one end. They are going to start some gambling game. They empty their pockets into the middle. There is a heap then of heterogeneous objects – mainly golf balls. The heap reaches to my feet. I hope I am not expected to be in the game. They start playing, to my relief without me. Then Lady X?, a beautiful, dark woman appears from her reserved position through a sliding panel. She indicates that she won't have such a game near her, too noisy, too masculine (?). I wonder if these 'male' men will give in to this 'female' woman. They do. But I see she is holding a thin object, a cross between a silver pencil and a fork – I thought it was her cigarette. She is pointing it at them like a revolver. They all have similar objects pointing at her. Very slowly and deliberately she does the action of pressing a trigger. There is an invisible shock. All the men's revolvers are put out of action. Their triggers won't fire. But they relight their revolvers from each other like cigarettes. Again the battle ensues. Again I am surprised the men do not 'fire' before she does, she is so slow in action. She fires again and once more the men's triggers won't act.

C. I am showing off about my youth to a lot of young fellows. Saying how wonderful things have always happened to me. My first headmaster was an entomologist. The first time I went out to look for orchids on the Swanage limestone hills I found a spider-orchid in flower. [This wasn't true, I meant a bee-orchid.]

Everyone showed astonishment and appreciation. I wanted to tell them about a fellow boy who found a wonderful butterfly-moth, but some other person (male) got in first, and began a story of his – speaking at the same time as me. I gave in.

[Except for Phyl, all these dream characters are strangers. These unconscious contents are as yet unknown and strange. In B. I am a fascinated spectator; not yet daring to be active.]

[Later remarks: In A. the half-crowns and pennies are the noble and base metals of equal size which will make up one day the new thing (?). The anima asks for more. I reserve something, hold it back – £5. Naturally what is reserved is found in the 'reservoir'. Water etc.

In B. the unconscious elements are strange and fascinating, i.e. necessary parts of the personality. I refuse contamination with the rest of men I don't consort with. The moral attitude of the ego again. So the ego is only a spectator of the drama, and the dark, unknown anima has all the man. In C. there is overvaluation of the ego and a lot of 'gas'. But the compensation mechanism substitutes 'spider' for 'bee'. In the end it is clear that the unconscious is determined, and succeeds, in having an equal voice. The ego gives in?]

Friday night, 3 February

A. (A string of adventures, wanderings, searchings.)

Begins somewhere on an Alpine height, in the clouds, cut off from everything human.

A scene in a sort of waiting-room during the night – a war is on. My family is sleeping one end of the square room. I am partially asleep at the other. During the night the war front is so much transformed that by the morning several 'nations' will have changed. Yes – I laugh over this. Towards morning, I find myself close up to my family – leaning on the bed of an aunt, close to her breasts. She tells me not to as I am 'hurting her bust'.

I am told some legend of a man like my brother who after years of adventures finally gets married – his one dream.

In a strange town travelling in an archaic bus to the station to go up North. A foreign (German) girl is beside me and some other ones, with her – trying to talk her language. The bus does an odd loop movement and the girl and I find our hands touching. We leave them there. She is ready for more but I am not.

['Die Wanderung ist die Begehung zielloser Wege, darum zugleich ein Suchen und eine Wandlung' ('Wandering is the actuality of a goal-less road, therefore at the same time a seeking and a transformation.' (Jung). Appears to descend from the clouds to earth or perhaps conscious to unconscious. The legend is of the Conjunctis, the joining of the two parts. The ego comes into contact with anima, which is foreign – ? why German?]

Saturday night, 4 February

A. On a station platform. My mother due to catch a train. A steam train comes in. When the engine stops the train appears to telescope, so that there is no coach – but it elongates itself again. On this train is due to arrive one of my musical manuscripts. I see it on a truck of luggage taken from the van near the engine. It is of phenomenal size – as big as a large canvas. I obtain it to give my mother to take for me to London. By this time the train has gone out. My mother is mildly annoyed. I am very much so, as it is Sunday and trains are few. But we are told the next will be 20 minutes to 4 – quite soon. In fact the train, electric this time, arrives at once. I pick up a few packages, but my mother is rather heavily laden and has difficulty with an enormous manuscript. Why do I make her take it? The train has stopped a long way up the platform. With crowds of others we have to run.

Then the coaches are all full. But up near the engine there are open coaches with table and chairs in pairs like a café. There are some empty – for mother and Peter (?) and others? I suppose the coaches are open because the train will go into a warm climate.
B. In a foreign town in the South. The girl with us starts exhibiting a grotesque dance in the street. But that sort of thing I imagine suitable to the foreign southern notion of things. I join in a half sort of way, by throwing (very badly) bread rolls at her, but she is too far off to reach.

C. A scene with just my father, mother and brother.

[There appears to be a regression to the beginning again owing to some failure

in assimilation – hence the return to the family images. The goods train brings an 'inflated' musical MS. The ego wants the unconscious to carry it.

The ego wants to dance with the anima but is too far away and still regards her behaviour as 'good enough for foreigners' – but not 'echt englisch!']

[Later remarks: The scene of the extra-large musical manuscript and the mother may mean that ego thinks the unconscious can do all the work now and so avoid the responsibility to get on with its own job – music.

Another interpretation would suggest that the square-shaped score is a mandala symbol, the opus in fact – the self, which is to contain the ego and the non-ego. A movement of the opus is finished but not the whole work.]

Thursday night, 9 February

A. War. Three 'scout' aeroplanes away in the enemy country. A landing field and lots of people and buildings etc. – the third 'scout' returns, circles round, lands by 'my' people and gets himself out of the cockpit by catching hold of a building. The plane's flight is spiral.

I see all this from a distance. Then I am close to. The third 'scout' meets the first 'scout', who had returned a year beforehand. There is an accusation, almost, from No. 3 that No. 1 had made no attempt to rescue him, earlier. And what of No. 2? A girl said, 'that's a different question altogether.' Apparently No. 2 had crashed and was dead.

B. Crowds of us doing [a] theatrical *[as on the actual evening before in real life]*. There are some tiny knickers, triangles etc. in a heap for us to cover the sexual parts for a dance (?). I do not take one – but eventually I see all the others (that is the men) with their trousers off in their shirts, about to perform. The 'triangles' have become a necessity. I see there is a very small 'something' left for me. I don't like to put it on in public. I try to find a dressing-room. Eventually I start to do it. But it is like a girl's knickers with longish legs and frills, and a split where it should join over the sexual organs. Although it won't work, though I concede that the girlish part of it may be the comic relief expected of my part in the theatrical. But my penis is clearly showing, though it is not its usual self, quite. It appears to have a tube over the balls end of it – like the sheath of a plant – or the container of the electric light in my bathroom. Then Iris Lemare [the conductor, a contemporary of mine at the Royal College of Music] turns up on the scene and other girls. I am a trifle shy.

['War' is still the fight in the psyche – 'the armed peace'. The spiral flight is the converging on the centre. The ego and the three airmen would appear to be the four functions (Jung thought that the human personality was made up of four functions – Intuition, Thinking, Feeling and Sensation – corresponding to the four seasons and four suits in the Tarot.) 3:1 in favour of the conscious: the one who has 'crashed' being presumed to be in the unconscious still (and hence the contamination to the girl). The 'garment' the ego does not like to take was shaped on the floor like a small circle, pinkish. The association is also to a 'triangle'. It would appear to be the 'jewel of great price' lying in the refuse heap – hence the 'girlish knickers' – the implication of 'cissy' etc. – the neurosis etc. within which when accepted in the proper relationship in the psyche, lies the key to the self. The ego puts on the 'knickers' but only in private, alone. They do not function properly, and so on.

It may be quite right at this stage for the ego to take the 'thing of shame' apart, privately. It is when the ego is wrestling with the problem alone that the clearest anima figure appears – though not the dark, unknown one.

From earlier dream material recollected from John's (analyst's) collection, it seems that the penis in the 'sheath' may be the returning to consciousness of the male function after a prolonged descent in the 'bog'.

Again, the penis hanging from the socket is exactly the bathroom light in the centre of the ceiling – so that perhaps the male function is to become the light (sun: see the sun penis in 'Psychology of the Unconscious') of the lower half, once the shameful knickers are accepted.]

[Later remarks: The crux of the question seems to have been the point 'the triangles have become a necessity'. But I do not understand the meaning of the small, circular pinkish garment. Hence the subsequent regression. It is possible that the girlish knickers (the feminine unconscious) should be inside, not outside. If they did cover the sexual parts that would be a worse state of grace. Because they are split open it is possible for me to see the vision of the penis, half born out of the feminine sheath that has up to now controlled it. Maybe the concrete reference is to the preoccupation with Wilf after meeting him on Wednesday. This is the for the present impermissible tendency to re-concretise the homosexuality on old tracks. The homosexuality has only 'inner' meaning.

Friday night, 10 February

A. Endless dispersed adventures: am conducting at one time the Morley College Orchestra, but with some new, unknown players. It is on a semicircular stage. We get close to the end of rehearsal. I am afraid the new trombones won't come again if they do not get enough to play – especially as they have to go just before the end – but they seem very friendly. Then I see that there is only a 'shell' of orchestra left – the centre is empty so I close the rehearsal a few minutes before time.

Am driving myself in a car but with difficulty and danger as I have my left arm round a young boy in the next seat – I think I have forgotten how to drive – especially how to get into gear again after free-wheeling down a slope – so that we have to stop at the bottom and start afresh. When we reach the destination by a change of scene, the boy does not want further embraces, so I let him go his way.

B. In a disorientated condition in my own music room. Sitting by the fire. On my left close to door and wall is Fred Emmery, the blind musician. I see him groping to find the table there, which is displaced to the right nearer the fire. Then I realise I have been forgetting that he is blind. I tell him this – thinking it might make his blindness more bearable.

He says it is all right but a nuisance when I am serving out vegetables – as he can't see what's on his plate. I tell him that I had previously been staying over Christmas with a deaf and dumb person (association with Helen Keller) – so I am fairly sensitive.

Emmery goes off down the garden path at a great rate – meets someone at gate and holds out his hand just as if he were not blind at all. I marvel. Then I see that the wind has blown holes in the woodwork of the south wall of the room – which is indeed in a very bad state and lumbered with contraptions of all sorts. I can't get to it. I think how rotten the materials must have been and think I must try another carpenter than the original builder. I go out to see what is wrong from the outside. I am barefoot – can only find one slipper – (left?) then I suddenly realise in a panic that it is 6 p.m. That I ought to have caught the 5.30 halt train for the concert in London. To catch the 6.30, which may just get me there in time for the show at 7.30, I must rush back and dress in ten minutes – I must show what I can do.

[*Wake and am glad that it is a dream, as I really have to catch the 5.30 today, Saturday, for the concert at 7.30*].

[*'Conducting' and 'driving' would seem to be the ego trying to grapple with its problems – but not very effectually. It may be that the two trombone players use the other two faculties, belonging normally to the conscious, which threaten*

71

to become unconscious again, unless given plenty to do. Is the music getting left behind again for too much fantasy?

Union with the boy seems difficult and dangerous under this condition, especially when it comes to the ascent after the descent ('free-wheel') into the unconscious. But union outside this seems impossible.

Emmery seems to be the negative Shadow. I have been blind to this, so it is 'blind' itself. It also gets dispersed. The wind ('spirit') is destructive because I do not understand it and can only blame the materials. Consciousness is unshod (ref. shoe lost) and there is an unholy muddle about the outside responsibilities: we must get back to work seriously.]

[Later remarks: The 'boy' cannot be embraced satisfactorily 'under these conditions'. The faculties of consciousness (trombones) threaten to leave again into the unconscious. The Shadow (Emmery) hurries away down the garden path because I cannot understand his remark about the 'vegetables'.

The spirit ('wind') is destructive, and the ego is (if?) late and must 'change' in ten minutes – that is to say, the ten minutes represent the amount of tension (Spannung) produced by the failure to 'read' the dreams properly (and act accordingly).]

Sunday night, 12 February

A. I am playing on a set of double-basses. They make a wonderful, rich sound like thunder: I have not quite learnt control of them, and there are unexpected 'bursts' or 'accents'.

B. In my new cottage which is nearer London. Evelyn [Maude] is visiting me. She says that it is not good enough to wait for marriage etc., that the adoption of children is an immediate duty. I think she refers to refugee children. She thinks I ought to adopt a boy-child now. 'Foreign?' I ask. 'No, English,' she replies. 'How old, do you think?' 'Two years old.' 'Have you some child in mind, then?' 'Yes.' It is a question of having tea – but when I go into the kitchen scullery where the three girls are who look after me, I find the kettle is being boiled for the washing up of lunch, and tea is premature. I am glad to feel that I am a bit easier in my dealings with the three young girls. The kitchen is at a somewhat lower level than the living-room.

I have visited a house nearby – in its garden – I have to go right round it to get it.

There are a girl and her father (?). I think that to get home I shall not go right round again but just step across the fence, back into the road –

the road is a new one, not yet taken over by the Council. I must get back to tea. The girl goes towards her house and I say goodbye on her doorstep. It is a quarter to four.

On a similar visit to another newly built house – further away this time – there is an aristocratic man, as my host – a Count? I am glad that I am in a nice suit which really suits me very well. I feel I am getting used to wearing proper clothes. I have to go. I take leave and put on a cloak – it is a little shabby – but I suppose my host will like me just as much in shabby things as in my good suit – the cloak buttons at the neck, but insecurely – I go towards my new cottage home. I like the valley – but I won't like the 'housing-estate', newly built houses – I like the idea of new country around, but I don't like the thought of being away from Oxted – I like the idea of nearness to London and cheaper fares, but I don't like being further from Evelyn.

[I wake with a feeling of anxiety – am glad when I realise I am still living in my real new cottage at Oxted.]

I then have a visual impression, rather blurred; I felt I must get all these dreams into a frame, and that my left hand was marking it out in the air, anticlockwise about two and a half or three times round.

(There was a second impression, but so rapid I did not clearly catch it. A man in a cloak is diving through a door – the door is too small – his black-haired head is above the door-posts and he gets flattened out, as it were into a shadow.)

[The first visual impression is of the 'circulation of the light' – only the light hasn't happened yet. There is just delimitation of the edge of the problem. The anti-clockwise movement and the left hand indicate the necessity of further descent into the unconscious, to find the centre and to set the light, itself, in circulation. Perhaps the second impression is of a difficulty of the head, the intellect, to bow itself under the door through to the unconscious fantasy.

The double-basses may be the first premonitory symbol of the 'basis' of the new thing. The associations of thunder, music, the feminine shape of the bass viol etc. are pretty clear. The good mother-anima (Evelyn) wants the ego to adopt the new self without waiting for 'marriage' (what is marriage the symbol of?) – she thinks the two-year-old baby boy should be English – that is to say, belonging to us, not strange, or foreign.

The first visit seems like the circling round the centre, towards the unconscious. A quarter to four would seem to show an upward movement again towards another attempt to solve the 'fours' problem.

73

The kettle boiling for tea is the power that has still to be used to 'wash'. It is still with the female images.

The clothes problem takes a slight step on. This is the persona question. But the 'Count' is still of foreign feint. The self-discussion on the way home is the problem of the opposites. The anxiety is the failure (and probable consequent regression) to solve this problem. The unconscious is expressing something as a move to a new house nearer to London, but the ego is of mixed mind about it. The trouble seems to begin with the shabby, foreign-looking cloak whose neck button will not remain clasped. The buttonhole and the button are the symbol of the failure to keep something joined.]

[Later remarks: It is still the masculine (conscious, ego) side that 'counts' against the feminine, perhaps. 'Marriage' would seem like a symbol for the same union – the advice then would be to adopt the new potential masculinity without waiting for the one transcendent function. The good mother-anima figure seems to say that something represented by the little two-year-old boy-child is ready for acceptance by the ego. But it is still obscure what.]

The spotlight is also a mandala symbol. It means at once that the self is to be illuminated, also that at present it is lighting up my back – unconscious, etc.]

Tuesday night, 14 February

A. Trying to find the right lines to draw a rectangle into a square.

B. On hike in Ireland with Wilf. We reach a sudden abrupt descent, a sort of miniature 'canyon', in blue-black slate. Wilf steps on this, and descends with a frightening rapidity out of sight. I think 'he's a goner and will hurt himself'. However, I have to follow. I find to my surprise it is not nearly so dangerous, that I can descend with almost full control. Wilf receives me at the bottom. Other island people (peasants?) ask us if we don't carry a map. We say 'no', because Ireland is so small and an island – one just walks round it.

I am conducting. I am on a raised set of semicircular platforms set on a rake, or tier. Almost half-way up. The orchestra or choir is below me in part. It is an uncomfortable position for conducting and I don't know the score very well and can't give everyone enough to do. At the break in the rehearsal I intend to get in a more comfortable position. I use a score I already know well and so get a better result for both myself and the players. On looking round behind me I see that the players are also balked by a spotlight shining from behind me, which therefore shines directly in the players' eyes, when looking towards me as conductor – but there were possibly some players behind and around me – very badly arranged.

Doreen Taylor *[unknown or invented figure]* and I on a couch – feet to feet – or my legs to the right of hers so that I am leaning over on my right elbow and side. Doreen has had a cinch [or crush] on two women, one Elizabeth Maconchy the composer. Both the women, I realise, are married – so that I wonder how women (like Doreen) can go so long without sexualising their fantasies – Doreen and Betty Maconchy become a mixed image at this point – this figure touches (or hits?) my behind, murmuring, 'Have I paid you back what you gave me? – it was difficult to hear, or understand – that I then hit her, some time? Then she is almost tickling my crutch, from the back – I am on my right side, turned away from her: this is sexually pleasant – I wonder as usual, how far it will go and what I shall do if it does.

[The squaring of the rectangle is still the problem. Some personal question is still on the way.

The Wilf image leads me down the difficult path to the bottom – there is no need for a map, perhaps, as the 'island' is the mandala itself, the land in the collective unconscious, the sea. Perhaps a further effort to analyse the Wilf image may lead towards a solution.

'The 'conducting' of the various parts of the psyche is still in a muddle. The ego has its back to the light, the shadow being cast somewhere in front. The 'map' must be the same as the 'score' – either one does need a 'map' and must find one – or one must learn to conduct without a 'score' – the use of an earlier, known 'score' is probably a false solution, a regression.

The anima figure on the couch is itself double – ('cinch' on two women) – and double image, behind the anima, is half contaminated (the women are 'married') hence the problem is to sort out the two animas lying 'behind' the girl figure. Betty Maconchy is the type of animus-ridden professional artist-woman, and has TB – so that is probably a correspondence to the anima-ridden ego and the neurotic complex, homosexuality. There is always reluctance of the ego – the anima makes the attack. But it is not clear, yet, what the reactions of the ego 'should' be. The learning over on the right side indicates a conscious bias and 'defence' of some sort. The reluctance or 'fear' of the ego before the anima must somehow be resolved and overcome.]

Friday night, 17 February
A. A game of tennis – myself and three men – the final game of the set is played on a very constructed court, enclosed in a room or building – and the net seems almost to coincide with the wall of the room and the doorway, so that while I and my partner are inside the building our

opponents appear as if outside and playing through the doorway. The service is with our opponents. The server is the only clear player to me, besides my own partner. The fourth man is never clear – (all are men) – they are unknown to me. My partner seems to miss his returns to the service, but I twice do a peculiar shot which lobs the ball up over the net and yet so close to the wall above the net (the doorway) that it is impossible for the opponent to get it – yet it faces each time on his side of the court. At the second shot I claim 'game' – but the partner on my left does not agree, though the opponent appears to: for the score is now 40:30 and in real tennis that requires further play till one side has two winning shots in succession.

B. A peculiar game of rounders. There is a centre post and two posts, rather like the focal points of an ellipse. The three posts are in a line. I and others (one or two) are at the centre post – two people are at each focal post. The game is to run from the centre to the focal post and touch it without being 'caught' – the players at the focal post going as far from their 'home' posts as they dare in good sport.

I run first to the right. I do not reach the post. I run next to the left, finding I can run very fast indeed, but good-humouredly failing to get by one man of the three round the post and nearly running off the ground.

C. Performance of *The Travelling Companion*, as at Sadler's Wells. Wilf and I sitting in one of the dressing-rooms (under the ground-floor level) talking to the 'producer'. Wilf on my left. It is a question of my taking part in the second act after the interval. The 'producer' is taking me with another man to show me the part I am to do (?) – he sends a call-boy for Mr Herne Hamburg. The boy replies: 'Herne Hamburg is here' and points to us. I indicate that I am not Herne Hamburg and the 'producer' is annoyed with the boy and re-orders him – the boy points once more to us. Wilf says 'Oh, am I known then here by that name?' – Wilf goes to get his dress for the show. When he returns with it and we are in another room I feel a bit annoyed with him that he hasn't brought mine from the wardrobe mistress. But he is unmoved. So I go myself to look for it – my jacket is already taken off and I have to use it (or a waistcoat?) as a sort of cloak – I hurry rather unwillingly through the crowd of audience (Sargent is conducting) coming out for the interval. This is the only way I know round to the back of the stage, but I don't know what part I am to play nor any of the music.

[The Travelling Companion *is the story of a mana-personality [someone*

76

with special spiritual supernatural or charismatic powers – eg or a priest] that helps the young lad, John, to get the Princess by dispossessing her of her magic power – de-potentiating the anima.

A. is the mandala again. There is trouble with the fourth as usual. And his opposite number, my left-hand partner, is 'weak'. There is a wall in the way. The court is restricted. There is some personal unconscious in the light, that prevents a proper play between the two sides or the four functions. My partner knows that 40:30 cannot be a 'game', but only 50:30.

B. is another mandala on three and twos. The name 'rounders' is significant after the square tennis court – but the circle is flattened to an ellipse and these are, as it were, three centres. Again the question of 'touching' and touch. The association seems to lead to the anima problem – but unclearly.

C. By the inclusion of the known Wilf – possibly in this case the Shadow – the problem is brought down to the personal question again – hence the problem of clothes and the persona – the ego felt uncomfortable in front of the audience and as though it were a great problem to make a join between the outside life of the audience and conductor and the inside underground, darker life of the stage and dressing-rooms. Again it is a question of not knowing the part and the music. The ego is 'at sea' – e.g. delving into the unaccustomed life of the unconscious. The meaning of Herne Hamburg is unclear. The association of Hamburg is to Charles Hamburg, a 'rural' conductor (in actuality a frequent conductor of the London Philharmonic Orchestra) – perhaps a hint of a shadow projection – or persona even. Herne, the world of mythology. [Herne was the legendary huntsman said to haunt the Forest of Windsor.]

Are these therefore the two sides of the Wilf image? The ego seems to fail to reach the wardrobe mistress (the anima) through the upstairs public part of the house route – implication that the ego ought to use the underground passages. The difficulty about joining the audience to the actors and singers is the same question as the wall in the tennis court.

Saturday night, 18 February

A. Have been in a holiday resort somewhere in a little town in the hills. Go out for a walk up the road and the hill towards some intended destination. Try to consider what has been achieved now the holiday is over: am reasonably comforted by the thought of the new slow movement (the Double Concerto for Strings). Towards the top of the hill-road I overtake (an old) woman. She thinks a storm may be brewing and this gives me the excuse to desist from the intention to go further and to return down to the little town.

Am back in the town in a baker's shop. There is some question of what I owe the man and wife who run the shop. I claim that I have regularly paid some weekly and usual purchases, though there may be special items outstanding. The man seems to doubt the weekly payments. The woman has some rectangular cakes (pastry-strips) on a bakers' tray – just freshly made.

She gives me one (for 2d?). I don't really want it but in good fellowship I take it and it is certainly nice to eat.

The records taken of the broadcast of the piano works [Sonata no. 1] [*on Friday, the day before*] have been left for me here in this shop. There seemed to be only three pieces of record – one for each movement, though the movements are really four . . . But the chief pieces were as if cut from one single large record. One, the largest piece, had sharpish edges where it was cut, or broken somewhat like glass, dangerous to the hands.

At the centre where the record finishes (though in the dream it seemed as though the record was to be played from inside outwards) the jagged edge went right up to the centre groove so that it seemed to me that the needle-arm would go round and round this groove and never get under way.

Besides these chief pieces of the record, there were smaller pieces laid out on the left, wrapped up in paper. There were nine or ten of them, more or less. The problem was how to pick them up in the right order so that when carried home I could replace them in order and so constitute a master-record. I realised that if the worst came to the worst the record as assembled could be played and so sorted out empirically. It seems in the dream as if I attempted to pick these pieces up and replace them in order as a test

[*The association is to a trick way of picking up and counting three lumps of sugar to appear not as nine but as ten, shown me by Wilf in real life the evening before the dream, in London.*

It would seem that the way up is not yet ripe. That the first and second movements have been done, but not the last. The elderly anima brings about a return to the problems left unresolved. The baker's shop is a symbol of change ('Das Feuer ist leidenschaftliche Erregung oder Triebausbruch, und ist ein Topf darüber gesebzt, so weiss man dass Wandlung im Tun ist. So ist die Küche ein Ort der schöpferischen Wandlung' *('Fire is a passionate excitement or a breaking-out of personal drives, and this is its essence: So is the kitchen a place of creative transformation'): Jung. Cf. the kettle boiling in dream p. 72.*

The problem is considered by the ego as 'paid for' or 'paid up' in its general sense, but with some special 'accounts' unsettled. It remains to be seen if this is too optimistic. The record is a mandala symbol, as are the cakes and the rectangular bakers' tray etc. The cake appears to be the same as the extra bits of record which are still tied up in paper, i.e. unpacked, unopened. The big piece of record is the extent of the mandala development so far, but the jagged edge, which is dangerous, means that the record cannot be played because of the trouble at the centre groove. The ego didn't want to consume the cake – but the anima knew better and the cake was tasty – similarly there was some question as to whether if the small pieces of the record were unpacked they would be found to be numbered in order. The unconscious seized on the trick of the sugar cubes to symbolise the problem of the unsettlement of the mandala question and the incompletion of the process.]

Tuesday night, 21 February

(A long series of adventures: not necessarily in the right order.)

A. [*waking impression, in the evening*] An empty earthenware double-handled elliptical casserole.

B. [*dream*]: A vision of a mosque-like, pillared and terraced building set in the cup of a hill – a 'square' or *place* in some aristocratic property in Italy – the road, running round the semi-circular cup of the hill, goes through the 'piazza' or terrace. It seems odd that the owner (the 'Count') should have taken such trouble to beautify the public road (right of way.

[*Either I woke or said, in dream, 'This is the portion of a mandala.'*]

On the way somewhere, with my mother (or Evelyn) in a food shop (baker's?) – if we take food here we may not have to go home to fetch it. The girl behind the counter has a biscuit tin of peculiar white pastry, bun-like biscuits with some sweet sticky centre to them. I eat one, but find it nauseating – over-sweet and sticky [*a constantly repeated dream image – as far back as I can remember since I have observed dreams in the last four years.*]

I have gone to fetch Evelyn's car for this outing. Am driving it back alone to fetch her (or my mother). I am glad to find I can still drive it. Double-declutching to descend the gears is not very good – but I successfully turn a right-hand corner and find that mother (?) has come to meet me, so that we need not go right back.

With Pam (Evelyn's daughter) – the car is waiting to be driven into garage – Evelyn is away for the weekend – it would be useful to use the car for that time. Have no licence. I told Pam how serious the fine is for driving without one, should I – as I would be certain to on that account on the journey to Oxted – meet with an accident. Decide that I mustn't drive any more and that Pam must take the car to the garage.

My mother and I in a room. Mother has been married again (to my father?) and there are another three babes. She is walking very heavily and out of breath with one on her arm – with a slight anxiety that it will wet its nappy.

C. Dr Sargent is conducting the *Mastersinger* overture in a desultory way – they are playing badly – but I am in a great admiration at the way he knows the music by heart and exactly how many bars each instrument should play. He says it is not a very good work. I agree, remarking that oddly enough I hadn't heard it again since my college days sixteen years ago.

A cliff-edge over the sea. We are about to go home. A little baby girl throws her toys (?) over the edge. I am afraid she may fall over. I take her on my lap – it is good to feel the living body of this tiny being.

In my cottage. Paul Dienes is on visit. He sees the card (written in reality the day before) on the piano to his wife Sari, with the message to him that I am engaged on Western Yoga [*Jung's description of dream analysis*] – he evinces curiosity – but I do not satisfy him – am a little shy of admitting the reality of the process.

Mrs Parvin [Dudley's wife from Oxted] comes in (I am alone and the room does not resemble the cottage of real life) in order to give some message to Wilf, who she has noticed is here – Wilf comes down from upstairs. He is dressed up to play the part of Old Moore. He is looking like the filthiest down-and-out imaginable – he gives a 'preview' of his part. He has a small white metal mug – he is supposed to be drunk. His nose is running with mucus and this falls into the cup. Then he pretends to drink and gives it also to the chorus (girls?) around him. I am the slightest bit disgusted – though I doubt if he drinks the mucus in actual fact.

[The vision of the casserole seems like the implement for the change, but as yet

the 'cooking' hasn't begun. The Italian palace seems to be what the dreamer says it is.

The sticky biscuits are some difficult personal problem that the ego can't stomach. It has associations with the homosexuality, but how is a mystery. That they have to be stomached and consumed or else to go back again to the beginning seems certain. This is the portion with the car. The ego drives the car till the problem of the licence (or morality, authority) is reached. Then the ego is afraid – so the car is given back to the young anima. To the extent that the ego attempts and succeeds in a 'double-declutching gear descent' the mother-anima comes to meet it. 'Double-declutching' seems to be a significant word and action.

The new babies seem to be produced by the remarriage of the mother and father – but the baby has certain 'natural functions' to be dealt with. Probably these are the personal problems still unsolved, necessary to the complete acceptance of the 'child' – the self.

Dr Sargent is the Mephistophelean intellect and persona image – showing the ego 'how to do it'.

The 'child' throws her 'toys' into the unconscious – the ego takes the child to itself to save the disappearance of the child as well. Natural satisfaction.

The ego, through the intellect, is still critical of the whole thing.

The Wilf image descends from the upper regions and is severely debased by the unconscious – the ego is almost disgusted.

Is this a compensation? Or is the masquerade an attempt to show the future (Old Moore), once the mucus has been accepted (consumed) – the mucus, the vile stuff that is really the bacchic drink. The ego in the dream takes no responsibility for having Wilf in the house; the mother-anima's message purported to come from the daughter (Betty). The ego is too aloof and solitary.]

The contents of the dreams gradually widened to include images and other material that seemed to be relevant to my work as a creative artist. It meant that I was having to deal with factors beyond the purely personal. A poem by Goethe that haunted me, from the time that Evelyn first drew my attention to it, was 'Magisches Netz:'

> Sind es Kämpfe, die ich sehe?
> Sind es Spiele? sind es Wunder?
> Fünf der allerliebsten Knaben
> Gegen fünf Geschwister streitend,
> Regelmässig, taktbeständig,
> Einer Zaubrin zu Gebote.

81

Blanke Spiesse führen jene,
Diese flechten schnelle Fäden,
Dass man glaubt, in ihren Schlingen
Werde sich das Eisen fangen.
Bald gefangen sind die Spiesse;
Doch im leichten Kriegestanze
Stiehlt sich einer nach dem andern
Aus der zarten Schleifenreihe,
Die sogleich den Freien haschet,
Wenn sie den Gebundnen löset.

So mit Ringen, Streiten, Siegen,
Wechselflucht und Wiederkehren
Wird ein künstlich Netz geflochten,
Himmelsflocken gleich an Weisse,
Die, vom Lichten in das Dichte,
Musterhafte Streifen ziehen,
Wie es Farben kaum vermöchten.

Wer empfängt nun der Gewänder
Allerwünschtes? Wen begünstigt
Unsere vielgeliebte Herrin
Als den anerkannten Diener?
Mich beglückt des holden Loses
Treu und still ersehntes Zeichen!
Und ich fühle mich umschlungen,
Ihrer Dienerschaft gewidmet.

Doch indem ich so behaglich,
Aufgeschmückt stolzierend wandle,
Sieh! da knüpfen jene Losen,
Ohne Streit, geheim geschäftig,
Andre Netze, fein und feiner,
Dämmrungsfäden, Mondenblicke,
Nachtviolenduft verwebend.

Eh wir nur das Netz bemerken,
Ist ein Glücklicher gefangen,
Den wir andern, den wir alle,
Segnend und beneidend, grüssen.

The Magic Net

Are they battles that I see?
Are they games? Are they wonders?
Five most splendid boys
Against five kinsmen fighting.

Regular, measured
As a sorceress commands.

They wield white spears
Which weave quick threads
In whose loops we feel
The iron will get caught.
Soon the spears are caught,
Yet in the light war dance
One after another steals out
From the delicate row of the sticks,
Which at once entraps one of the free
As it lets go one of the bound.

So with struggles, fights, victories
Escape alternating with return
An artful net is woven
Sky flakes that of equal whiteness
That draw from high in the thickness of the weave,
Intricately patterned stripes
That you could hardly do with colours.

Who receives now the most desired
Of garments? Whom does
our much loved lady favour
as the acknowledged servant?
Sweet Fate's token, longed-for
in devotion and silence, favours me.
And I feel myself embraced
Dedicated to her service.

Yet while I do comfortably
strut in my finery
Those fates, secretly working
and without dispute, knot themselves
Other nets, finer and finer
Weaving in twilight threads,
moonbeams, and the fragrance of night violets.

Only just as we notice the net
Some lucky person is caught
Whom we all reluctantly greet
With blessing and with envy.

The sorceress in the poem was Goethe's lover, Henriette von Wolfkehl
(the wife of a minister in the Weimar government); and the nets in which

lovers became entangled apparently referred equally to the woollen vests Henriette had made for Goethe! This poem, which I only half understood, crops up in the 24 February dream. By the time I reached my third opera, *The Knot Garden*, in the late 1960s it had been transformed (in Act 3) into:

> We sense the magic net
> That holds us veined
> Each to each to all. . .

– and provided the opera as a whole with its most fundamental metaphor.

Friday night, 24 February

A. Performances of choral works in a big stadium in the distance. The choir etc. is out of sight, but a woman is conducting, possibly the composer, with very expressive gestures of the hands. She 'nets' her fingers together at one point to express a reference to nets in the music. The final sentence of the chorale is an Italian one about the sweet South – a strange ending it appears to a rather grim work.

With Layard [analyst] who is on a bed facing me – on my right (and his left) is a youngish fellow – a colleague of John's, perhaps John's analyst – behind him is a railway line or a river – he is leaning on a fence, within which are John and myself.

John is describing to the young fellow how he is getting on all right, but that he is a little worried that a strong dream or nightmare impression might cause him to get up in his sleep and fall over the fence on to the railway line (or into the river). I think this very unlikely and am rather sceptical of John's apparent sincerity. I am looking at him with very clear eyes. John remarks that it is just as unenviable a thought as my eyes – meaning to have to look me in the eyes. I am a little surprised at this reference to the clarity and truth of my vision, and am a trifle pleased at it. Everything was very friendly, leisurely and warm.

John goes. The young fellow talks to me. He refers to a concert (the one in the same dream, but now in feeling some months in the past) where he had heard some work of mine, that I had myself forgotten. I hope there will be a chance for him to hear it again, as having been reminded of it, I will see if I can get it performed. But he brushes this aside and speaks of the woman composer's work about nets: the *Magisches Netz & Fischeres*. He then describes in detail (unfortunately forgotten) how the metaphors and so forth used in this choral work

84

had appeared in such and such a way in a dream of his. Particularly some double antithetic pair of metaphors had appeared in the dream as two antithetic animal symbols.

B. Looking at a trio for female voices and piano (association with John Ireland and song I used to sing as a young lad of 17–18). Surprised at the instructions (in Italian?) for the singers to sit together. Imagined a round table with three women and a piano and pianist to one side of them. Noticed that the music had the usual tricks of verse repetitive accentuation, showing a good technical sense, but the harmonies seemed meretricious.

I am watching Miss [Elizabeth] Maconchy consulting a colleague (Dr Sargent?) about some music. (Same relative positions as myself, John and John's colleague.) Associations in the dream are to the question of socialist music etc. I feel a little superior – that Miss Maconchy has not succeeded in disentangling this question. I see, close to, the last two bars of a work of hers. I have to look closer for what I expect to be double dots. The small note on the right top corner of each bar, if an integral part of a whole-number bar time signature, would mean a double dot after the minims. On looking closer I see that the small notes are bracketed and as though extra grace-notes.

[The sweet Italian ending to the serious choral work is the problem of opposites, etc. Perhaps also a foreshadowing of a satisfactory, still unexpected ending to the process – the Opus – the work. The music is still being conducted and possibly composed, by the unconscious (anima) figure. The netting together of the two hands is a symbol of the uniting of left and right in the magic net. 'Magisches Netz' is a poem of Goethe's that has always fascinated me. Yet I do not understand it. It also has associations with Evelyn. The choir in the stadium is the mandala.

The scene with John and the stranger is the mandala question. The bed is the feminine unconscious thing. Showing that John is a contaminated image. What of? Hence it is uncertain what he might not do under the influence of the unconscious (sleep-walk on to the line): e.g. the image might disappear altogether again into the unknown. But the ego is sceptical and seems to become positive through this clear sight, e.g. the contaminated image is about to be, or is being, looked at straight in the eye. The problem is being faced. The danger will be that of inflation. The ego, on carrying out its own analysis, becoming its own analysis, seeing clearer than John in dream symbol, will stand in danger of assuming mastery of the unconscious, especially the mana. This is probably the false assumption of the stranger analyst's interest in the ego's own composition, rather than that of the woman (the unconscious).

The composition which the ego had forgotten, and which does not exist in real life, is the same as that of the woman. The ego would possess it if the unconscious is come to terms with, etc. The 'Magisches Netz' can become clear through the dreams of the analyst. Appears like a confirmation of the good effects of growth through this present method.

The trio of three female voices and the piano is a mandala – the three and the four problem. It seems like a reference to personal problems in the way of a complete quartet – hence the association with adolescent Schwärmerei *(the John Ireland songs).*

The last scene seems like the dangers of inflation becoming fact. The ego feels superior, but the social question is not so easily set aside. The minims and double stops etc. are as yet puzzling mandala symbols.]

Monday afternoon, 27 February

A. Hypnagogic vision of a woman's naked body without head and arms, or calves and feet. The hips and thighs well modelled and the vagina like a very dark blue rectangle. (Feeling of having seen something more than ever before – the rectangle in the feminine curves.)

B. Am talking with Phyl and suggesting to her a plan that she, I and Evelyn club together to support Fresca. Phyl is incensed 'And fall all on me,' she says. I tell the truth of this remark – she had helped Fresca once before to no purpose. (I wake and realise that it is *umgekehrt*. Fresca has in real life helped Phyl.)

[This seems as though the fourth thing cannot be obtained at the price of one of the others. That that would simply be an umgekehrt *(a substitution). Also the ego must take full responsibility and pay up everything for itself. (Association to the words: 'And thou shalt not by no means come out thence till thou hast paid the uttermost farthing' (fourth-thing) – spoken of the forgiveness of brother to brother: St Matthew, 5: 26).]*

Monday night, 27 February

A. Crossing an open common (on way home?) – there are a group of gypsies in a cart which they have stolen or are in the process of stealing. I see that Rose Turnbull [wife of the Oxted signalman Fred Turnbull] is surreptitiously assisting them. She is in the cart too. Her father must be on signal duty, perhaps. There is a difficult moment when some person calls 'Rose, Rose, Rose' – and the gypsies hurry across to the left with the cart. I imagine Rose will come back after. The gypsies get away – I muse on the fact that all the same I have noted the event – yet I have no intention of getting Rose into trouble. I wander on towards the right, down a road on the right side of which is a dirty greenish shallow ditch of water, pretty wide. I want to shovel stones into it to make it dry. I find that the shallow water is really only covering granite stones already.

B. A performance of a show is going on downstairs somewhere – Margaret Barr's group *[a professional opera producer who worked with my amateur operatic groups]*. I am included. I go downstairs to find a costume – for I have on some fancy-dress style of costume which is for the very end of the play, but have to appear between now and the final act in some costume I have not yet been given. The one I have on is, as it were, premature yet I think it can be managed somehow. When I get downstairs and on the stage level I am told that it is Meg Masters (Wilf's girlfriend) who has charge of these particular costumes – everything has been given out, it appears, except there is a large yellow silky piece of cloth somewhere which might of course be mine.

Meg has gone up to her room to rest but it is time for the final act. I decide I shall have to go up and find out from her, though it worries me very much, as I had firmly decided not to go to her so soon etc. since Wilf's taking up with her and my retirement into myself. However, there is nothing for it. Wilf is away somewhere else. Mr Morris [unknown] shows me the way. We go out to the right on to the bus road where buses run to the timetable down to the town (seaside?) – We then turn right again and begin to climb up the hillside towards the level where the funny old-fashioned railway runs in its own time to the town. I remark that this must result in two different sections of the village. Those who live on the dot and go by bus, and those who live according to chance and go by train. When we reach the railway level there are a lot of people waiting for the train and we turn left and walk through them – it is now very high up and I remember how Wilf told me they lived high up and catch a wonderful view.

It is the nose of a very steep promontory in a narrow gorge, far down in which is a great river, very fast. I admire the grandeur of the outlook with a certain envy and jealousy, but it is so high that I have slight mountain sickness. I decide I would not live here if I could. Then we turn right towards a village school. I remember this accords with Wilf's descriptions. It is a question of opening the door unobserved.

Mr Morris puts his hand through the bars and turns an inside key – I notice a boy and his mother approaching – but really the door is unlocked and opens of itself – we go in and I think the boy and the mother will follow. We go to the right to a narrowish staircase up the side of the wall – half-way up is a right-angled turn to the left. Meg is not resting, because we heard some visitor taking leave. We stand a moment on the stairs.

Mr Morris ascends and I stand longer at the turn, where it is slightly wider. It is a woman (like Sheila) [Larema Ayerst's sister] who knows me, descending, and with a dog. Now I shall be recognised and what will Meg think? When the girl reaches me I lift my head, which I have held down deliberately – she says: 'Why how you are becoming handsomer and handsomer.' I realise that the fancy dress, some sort of hussar-like costume, is becoming to me. I follow Mr Morris now up into the room and then turn right. It is very small and a square table practically fills it. Meg appears as a middle-aged motherly woman (not Meg at all, but a Mrs Povey). I am surprised somehow that she needs the relationship with a young fellow like Wilf. I am a little embarrassed because she says something in which the words 'physical reactions' are audible. I look under my eyelids to the left to where there is a little bed – it appears too small for them to share. I wonder if there is another room further upstairs, or if this is where Wilf sleeps when they sleep apart.

I am a little ashamed at myself. Also I am not sure that I am not playing a part and trying to be more subdued and heart-broken about the affair than is really true. There is a woman on my left, too, with a great blue dog in her lap. I look intensely at the animal, which begins to growl, and his face becomes that of a bulldog. The two women think nothing of it, but remark that earlier on it would have flown at me – now it is quite safe. (Before this I had noticed that Mr Morris was about to eat two large sausages on a plate, and that to my surprise I had nearly finished consuming two cold ones). I am suddenly a trifle weak-kneed and tell them to keep the dog in hand as I am not quite myself and am likely to disturb it. It is a moment of self-pity.

A spiral-sort of path up the hill.

The room in the school: the room had a window facing me, behind Mr Morris, through which I could see a lovely peaceful farming countryside, the very opposite to the river and the gorge.

[*This question of costume is the fancy dress (fantasy, unconscious, distressing*

*to the conscious attitude) the ego is learning to wear – but it is 'premature' –
there is something still to be dealt with – this is in the hands of the anima – so
the intellectual conscious function leads the ego up towards a confrontation with
the problem. And it is the upper level of the village that is travelled by
'chance', by fate, instinct, the unconscious. It appears as though a reversal of
values has happened. The ego finds these dazzling heights enviable but sick-
making. The door into the school of the problem is not really locked, there is no
real censor, once the intellectual function is asked to open the door and turn the
key from the inside. The problem narrows and becomes more personal. The
conscious function continues to ascend. The ego wants to hang its head and
hang back half-way up on the turn, where it is polite to await the downcoming
anima figure. It is then assured that the fancy dress is 'becoming' – the process is
going forward – so the ego goes up into the final narrowing of the personal
problem. The anima is not a young girl of 17 but a motherly woman of 45 – a
friendly and kind mother-anima. From this room the view is not a terrifying
one and too grand and 'collective' to be lived with, but that of a peaceful, fertile
countryside.*

*The ego is unable to accept easily the amoral connection between Wilf (the
ego himself) and his older woman. Hence the doubt if there is not another room
further up yet, with a double-bed, the bed of union. The conscious function
shares the proper expected behaviour: to eat the hot sausages (possible
association with heterosexuality?) The ego wants to pretend to be heart-
broken and jealous, etc. – but has already nearly eaten the cold sausages (assn
with homosexuality?) The two pairs of sausages refer to the Zweideutigkeit
of the symbol – the sausages associate to penises, the [number of sausages],
two, is however feminine (hot and cold, etc – problem of opposites). It appears
as if the ego falsely tries to arouse the dog (the animal instincts, functions) – but
the wise mother-anima knows that the dog has already been trained.]*

My confidence in the value of the dream therapy quickly grew. I
began to feel free to interpret the dreams using the widest range of
references. The wonderful mandalas in *The Secret of the Golden Flower*
(by Jung and Richard Wilhelm) became embedded in my mind, and I
found Jung's studies of them in *Psychology and Alchemy* and *The
Integration of the Personality* absorbing. Phyl had introduced me to the
translator of Chinese poetry, Arthur Waley, and his mistress Beryl de
Zoete (who gave me her book on Balinese dance). Waley gave me his
copy of Richard Wilhelm's translation of the I Ching, but was very
dismissive of it all: he said it was mainly a collection of folk- sayings,
just like, 'Red skies at night, shepherd's delight'. (I met Waley off and

on over the years; the last time I saw him was at a performance of Beckett's *Endgame* in the Royal Court Theatre.) The I Ching suggested various possibilities, at that time, for the masque that was finally to become *The Midsummer Marriage*. I found, much later, in discussion with a scientist friend about *The Mask of Time* text, that certain concepts in the I Ching corresponded with the latest notions in molecular biology; and in this last big work for the concert hall I made more than one significant reference to it. The point was that I was always intrigued as to where poets and other artists obtained their metaphors. Prompted by Eliot's *The Waste Land*, for instance, I obtained a set of Tarot cards:

> Madame Sosostris, famous clairvoyante,
> Had a bad cold, nevertheless
> Is known to be the wisest woman in Europe,
> With a wicked pack of cards. Here, said she,
> Is your card, the drowned Phoenician Sailor,
> (Those are pearls that were his eyes. Look!)

Both the dreams and the interpretations that follow draw upon all this experience.

Sunday night, 5 March

Having to descend cliffs to the sea. The way down to the right is too precipitous, but I found a possible way round behind to the left, and manage to get my mother down as well, to the surprise of some other people. The seashore is hot mud, with thousands of horse-flies basking in the mud. Will they begin to sting us?

Mr and Mrs Morris [invented] and I catch a bus. In the crowd and rush when the buses arrive I do not see very clearly which bus they get on ahead of me. The one I get on goes off first and I realise it's the wrong one. It is a No. 2. I should be on a No. 9. I must get off at the first possible stop and hope that the Morrisses will not have gone back for me. When I get off it is in the country and the road straight onwards, which the No. 2 bus is to take, seems too small to be a real bus route – the 9 has to take one to the left, at the crossroads, to which I walk back. There is a dip in the road along which we have presumably just travelled and up which I hope to see the 9 bus coming. I see instead a woman figure with a '9' placard on her head and behind her a man. It is the Morrises. She cries out at the sight of me that I am a ghost, a revenant – but I shout to her that I am quite real.

[In the Tarot card pack the 2 is 'La Papesse' – the secret polarity – the woman emanation following on the man – the striving in two directions after the spring is only one. The 9 is 'L'Ermite'. The lantern of consciousness in the middle of the eight heavenly directions.

The consciousness is at first 'alone', 'hermit-like'. This would seem to concur with the '9' placard on the head. A placard shaped exactly like a playing-card. It would seem like an indication that the ego cannot rush ahead on the '2' bus – the female polarity, but must continue to develop the lantern in the middle of the eight directions.]

Saturday night, 11 March

A. The garden outside my window again. The ditch or drain which should run down the right-hand side of the square had broken bounds and is running along the top of the square (parallel) to the house and window and so swiftly that I notice it has washed away a lot of the bed of flowers, with a sea of bulbs (?), so that at the left end of the line the row of plants has fallen into the water and crumbled away. I go out to see what is really happening. Go inside the square and see how the water is flowing thus because I fancy it can't get away properly down the very hard side ditch and I go to the bottom right-hand corner to see – and find a swirl of dirty water and sewage (?). There is a schoolmaster, oldish man there (known) (assn: Major Payne, *[the headmaster]* Irving's partner at Hazelwood) who says that it must be dealt with by the sanitary people. I say that it costs an awful lot. That I only got the house drainage (at the top left-hand corner) done at all through my friendliness to the sanitary people. *[This was an exaggeration in the dream – and not actual in real life].* The idea being that I could with patience get round the sanitary people again to do something cheap, but that I couldn't afford immediate payment of women, etc.

B. At the childhood preparatory school – in the big classroom. A sort of informal concert being given at one end by Oxted musical amateurs. Some music is played and conducted by ? – then it becomes my job apparently to conduct the final item. Some woman tells me not to expect too much as there are only seven real players, one being a virtual passenger (making, I think, eight in all). I go to where the small group of instrumentalists is getting ready round a grand piano. There is no baton except a very heavy and ugly one used by a previous conductor (a woman, I think). Someone gives me a slightly better one (i.e. thinner and longer), and a man takes the ugly one away, because it appears in the dream to belong to him and at the same time he seems to understand its unsuitability and unaesthetic-ness. I am just about to start conducting when Miss Douthwaite [a local rather good-looking professional singer] comes across from the left carrying a beautifully made baton in her hand. I hope at first that she is going to play and hand me the baton. But no: she indicates with a smile that she is going to conduct. I go away as she starts singing strongly. I go out of the hall and decide to go home – partly pleased to be through with it all, partly uncertain as to what I really want. I go upstairs to find my overcoat.

[The garden outside the window is the mandala symbol, this time ringed round by water – because the new path of the ditch in the dream completes the square, more or less, as the garden actually is – there being a ditch on either side running down the slope and a stream along the bottom. I am almost certain that the dirty sewage water is really the life-giving drink in its 'vile' disguise, as by a curious coincidence this morning, Sunday, 12 March, I have just read the parabola at the beginning of Silberer's book on Mystical Symbolism, *where the Wanderer has to get into a square garden and where the black, swirling water under the mill-wheels becomes the life-giving drink to the regenerated 'prince'. I can't see what the schoolmaster is, or rather who has the rights of the discussion. But I am inclined to believe that the ego ought to 'pay up', whatever that may mean. The 'final piece' in the programme is a constantly recurring image. Like the eighth player who is a passenger, 'passenger' has from childhood schooldays, at the very same prep. school, had a derogatory sense, associated with football, but even at that age my subtle mind saw that the word might also mean 'one who passes the ball' and so lose its derogation. The last piece is really in the hands of the anima – a somewhat resplendent one – and who has the beautiful baton. Are the batons sexual symbols? Partly, in all probability. Really it looks as if the ego ought to have brought its own baton and that this is the constant trouble with the last piece. And somehow the ego's own baton is really there all the time in the unacceptable unaesthetic form (B. is the personal form of A.)*

Miss Douthwaite's Christian name is 'Blanche', also the daughter of a chemist (alchemy; hermetic art). Silberer [in Problems of Mysticism and its Symbolism] *has the following: 'And there went by the rose garden the most beautiful maiden arrayed in white satin with the most stately youth who was in scarlet . . . "This, my dearest bridegroom," said she "has helped me over and we are now going out of this lovely garden into our chamber to enjoy the pleasures of love".' And further: 'The garden is . . . one of the oldest and most indubitable symbols for the female body.' (The Mother) standing in the*

*garden, is to be in the regenerating womb again. 'In the symbolism of dreams
and of myths the hat is usually the phallus.' In August 1937 there was a dream
of a young boy taboo because of the homosexual censorship who asked me 'have
I a hat?', and I produced one on a string, magically from behind him. There
was a dream about being carried magically backwards by the 'homosexual
poets' i.e. Auden and his circle to the round table under the tree and the
woman. Union with the boy is necessary – even to make him 'come' (to become
the new youth) or to penetrate the 'behind' (to get through the homosexual
phase towards the goal behind) – the incest problem – Mother rebirth – against
the Father. 'That the masturbatory period precedes the subsequent garden
episode can be understood if we realize that the masturbation phantasy
animates or predetermines the immediately following incest' (Silberer):
'. . . the wanderer put this aside' – so at the present I find masturbation has
ceased. The rebirth takes place ('Inter faecem et urinam nascimur' in the black
waters of death and life – Silberer gives the following: 'Mucus = blood = pus
= urine = stinks = semen = milk = sweat = tears = spit = air = breath =
speech = money = poison.' Cf. the mucus from Wilf's nose – joining of nose
(breath) to mucus and through Wilf image to semen consumed and mother's
milk, etc. etc.*

*'In the concept the seed corn has the same value as the spermatozoon. The
man is the miller, the woman the mill'? (Ibid.) Cf. the initial dream of the
rucksack of grain. Also the dreams about bread- rolls. 'The newborn, milled
grain.'*

*As the last writing was finished I found myself humming a phrase from the
duet of* Robin Hood; *I then looked up the words:*

She: When cockle shells turn silver bells
And mussels grow on every tree:
When ice and snow turn fire to burn;
Then will my heart be turned from thee.

He: When men and moon come tumbling down
And waters flow into the sky,
When lilies grow within the sea
Then will my love grow cold and die.

*Also the question of the batons – if the sexual symbolism is accepted the old
baton is the father's (the schoolmaster) and the new one the regenerated phallus
in the anima's possession. (Isis and the wooden phallus.) Also the
schoolmaster figure in the garden dream is a father symbol in antagonism to the
ego, who must displace the father and reach the mother.*

Naturally the father wants to call the 'authorities' (sanitary, moral etc). and make the ego pay money – lose power etc. The authorities cannnot be cajoled – must be fought.]

Sunday night, 12 March

The childhood orchard. Wilf is making a new flower-bed on one side and I am surprised that he has dug up a whole quantity of the orchard all the way round. I can't imagine how we shall be able to find time to keep it weeded. I am helping Wilf to level off a path or road, i.e. take off about a foot of the top surface. It is very hard and strong – one end is like a sudden drop down, so that when I try to level off the top surface all I really succeed in doing is to dig away his end so that it all falls into the dip – like digging at the top of a cliff. I don't know whether I am doing the right thing.

I have been to choose four different corn grains from somewhere – and I have them in a square receptacle, planted in four sections. They are growing up very well and bearing grain, the problem is whether they can support the winter and become self-productive – perennial in my garden. Some expert asks where I got one of the four. I tell him I chose them at random – he says that this grain is rare and not indigenous to this locality and will be difficult to rear.

A sort of cottage of dwelling place (bungalow) where four of us are sleeping – at first, it appears, in separate beds – and not, as far as I can remember, in any order. I go into a little room where I piss against some sort of drain – then into the bathroom – Betty Gates (aged 16–17) is there doing the beds. There is a biggish one for me and beside it a camp-bed for my wife(?) – I wonder at my having the bigger bed and she having to sleep on the camp-bed when we were not together – but I am not certain if we ever sleep together. I turn on a cold bath; I get undressed down to pants and vest. I have been unwell and in bed – perhaps it was really flu. I think a hot bath would be nicer; I let the cold water run out – it takes a long time. Betty speaks of someone who has an electric boiler – but she agrees that our coal boiler is really much better for my needs etc. – as the water has to come a long distance to the bath – this is what gives one the idea of the hotel bath. I think I might catch cold in the bedclothes, though I feel very warm, and then see I have still a pullover on the top half. Then I feel the water in the bath that is so long running out and find it warmish, but see that I seem to have forgotten to turn off the cold tap – very mysterious – I am in another room, making up my(?) bed – there is a slight shortage of blankets – if only we slept in pairs (I think, boy-girl, boy-girl).

[The childhood's orchard is a clear rebirth symbol. The Wilf image is doing the cultivation – the problem is to make a balance between grass-orchard and flower-beds. Wilf is also making the road, but the ego is muddled by it, doesn't know the right level.

The four corn-grains in the square is the mandala with a lot of rich associations – it is a much completer form than the orchard. The corn being rooted and growing etc. But the wise man (alter Weise: Jung) knows that one of the four is not indigenous to the locality – (contaminated by the unconscious).

The scenes in the bungalow are the personalising of the comic grain symbols. Here are the ego's personal problems – marriage etc. Bath is rebirth. Washing etc – after illness (introversion). The hot water choice is good – but the fear of catching cold puts on an extra bit of top clothing and leaves the cold tap on – also because of impatience at the slowness of the cold water running away. (Impatience at the disappearance of all the Wilf-homosexual transference etc).

Probably Betty Gates (note the surname!) is a substitute in the dream for the 'wife', so as to be permissible to the old homosexual mask. This appears all the more plausible that in reality Betty Gates is Betty Barnes (an illegitimate child of a man Barnes by a woman subsequently married to a man Gates). The long distance of the hot-water pipe to the bathroom seems to indicate the considerable personal difficulties intervening. An electric (modern new, exciting, dangerous, etc.) water heater is only possible when the distance has been reduced and Betty Gates can appear in her own right – as the anima, wife, mother, etc. etc. Feat of catching cold during the waiting for the new (hot) bath results in a lack of balance in the clothing – the top half becomes accentuated, as it were. It is possibly the lower half that needs really to be warmed up. (Academical 'cooking' – in the bath, 'philosopher's egg', etc).

The seven years with Wilf has not been merely a 'waste of time', but also a ploughing of the ground preparatory to growth (Wilf image digging up the orchard). At the same time the digging into the Wilf image etc. is a ploughing of the ground for growth, etc. Also a levelling of the road.]

Wednesday night, 15 March, London

An examination of a screen performance of something of mine for publication, e.g. that I had appeared in a film somewhere of my own work. This was to be re-shown. There was a young fellow who was the 'publisher' and producer. Also an assistant of his. The screen itself was on the left of the room and from its base was an inclined plane down to the floor – the following is a side elevation.

When the important moment approached the assistant rushed up the inclined plane and as it were dragged something out of the screen, while the 'producer' did a wonderful dance rather like the Blake drawing of Elihu in Job. Then the assistant slid down the plane in a sort of osier basket, remarking in an American voice with regard to the producer's dancing that he must do something (I can't remember what) with his 'Hoboken'. Then the whole thing had to be done again with my making the assistants remark in an American accent as if playing a part. I was a little dubious of my doing it well, but I was very keen to have a shot and the whole atmosphere was very jolly and I was in constant laughter at the antics of these two.

[Elihu's was the dance of youth and beauty – 'I am young and ye are very old' – a sort of premonition of the new man to Job. 'Hoboken' is a district in New York, and associated in my mind therefore with the Negroes. The osier basket was somewhat like a cradle, or even an association to Moses' childhood and discovery by Pharaoh's daughter. American accent might mean extraversion – examination for a fresh period of publication, or turning outwards again from introversion.

This is possibly also the very fantastic boy player who tended to get too 'self-conscious' – is this a warning of too much introversion in fantasy? Perhaps the ego was really right to skip to the end of the play and so finish rehearsal; and be ready for 'the show'. Further dreams should clarify this; also the crises events (Hitler marching into Prague) may dominate the fantasy life for the time being, exclude preoccupation with it by outside necessity.

To show the film on the screen is to examine the past by the light of intellect, intuition, etc. The screen is on a higher level. The producer or examiner or publisher is on the ground level in the darkened room. The assistant slides down in the 'cradle' from the screen level towards the floor, having 'torn' something out of the screen. Perhaps the problem is to turn the ego from observer into 'actor' – to come to complete grips with the process which might be bearing towards some point of fulfilment.]

Friday, 17 March

A. Question of using choruses from Eliot's 'The Rock' in my new oratorio – (Possible figure of a woman playing on a big organ – but details have gone out of memory.) A girl composer brought a review copy of one volume of *Grove's Dictionary of Music*. This was to be sold at 4/-. I bought it, thinking that though it was heavy to take home, alone with the two big books in my case already, it was too much of a good chance to miss. Also the *Grove* editors ought to send me the volume containing my own name, thus I would have two.

Early morning dream:

In my own room – a lot of visitors – first of all, mostly men (the composer) Alan Rawsthorne (another contemporary of mine at the Royal College of Music) and some friend of his. I am glad to see so many (there were five or six in all, perhaps) but a little uncertain how I am to feed them all. At first I am at the back of the room away from the fireplace. Alan Rawsthorne is discussing the exposition of one of his own works. I put forward an explanation that between the first and the second themes there must be a bridge passage, which really lifted the music into a higher level and showed what I meant by a gesture. Alan Rawsthorne asked me if I have learnt to do this – I said I had. He said that was wonderful – the music then really grew into its next phase, instead of a scheme being imposed on it by the composer from outside. I thought for a moment of showing them my new string concerto in which it had happened, but decided I could not play it adequately on the piano.

[The dream on waking seemed definitely reassuring – as against the external political situation.

I think 'The Rock' is an association to the necessity for reaching rock bottom. The new oratorio [A Child of Our Time] is the opus – the synthesis – Grove's Dictionary is the same thing, probably. It is thought of in four vols. It might seem as if the ego has one in its own right and now tugs another from the unconscious. The dream in my own room seems to suggest that the ego is glad underneath to be giving hospitality to lots of its components. Rawsthorne is the persona Shadow. The ego seems to be taking the right lead with regard to the Shadow and the Shadow willingly assents. But the ego isn't ready to demonstrate its newly won 'artistic' power in public.]

Sunday night, 19 March

A. Myself and an older companion playing on double-basses. His is the larger, but two of its strings are broken. (A similar idea but in other symbols recurred during the night, but has been forgotten.)

On a sort of launch or boat, which for some reason needs to be kept in a certain position in the stream of the river while the 'driver' goes back for something. I take over the motor with some trepidation but also pleasure; I have to drive the motor just enough to keep the boat from drifting downstream. There is no anchor possible. But there is difficulty about reaching some gearing or mechanism of the shaft down in the water, or bottom of the boat, and I get into a certain amount of difficulties.

Then the boat becomes a dredger and the mechanism begins to heave up buckets of riverbed slime. I can't hold them back waiting for the return of the 'driver', so the boat threatens to get over-full of the dredgings.

In some sort of country open-air school – Have eaten an apple and just begun another. The headmaster calls for a restart of the morning's work but is most apologetic when he sees I haven't finished the second apple – he is anxious I should have proper time to finish it. But I indicate that I will catch the others up, as it were, so they all go off to the left and I walk down to the right finishing the apple and running a sharp cutting hoe through the right side of the path through the turf. I think this has some possible use. Then I come to where the headmaster and the others are throwing hay across the wall from a wagon. I help.

The head has a forkful of hay, does a complete circle and throws it over his head, it falls on the road. I help it over on the further side. 'Not across the road,' shouts the head. But I indicate it is so – then he realises that he has got giddy from the circle he turned.

I and another are play-acting at being asleep(?) during an elaborate three-day (?) dance of the school. It is really a mimetic dance in ?*Kinder* fashion. I feel that actually this unusual sort of school performance will be very original – it is under the guidance of Margaret Barr. It seems that we shall have to remain lying down (asleep?) for a whole day perhaps. We have gone off up-country: in the end we come to a barn and a farm where someone suggests that I might take a wonderful jump out of a barn window. Then we go back.

B. (*waking dream*). The second verse of a children's song – one child has the verse and all the others the chorus, down on their hands and knees and with heads on the ground – 'asleep' or make-believe dead. But the entry of their voices at the second verse is very bad. An observer makes me worried about it and I try to stop them to go back. But I can't – so I decide to give into them and go ahead – then they do stop and decide the time has come for a break, and go off. I want to find out why the older girl is not singing the verse, but a younger one, not so good.

There is Wilf in bed. I sit on the bed and put my head on his breast and he seems not to mind. I even put my arms round him. I speculate how curious it is to feel so much natural pleasure which is really taboo and whether this experience with Wilf will make all future emotional experiences self-conscious and impossible. By accident our lips touch, as in a kiss. Wilf draws back as if shot. I put my hand on his mouth as if to wipe out the accident, and say in a bantering tone – 'You will die of that' – I feel the reaction is a bit exaggerated.

[The boat that has to be kept stationary on the stream without an anchor is a typical symbol of the two-way libido. The mechanism is not perfect yet – there is further 'dredging' to do. It seems possible that the 'older' double-bass must give way completely before the younger. That perhaps all its strings should be broken. That disbelief really must 'die' from the kiss. The 'second verse' and the 'second apple' (of knowledge) seem symbols of the same idea. Is a second lap starting or is the starting of a second lap false and unnecessary? Further dreams will clear this up.

Another possibility is that the 'second' thing is simply the beginning of the new – the 'new' relationship, the 'young' double-bass, etc. Perhaps the children's bad start in the second verse is not a serious matter at all, but only considered so by the watching censor. Is it too that the 'work' is really to begin again after the 'break', and the ego is still eating apples, instead of being ready for some action?]

Monday night, 3 April

A. A sexual dream with [Aubrey Russ's friend] Neville New. There are two beds, but I wish to leave mine to go into Neville's. I am in a state of great sexual excitement. I think in the dream that I have already had one orgasm. There are obstacles to the fulfilment of the desire – and sometimes I am on the point of deciding that it is not meant to happen – but eventually the obstacles are overcome and we are together. I am on top of Neville, who is on his back. I feel we have no need of the pyjamas we are both wearing. I undo his pyjama jacket and delight in passing my hand over the naked flesh – but the excitement is such that I reach the full orgasm, and awake.

B. Watching the old childhood's house in the early morning – the east side from the yard. I am surprised that all the windows are shut up, none of them sleep with wide-open windows as I do – only [Larema Ayerst's brother] Bryan [Fisher] (in my father's dressing-room, where I slept as a child) has a top section of the window open. All the other windows are tight closed and look very dark and blue-black in the half-light.

C. Getting up in the morning. Having to piss in a chamber-pot. Arguing with myself about my future. [The head master at Hazelwood school] Irving (imagined in the dream as somewhere offstage) states that my school period will not end till the summer.

[In the sexual dream it seems as though the obstacles should really be overcome, that the contact is necessary, psychically. This is backed up by the choice of images – Neville New. It is the new self. The equivocation on sex arises from the male figure taking the female posture on the female bed. In real life Neville New is a much depreciated figure. Perhaps once again the 'new' comes from the despised old.

The dead house seems like The Family Reunion – *only the young fellow (really the ego) in the father's dressing-room has the top section (like the pyjama-top the ego undoes) open to the east, the new!*

It would appear that analysis must go until the summer. Nine months.]

Wednesday night, 12 April

Going to see Kennington one evening – when I got off the train, decided to go direct up the back way and out into the studio from the lane at the back – this lane is like the backs of houses in London and the North, where the old sanitary tins used to be collected. The little doors in the wall towards the houses and the street side (right) were much like such sanitary doors. I had some difficulty in being certain of which house it was, but 'No. 16' was marked in chalk on a very small door – trap-door size – and except for some moments of doubt – ask which exact door the '16' referred to.

I eventually got it more or less open and could look down into Kennington's studio – nearly heaving over some obstruction as I did. Kennington at once called for his daughter (?) to go round and fetch me in. I had arrived, I think, just on time for the appointment. (Nothing of the dream pictures at all like Kennington's real house.)

Somewhere upstairs. I have sent a lot of children from one of the choirs off to bed (?); when I come back into the room there are some of the older, difficult ones from Malden. I wonder whether to begin to deal with them and pack them off (with great uproar, of course!) in fairness to the others.

Some girl child has made some soup and it is ready – we sit down to table but are not sure to begin or not – waiting for someone from downstairs?

All the kids go down – I delay upstairs to pee.

A scene in shop with my mother in some strange town. It is a question of buying something in this shop and taking it to eat in a shop to the left or right, or buying in one of these shops and bringing to eat here. But my mother goes into great particularity about the cleanliness of various green salads for sale, and thereby makes me a little embarrassed.

[These dreams of children's choirs are symbols of the ego's efforts to bring the autonomous amoral elements under control, or into some possible scheme of life. The ego is still too hard-bitten a moralist to have come to final terms with the anima manifestations. The moral problem leads back at once to the mother – (the dirty lettuce, etc).

Kennington and Owen, the dead poet and this living brother artist must be figures I think for the 'Alte Weise' (wise old man) archetype in some degree. In the earlier dreams Kennington is still a foster-father figure. Perhaps it is gradually clearing itself up.]

Tuesday night, 2 May

Some questions of my father having really been in love with one of my aunts, his sister – then in the dream this seems to get 'censored' into his cousin (?) – the idea was of a physical relation. [On waking in a half-dream state the idea of incest came to mind – association to reading, during the evening before, Jung's Psychology of the Unconscious].

With my father (?) in some foreign land in the sunshine – there was 'over there' a beautiful palace, four-square and with lighted windows – and guarding it, or assulting it, were two kinds of soldiers in beautiful red uniforms – some were native soldiers, others 'British' (?) with uniforms as from the last century. I discussed with my companion which sort were 'ours' – I thought them both very handsome and aesthetic. But then the fighting began. The 'British' gathered together on the right and the natives on the left in front of the palace – they levelled the bayoneted rifles at each other. I was distressed to see how little cover they took – also one man on the British side simply turned his back, stuck his bayoneted rifle into the ground and was pulling it over like a train lever. Meanwhile we began to circle round to get behind the British – (anticlockwise movement).

I was a trifle scared at the firing and amused at having to get behind 'our' lines. When we got there it was all over and the question was now of looking after the wounded – my father talked to an army doctor. I looked at one of the wounded more closely – he appeared to have some of his left breast shot off and forming apparently the head of a small baby – it was too revolting to look at closer.

I am with Mr Bingham (in real life my employer through the Co-op Education Dept) transformed into a doctor. I have some scratches on my right knee and thigh. He says, without looking at them, that he has been told that they are like a purple line – that they will never heal unless opened deliberately and made to bleed. I do not entertain this idea. He then examines them. They seem to me nothing at all. I can't see the necessity of the surgery. He has a pair of scissors in his hands and makes a movement to cut into the thigh, just above the knee, with one prong of the scissors. I resist and refuse – in any case I feel it ought to be a sharp scalpel – but then perhaps of course it will be so sharp it will go too deep. He gives up the scissors and I wonder what he will do – he takes some cotton wool and with some liquid starts to bathe my forehead – is there a scratch there too then? Then he extends his hand over my closed eyes and down to the mouth. I feel the liquid nestling cold against my cold lips. I realise he is giving me an anaesthetic and that therefore it really is vital that the leg should be cut and that now I shall go under. I begin to study the effects as I lose consciousness. [Wake].

Some scene of climbing up a staircase to a flat to see if Fresca is back. At the door is a strange woman who says she is out and that it is midday. I am still in pyjamas and feel ashamed at being up so late in the morning.

[The impressive dream is the one with the doctor. The ego resists being cut in the leg and has to be 'put under', to 'lose consciousness'. It really is a vital matter after all. The previous dream battle is a symbol of the struggle between conscious and unconscious: the ego trying to get shelter behind the conscious collective uniformity – but as in a similar dream annotated by Jung, the uniform is an old-fashioned one – it is out of date for the new situation. Perhaps the soldier on his back with his left breast torn into a child's head is a grim symbol of the rebirth.

The moral question is still the balking one. In the dream the ego thinks it can heal itself. But the problem of the necessary imperfection still remains unsynthesised. 'Das Leben bart zu seiner Vollendung nicht der Volkommenheit, *sondern der* Vollständigkeit, *Dazu gehört der 'Pfahl im Fleisch', das Einleiden der Mangelhaftigkeit, ohne die es kein Vorwärts und kein Aufwärts gibt'* [*When at the end of life and looking back, this is not perfection but completeness. This brings along with it a thorn in the flesh, the presupposition of imperfection; without it there is no forwards or upwards.*] (*Jung*). It is not enough to comprehend this paradox in the intellect: it is the actual experience and satisfaction in it which is difficult. At present the conscious holds rigidly to the single truth of perfection – hence the continued struggle. The unsurgical scissors are a good symbolisation of the Pfahl im Fleisch!'!)

Sunday night, 7 May

Reading out of a pamphlet book to a few people. Came to the chapter headed 'Homosexuality'. Evelyn Maude who was facing me (we were all seated), indicated me to pass on and not read this chapter. She mutely appealed to the other listeners. I realised I was the only person to whom it had any significant interest but was reluctant not to read it. Evelyn came round to make it quite clear and placed her hand firmly and affectionately on my shoulder like a good mother. I turned over on to the next chapter (title forgotten): this was illustrated with pictures, which I described to everyone in great detail – but the print was partly of a sort of James Joycean German and almost gibberish. I read it all as best I could, a shade resentful.

[*It would seem that the mother anima makes it quite clear that the homosexual chapter is closed, or at any rate it has no general significance, but only personal.*]

Tuesday night, 9 May

The war. In a sort of barrack shed. 'Our' side (British) go out to the fray. I remain standing by the hut door watching for the (German) spies or hidden batch of the other side who come out into sight, reaching the hut as our lot go out of sight. They pass over to their right and my left. I notice that some of the young men are being impersonated by girls. It is a film. 'Our' lot come back and the Germans go in again. Then 'our' lot go off anew and the Germans have a brainwave, to attack a building over on their left and my right, which is left unguarded. (I wonder by the way what they will take me for when they notice me. I decide 'the journalist'.) They go off to the attack.

The building is not a building but a huge table-box, with a stone

103

slab on the top (association to the Tibetan story of the bodies left to die and putrefy in such a box). I manage by accident to learn the trick of setting this upper stone slab as a swivel. It swings round, to and fro, alternately squashing and elongating some sort of special glue-like mortar. The idea is to get as much of an opening into the hollow table as possible. (There is some notion of the relation between covered and uncovered hollowness to be that of Trotskyism and the reverse.)

Suddenly I find I have swung the whole slab off to the side. When it is to be closed up again there is to be an inner top fastened down or built solid of concrete or mortar and then the slab swung back into position. Somebody or something is to be secretly immured (association to Mithra Heddernheim picture given in *Psychology of the Unconscious.'*)

Two beds. David Ayerst alone in one. [The poet] Norman, myself and Wilf in the other – both single beds. I have my back to Norman and face Wilf, who has his head and hands on my chest – like a child. He decides suddenly to go to his own bed. Norman agrees that to separate gives more chance to rest. As I go by David in his bed alone, I think that only wives are 'allowed' to share beds. My bed is somewhere close to the hollow slab.

[The Mithra association gives the hollow slab to be the death or rebirth in the mother. There are virtually four beds and four males. Actually in real life Wilf has his girl, and both Norman and David are married. The ego goes to the 'Mother'.

PS: In the dream I remarked about the young soldiers impersonated by girls. Wilf said that they were the film beginners. Had never been in a film before.

In the Tibetan story, the decomposed bodies of men became the drink of immortality. Hence a further rebirth connotation to the hollow slab, but also a horrible one.]

Sunday night, 14 May

(After laying down the Jungian law to Wilf and his girl)

John Layard and his wife [Doris] and Fresca and I. Doris and I facing each other – John on my left, Fresca on my right. Doris asks me what dreams I am having. I say they are about the head separated from the body and the head only is to be illuminated (?). She says this is quite wrong: that she has taken to being an analyst lately and finds it very interesting – she can say definitely that the body must be dealt with (?) as well.

[This represents some definite compensation for a certain inflation and superiority in my behaviour to Wilf's Meg. I have tended to depreciate an artist's relations to a woman. Thus, by implication, Wilf's to Meg. The anima-mother image as a woman analyst administers correction and advice.]

Monday night, 15 May (Nightmare)

At night in the country. To the south of the cottages here, but with the topography of the childhood's home. The end of a lane, leading out into the open, facing back to the houses. I leave a table (?) in the lane. I have got to go and see to something back near the cottages. I grope for the little electric torch. I find a much fatter one. At first its light is very feeble against the dark and damp mist. I have difficulty in finding the cottages. I am too far to the right (east). I find first mine (the middle one) then the double one on its left. I pass between them. My mother appears in a shadowy way and asks what the trouble is. She agrees I must go further to the bottom of the garden to see what it is. I must not wake my father. She will see after him. I begin to go further down towards the bottom of the garden. The feeling of nightmare arises. I am not, however, really frightened to do what I've got to do. There is a light suddenly down at the bottom. Also a sense of an explosion or noise, and of a big building like a school where the houses were – just behind me – also of lights in the building. Mrs Henderson's voice comes very sharply from the bottom of the garden: 'Is that you, Michael? Are you the cause of all this affair?' 'What affair?' I ask. 'There is someone on the roof – just above Gander's room.' At the name Gander I feel the full force of the nightmare. There is some terrible responsibility or connection with the figure on the roof above Gander's room which I am evading.

[Wake as the dawn is coming, in great anxiety. Have a disinclination to go into my work room and, say, write the dream down at my table. Perhaps this is the table in the lane end. The torch is a libido phallic symbol and associates in my mind with Wilf and my behaviour to him – my doubts if I ought not to try and come close to him again. It seems that the phallic light shows the way to the real mother and then behind that again to the 'terrible mother' and the nightmare. Does 'Gander' refer to the nursery rhyme and so to libido – perhaps incest etc. that has got loose again – out on the tiles? Or is the responsibility to take stock of the sexual-sociological demands? The momentary inclination to return towards Wilf may have provided the 'terrible mother' image – the repressive longing that must be overcome for adaptation.

105

Goosey, goosey, gander, whither shall I wander
Upstairs and downstairs and in my lady's chamber.
There I met an old man who would not say his prayers
I took him by the left leg and threw him down the stairs.

The old man is presumably the old sun.]

Tuesday night, 23 May

At the back of this cottage unexpectedly – startled to notice someone in my bedroom through the window at the back. Looking more closely, I see it is Florrie putting away clean clothes. [*Wake*].

Upstairs in the Co-op Education Dept office I am handling, just inside the door on the right, up against a window, a typewriter which I every now and then make ring or do some movement by accidentally touching a switch with my elbow. The chief girl secretary asks by glance if I want to talk to her in the inner office. I am quite *persona grata* but this is not what I am waiting for.

Later I am sitting on a seat to the left of the door and further in, talking to the Education Secretary himself (or herself?). A little tiny boy comes in – he is very white and nervous and I put my arm round him to make him feel more 'at home' and to ask what he wants – he is so small that it is surprising to see him about by himself. He says something about 'Ilka Moore'. I ask him, he [*?sings*] 'Ilka Moor'baht 'at' – I say that was the usual thing up in the North – perhaps, though he really comes from the North and is not a real Londoner. I feel a great affection for the little person and he is standing in my lap facing me, supported by my arms round him.

I wonder what the Education Sec. thinks of me and also realise I shall be late for the midday meal downstairs, but I am so happy and moments like this are so rare – I shall have to break it up all too soon in any case. Meanwhile I realise I get almost a sexual excitement produced by his feet in my lap, but I realise that he is too young for any feelings of that sort and is just happy on its own account. Eventually, I break it up as gently as I can and find myself in the dining-hall below. The meat course is almost finished (it is a school of boys, only few there, on this day, at two long tables); the boys eat quickly. Also there is no head of the table chair for me (all occupied) but a seat at the end of one long side facing Mr Irving [Hazelwood Headmaster, he became Education Sec.] I hope they are not too annoyed at my being so late.

She [Mrs Irving] indicates my place but asks me first to take a second helping to some boy at the other end of a table (these seem to be now three) – and then I take another plate and another – till I do get my own plate, partly because I see that all the meat course is already gone. I can't quite make up my mind if I think Mrs Irving has forgotten to serve me in carelessness or to administer a slight corrective for having been late. I am not much worried by it, anyhow.

By looking through the back into my sleeping room I see the woman, but depreciated – as a servant – who left my service to get married to a groom – the figure comes from the past.

[The office is my 'upper', social life. The typewriter is a mechanism I don't know how to manage in real life. The tiny boy is supposedly a figure of the puer aeterna *who appears jolly and strong when the ego takes him into his arms.*

The story of the song 'Ilkley Moor' is of some fellow who caught his death of cold on Ilkley Moor without a hat and was buried, eaten by worms, which were eaten by ducks and then the ducks eaten by us, his pals. No doubt exactly the song this child should sing!

There is still some bafflement about the concretisation of homosexuality – the conscious does not easily give up this habit and the moral entanglement that ensues – but it is getting easier. The ego knows that such moments are rare and precious in the dream symbolism. The school dining-hall is the 'lower' social (?) life – or the past, perhaps. Here the woman is a mother and the ego is uncertain of his relation to her, and of his 'place', and eventually of his 'meat'.

There is regression to the past because of the inability to adapt to the present somewhere – is the partaking of a 'midday meal' a figure for a present difficulty? – or is the 'duty' to go downstairs a reflection of the remaining uncertainty about the relationship to the wonder child?]

Thursday night, 25 May

A scene in which I am trying to masturbate a young man (Wilf?) while his girl remains close by. I do not bring it to any conclusion.

I am watching Oliver [Morley] get into trouble with Wilf (?), who is responsible for him. Oliver has to have his right hand caned. He does not understand what it is about. Afterwards Wilf seems to want Oliver to shake hands and close the affair.

I feel that Oliver thinks that Wilf's outstretched hand is in order to inflict further pain on his own sore one. He cries desperately and says tearfully he will 'begin to cry again', and is so tearful that he can't find

107

Wilf's hand with his; constantly misses it, in the air. I feel moved to say – 'Don't be so cruel, Wilf.' Oliver is staying the night with me. He has gone upstairs to sleep. I want to get hold of John Layard on the phone. I think also that I could perhaps take Oliver round to see him so that John would be able to say how Oliver's present condition strikes him – but I can't get any connection on the telephone and have to give it up.

[Oliver comes into the dream as the result of last night's postcard to say that he is ill. I fancied that this might mean that his introversion at school is taking a serious form. Oliver must, I think, stand for 'the complex'. The figure that has no social sense and does not understand the moral punishments. I can't remember, but it is possible that I tried to masturbate 'Wilf' with my right hand, which in Oliver's case is caned by 'Wilf'. It is presumably the 'Oliver' in me that causes the outward trick of homosexuality and the 'Wilf' as moral mother in me that wants to cane it or punish and suppress it. It is possible, on the contrary, that 'Wilf's' method with 'Oliver' is correct, though cruel – hence perhaps my feeling I ought to consult John Layard when 'Oliver' is once more 'under my own care'. But I cannot get through – perhaps the ego must wrestle with it himself.

To cane Oliver's hand is an act of the Shadow side: it is impossible to assimilate to my conscious attitude – yet presumably what I am doing inside myself.

Perhaps my exaggerated sensibility to Oliver in real life is a compensation for the terrific resistance to permitting any 'right' to the complex in my own case. It seems a tremendous plunge to admit 'forgiveness' to oneself. There must be no measure of 'escape', but as yet it is not clear how 'forgiveness' at all can be held out to the complex without permission of 'indulgence'. The answer I know lies through understanding – just as with Oliver in real life.

Really somehow the 'Wilf moral-mother' must shake hands with the 'Oliver' complex: there is a deeper meaning underneath the surface 'cruelty'.]

According to Jung's theory, the 'Shadow' world of the unconscious is telling you something which the conscious doesn't wish to see. But it didn't seem to be working out that way for me. I had a deep guilt that came in my final relations with Wilf, which had led me to think that everything I was doing was wrong and I must aim to be married –I should not be what I am. I went into the dream therapy anticipating that what would come out was the possibility of marriage. But then I began to realise half-way through that something else was being said. That came in the extraordinary dream (27 May) in which I was contrite and Wilf forgiving, and a mystic marriage took place. This I rejected. I turned away for some reason (moral?) from Wilf's shining face, knowing that love had to go deeper. The image of the shining face later appeared transformed in the alto aria in Part 3 of *A Child of Our Time:*

> The soul of man is impassioned like a woman.
> She is old as the earth, beyond good and evil,
> the sensual garments.
> Her face will be illumined like the sun.
> This is the time of his deliverance.

Saturday night, 27 May

In Stamford Town (where I was at secondary school) – trying to help my mother find her way back to the school by herself.

A curious contraption for a performance of some scene imitative of Venice (?) – it was like a boathouse – there was a stream running through down one long side and a boat on it with someone (girl or boy?) on it. The problem was the question of lighting up a sort of backcloth in one position; the effect was suddenly very exciting as though of very great depth and scintillation of light, but it was not large enough and so caused confusion in those parts of the background where this effect did not happen. Then the stream etc. seemed to get reversed and we were looking at it from the other side of the boathouse. Now I suggested that we ought to put a dark background behind to show up the boat, etc. The occupant of the boat put a big coat behind the head and spread it out so that the background went dark – but the effect was quite wrong.

In a sort of church: we had to go into the chancel across a line under an arch and there part to either left or right. We were all young men. I was told quite clearly to go the left and I thought that Wilf would go to the right. I crossed the line and went to the left, turned and faced back. Wilf also came on this side and for the moment I was puzzled and in doubt, but held on to what I had been told. It appeared as though too many would come to the left, but then it seemed that there was too long a line to the right. Anyhow, on facing across the line again, the other line was on the left, and my line on the right. Woodbridge was the first on the other line and Wilf (?) just behind – at any rate I was again a little uncertain who was to be my partner. It was some sort of mystic marriage – but there was nothing sexual implied or felt. The fellow on the left of us, our partner, was to make some sort of an act of contrition and we were to make some sort of act of forgiveness – Woodbridge (or a mixture of him and Wilf) made the contrite act, to my way of feeling. I did not know what I was to do to show forgiveness and also I was quite certain I was not 'fit' to do such a thing – so I hung my head and waited a bit – it appeared then as if a Bishop came from the body of the church and indicated that we were as one – and that I put my arms round him in a brotherly way. (The chancel of the church would appear in feeling to be at the west end and so upside-down to the usual Christian practice.)

This was the turning point in the therapy. Running parallel was the worrying affair of what had happened to the imaginative life out of which the music must come. If I succeeded in analysing myself totally, I might lose the music. I was also concerned about the matter of individuation – about the four sides to yourself, as Jung would have depicted them. Then, three nights before war broke out, I had the classic dream of a forced death: I was going to be strangled by four men. I accepted it – I said, 'Let what must, happen' – and realised afterwards that I had turned a corner. A kind of rebirth was now happening. I stopped writing down my dreams. Three days later, on 3 September 1939, the war began: simultaneously, I started writing the music for *A Child of Our Time*.

Special Dreams during Holiday, 22 July-8 August

In a sort of bureau with a glass partition. God was on the inner side and more particularly one of his women analysts. Connection through the partition was by telephone. Nothing however transpired. So I turned about and there was Cox-Ife, one of my colleagues in music, who told me that the way out lay through the elucidation of a list of sybilline aphorisms which he showed me. But I could make nothing of them, nor could he. However, he hummed or sang the first two longish sentences. I asked him excitedly to sing them again. He told me such foolery was a waste of time, but complied.

I told him then that he was singing two musically complementary phrases and that this was the real answer. Whereupon he dipped his finger in some liquid and marked my face with a large cross, like baptism, only it didn't register or mark in the middle, but mostly the four ends of the cross at forehead, chin and the two ears.

[I understood God to be saying that he could not accede to any request to do a

miracle for me or mankind, because however much he might wish to, any push
in one direction forced him to a complementary pull in another. His reality was
actually that of 'Impotent Power'.]

[A dream remark: 'The Queen of Holland lives sparsely.']

A quartet and myself, my brother, father and mother. My mother was
saying that the real safeguard was the fact that my brother wholly, and
I in part, were instinctively led towards relations with the other sex.
But my brother broke in loudly and said that this was just the problem
– that I was not safe at all and my relation to a certain man (he meant
Wilf) was proof of this. I got up and walked nearer to them and,
speaking mainly to my mother, said that whatever else was in
question it was definitely wrong to give up a true friendship for such
moral equivocation. My mother, to my surprise, nodded her head in
agreement. 'In my case,' I said, as I returned to my seat, 'Wilf has set
up house with a girl and it is all over – so you may as well know.'
    A question of my brother and I sharing a house – on his side of
London. East not south. But the difficulty was that of his wife and my
boy (or girl?) – there was not enough room.
    [*Late in the same night*] A vision of a sort of solarium – a model
heaven – in the east was the King – in the north was the Queen of
Sheba – but the solarium would not move round properly beyond the
great flourish of THE KING, followed by the Queen of Sheba, because of
two figures in the west – sort of puppets – the nearest was a very
beautiful Indian-looking goddess – like a statuette of Shiva. These two
puppets were caught by string – hitched up at the back somehow.

Thursday night, 31 August
[After visit to London in full preparation for war nightmare.]

At first in childhood's home – remarked to my brother how close to
the group the upper-floor windows of the little cottage were in reality
as seen by our grown-up eyes – one could easily step out from where
we were on to the ground. Later alone at night, early morning in bed
in a strange room in a strange house, unable to sleep. There was a lot of
movement outside on the stairs etc. – eventually a young fellow came
in with a tray of some sort of breakfast – he said it was 5.30 – he had
woken me early because all the groups of men were awake downstairs
and knew I had the money to pay them off – he came and stood on the

left of the bed by my head (my feet were nearer the door opposite). I saw he had what looked like a very fine medical syringe with a long prong – but I saw more closely that it was a revolver.

I did not have to pay out and retained the money myself, of those of the comrades who had been killed during the last week, or period. This was at once both a satisfaction and a fear. Then one of these 'dead' men came in through the door, and another, and took their places alongside the first man. I realised they were spirits of some sort.

But I knew there was a fourth missing – the last to 'die' – he came through the door then, which closed behind him – his face was white and blotched and aweful. I said mentally, or aloud, 'Let what must be happen.' The fourth dead man gave me both his hands. I gripped the fingers curled into each other's palms – then at a signal from him the other three began to strangle me with their hands. I realised with relief that it was a dream – then the strangling became more realistic. A bell began to ring – an alarm clock out of which I was to awake. [*Woke – wondering if I ought to have let the dream go further*].

POSTSCRIPT

A few years back the psychiatrist Anthony Clare asked me (in a BBC radio interview) the curious question, 'What died?' Probably some fear died. In the final dream, death is confronted – in other words, I accepted the invitation, whatever that was. The vital thing, it seemed to me, was that the therapy had reached a conclusion: the quarrel inside myself, instead of interfering with my creativity, now enhanced it – I had greater control of my powers as a composer. I also realised the human imaginative power of the dream-life: and that is something I find absorbing to this day. Meanwhile, the process of 'individuation', as Jung called it, produced an acceptance that I would not be married. I was thus ejected out into the world as a loner.

CHAPTER SEVEN

THE HEART'S ASSURANCE

THE WORLD TURNS ON ITS DARK SIDE

Alone in my cottage, on the day war broke out, I sensed that it would be a long-drawn-out conflict and worried that I might not be alive at the end of it. I had none of the confidence possessed by some people that the good Lord would ultimately protect me. Of paramount importance was the need to write *A Child of Our Time*. I was then working on the *Fantasia on a Theme of Handel*, and decided to put this aside, in order to compose the oratorio (whose text was already finished). In my naive way, I wrote to Fresca saying that I might not survive, but at least English recitative would have a new lease of life!

If composition had been threatened in the past decade by conflicting personal drives, now it was at risk because of what I believed to be my public responsibilities. My self-assurance as a composer and my technical skills meant that I could now stand by anything I had written: no more large-scale revisions, no more withdrawal of ill-conceived efforts. I was currently beginning to get a few professional performances of my work and there were signs that the music might be published and recorded. At the very least, the war was a damned nuisance.

I was nevertheless frightened by it all. If I had to go to London, I tried to get out again as soon as possible. Fresca had a house in Mornington Crescent, which she rarely used at that time – it was looked after by an old nurse. Sometimes I stayed there, but I was ill at ease in it: eventually, it was blown up – mercifully, without anyone inside. Once, during the bombing, I wanted to return home and it was too late (or impossible) to reach Oxted. David Ayerst and I took a train instead to Caterham, walked from there up on to the Downs and looked back at London burning.

At the outbreak of the war, the South London Orchestra disbanded.

My adult education choirs were also suspended, and in order to earn some money I had to teach Latin for a term back at Hazelwood School. Through Wilf's father, Dan Franks, however, I had met the Morley College Principal, Eva Hubback, and had grown to admire her enormously. When Morley College was blown up in October 1940, and the Music Director, Arnold Foster, had to leave London (he taught at Westminster School and, for safety's sake, had to take his boys out to the country), she asked me to rebuild the musical life of the College over again. I was only too happy to do so. I started with a choir of just eight voices, but this grew to 30 by the 1941–2 season. I did no teaching, preferring to delegate and merely supervise the overall running of music.

Back in 1938, at a concert performance by the BBC Symphony Orchestra of Hindemith's *Mathis der Maler*, I had been introduced to a tall, distinguished-looking gentleman in tails – Willy Strecker of B. Schott Söhne, the German music publishers. He had given me his card and asked me to send him scores of my compositions to date – including immature ones, so that he could observe my development over a period. I was taken aback: for works like the Concerto for Double String Orchestra had been turned down by the BBC and Boult, by Boosey & Hawkes and Oxford University Press, the International Society for Contemporary Music, and so on. I had sent Strecker a number of pieces, which reached Mainz a few weeks before war was declared: and shortly afterwards I had gone to meet Willy's son, Hugo, the director of the London branch of Schott, and the executive manager, Max Steffens. They had told me that the Concerto and possibly the Sonata had been accepted for publication. In the event, I had to wait until the war ended for anything significant to come of it; but having received such a favour, I remained loyal, even though the scores were destroyed when firemen pumped water into the Schott Mainz cellars during the winter of 1943–4. Steffens asked me if I wanted a contract and I replied, 'Of course not!' What mattered was that I had received a first hint that I could belong to the European musical scene.

The accident of war brought me into contact, meanwhile, with a number of distinguished refugee musicians. Some I managed to attract on to the staff at Morley: others I persuaded to participate in the Morley concerts. Chief amongst them were Walter Goehr (a Schoenberg pupil), who took over the conducting of the orchestra, and Matyas Seiber, widely versed in everything from dodecaphony to jazz, who came to teach composition.

114

(*Left*) With my mother and brother Peter (left), circa 1908

(*Below*) A rather serious seven-year-old

(*Below left*) My cousin, Phyllis Kemp

(*Right*) An amateur ballet performance at Stamford School – Tripping the light fantastic on the right

(*Below*) From pupil to teacher of French and Music: the school photograph at Hazelwood in 1928; and (*foot*) with the London Labour Choral Union in Strasbourg in 1935, extreme top left . . .

(*Below*) In 1943 press interest was increasing: the *Daily Telegraph* praised my second string quartet; meanwhile Ralph Vaughan Williams tried, unsuccessfully, to keep me out of prison

(*Left*) R. O. Morris, with whom I studied at the Royal College of Music on my second visit (1930)

WORKS BY YOUNG COMPOSERS

The Boosey and Hawkes concert of new works of young British composers given at the Wigmore Hall yesterday was on the whole disappointing.

Although Bernard Stevens's piano trio is a profounder piece of writing than Noel Mewton-Wood's string trio, both works proved to be little more than competent essays in note spinning.

The really bright spot in the programme was Michael Tippett's second string quartet. It is the work of an alert and imaginative mind, whose individual approach to the problem of form, and keen feeling for rhythm, and extraordinarily melodic sense are extraordinarily impressive.   R. H.

MICHAEL TIPPETT SENT TO PRISON

DR. VAUGHAN WILLIAMS'S PLEA FOR COMPOSER

MICHAEL KEMP TIPPETT, 38, director of music at Morley College since 1940, whose compositions were described by Dr. Vaughan Williams as forming "a distinct national asset," was at Oxted, Surrey, yesterday, sentenced to three months' imprisonment for failing to comply with the conditions of his registration as a conscientious objector.

Mr. Howe Pringle, prosecuting, said that the appellant tribunal decided in May last year that Tippett should take up full-time A.R.P., N.F.S., or farm work. He was directed into farm work but failed to comply with the directions. When interviewed in April, he stated that his views were such that he did not feel he could comply with the conditions.

Dr. Ralph Vaughan Williams, called for the defence, said, "I think Tippett's pacifist views entirely wrong, but I respect him very much for holding them so firmly. I think his compositions are very remarkable, and form a distinct national asset, and will increase the prestige of this country in the world. As regards his teachings at Morley College, it is distinctly work of national importance to create a musical atmosphere at the college and elsewhere. We know music is forming a great part in national life now; more since the war than ever before, and everyone able to help on with that work is doing work of national importance."

Mrs. E. Hubback, principal of Morley College, said that she had always known Tippett as a pacifist and was convinced of his entire sincerity.

In replying to this letter, please write on the envelope:—

Number ...5832.... Name ...M. K. Tippett...

...WORMWOOD SCRUBS... Prison

The following regulations as to communications, by Visit or Letter, between prisoners and their friends are notified for the information of their correspondents.

The permission to write and receive letters is given to prisoners for the purpose of enabling them to keep up a connection with their respectable friends.

All letters are read by the Prison Authorities. They must be legibly written and not crossed. Any which are of an objectionable tendency, either to or from prisoners, will be suppressed.

Prisoners are permitted to receive and to write a letter at intervals, which depend on the rules of the stage they attain by industry and good conduct; but matters of special importance to a prisoner may be communicated at any time by letter (prepaid) to the Governor, who will inform the prisoner thereof, if expedient.

In case of misconduct, the privilege of receiving and writing a letter may be forfeited for a time.

Money, Postage Stamps, Food, Tobacco, Clothes, etc., should not be sent to prisoners for their use in Prison, as nothing is allowed to be received at the Prison for that purpose.

Persons attempting to communicate with prisoners contrary to the rules, or to introduce any article to or for prisoners, are liable to fine or imprisonment, and any prisoner concerned in such practices is liable to be severely punished.

Prisoners' friends are sometimes applied to by unauthorised persons, to give or send money, under pretence that it will be for the benefit of the prisoners. The people who make these requests are trying to get money for themselves by fraudulent pretences. If the friends of a prisoner are asked for money, either verbally or by letter, they should at once inform the Governor of the Prison about the matter, and send him any letter they have received.

Prisoners are allowed to receive visits from their friends, according to rules, at intervals which depend on their stage.

When visits are due to prisoners, notification will be sent to the friends whom they desire to visit them.

No. 243 (15717—19-4-23)

Evelyn Maude, considered a 'respectable friend', was the recipient of many of my letters from Wormwood Scrubs – cover notes like this accompanied all my outgoing post

arch 3 1945, the *Picture Post* documented the BBC performance of *A Child of*
ur Time with the original soloists Joan Cross, Margaret McArthur, Peter Pears
d Roderick Lloyd

Picture Post, March 3, 1945

In the Corn Exchange, Bedford, Michael Tippett, a Lonely Figure, Listens to a Rehearsal of His Work
s left, the four soloists, Joan Cross, Margaret McArthur, Peter Pears, and Roderick Lloyd, standing among the choir, are singing the Spiritual "Steal
y to Jesus," which the composer has woven into the Oratorio. Performing with them is the B.B.C. Symphony Orchestra, conducted by Walter Goehr.

A COMPOSER LISTENS TO HIS OWN ORATORIO

**Michael Tippett's Oratorio, a "Child of Our Time"—one of the most interesting achievements in music produced for many
years in Britain—is being performed at the Albert Hall on Wednesday, February 28, by the London Philharmonic Orchestra
and two choirs, in aid of the children of Warsaw.**

Photographed by H. MAGEE

oratorio is to music what the Miracle Play as to drama—a representation of the conflict in an's soul, and of his redemption through faith. its simple opposition of good and evil, the le Play died, giving way to a more sophisticated in which modern man, sceptical and mate- ic, looked for other answers to his problems religion. By the twentieth century, the Pas- of Christ, which ormented the con- e of Europe for 2,000 years, no inspired oratorios those of Handel, and Mendelssohn; suffering of the y, the tortured, he dying, had be- commonplace— theme of living than of art, a lus to revolt rather to music. Both s and people d to have become to the world's n, because it was ound them. And ratorio, with its voices crying out against the s of the mob, with its soprano of pity and its of defiance, answering the bass of tyranny and eemed as dead as the Miracle Play. chael Tippett, raising the form from its recent t, has written an oratorio of our times. He scarded the "sacred" conventions of his pre- sors, but his secular theme has the deepest ual purpose of religious music. don't remember precisely how a *Child of Our* first came into my head," he says. "I can nber being much affected by Grynspan's ng of von Rath at the German Legation in

The Score of a "Child of Our Time"
This is the original score, since published for the use of Choral Societies by Schott & Co., Ltd.

Paris in the autumn of '38. And I remember listen- ing, on Christmas Day of that year, to the broad- cast of Berlioz's lovely *Childhood of Christ*, and afterwards trying to think out what had become nowadays of the emotional power in the once uni- versally accepted image of the Christ Child, a power which at one time could make all Europe bend its knee—at least for a season. The real beginning of a *Child of Our Time* was the moment when Grynspan's act and Jesus, who *voluntarily* died for sins, became the strands which formed, as it were, a new-old pattern. And this pattern seemed to me expressible only in an oratorio—which is, by convention, a religio- dramatic musical form. Bit by bit, the drama sorted itself out into chorus, scena, airs and recitative. But there was still something miss- ing which was traditional for the Lutheran Pass- ions—and that was the chorales, which the composer chose from the great hymnals of the time, accord- ing to his needs as to words and music. The effect of the chorales was something like a popular commentary on the divine story.

"Now, I didn't imagine that any such general melodies existed in our time, until, by chance, one Sunday I listened-in to a man singing negro songs. I remember he sang them very badly, but when he came to a phrase in the spiritual 'Steal Away,' I was shot through with the sudden realisation that the melody was far greater than the individual singer, and had the power to move us all. So I got hold of

Continued overleaf

Tippett Beats Time With His Finger
The thirty-nine-year-old composer listens in rapture to his work, murmurs "Heavenly music, heavenly music!" **19**

THIS OPERA BAFFLES US TOO, SAY SINGERS

TREE TAKES A BOW ...

Bewilderment at Covent Garden

By JAMES THOMAS

NOT since Salvador Dali tried to introduce a flying hippopotamus into the cast of Strauss's "Salome" has the Royal Opera House had such a baffled cast on its hands as the one which will launch Michael Tippett's "The Midsummer Marriage" into the world tomorrow night.

It is the first opera in (more or less) modern dress which Covent Garden has staged. Its villain is a business tycoon called King Fisher, and it has a flight of stairs which leads up to heaven, with another which leads down to hell.

And the cast, after weeks of rehearsal, are still wondering just what it's all about.

The prima donna, Australia's Joan Sutherland, said yesterday: "Mr. Tippett told me not to worry if I didn't understand it. He said just to sing it as well as I could, and to leave the audience to work out the significance for themselves."

Not a timber yard

The Covent Garden official who showed me around at rehearsal yesterday tried desperately to give me an idea of the story, but finally admitted total failure.

On the stage the action appeared to be taking place in a timber yard encircled by a bright blue cyclorama.

I asked: "What are all those planks standing up on the left?"

"A wood," said the Covent Garden official miserably.

"And what do those dancers represent?"

"Trees, I think—dancing trees," said the C.G.O., plucking at his collar forlornly.

We met Otakar Kraus, the big businessman villain in a short black jacket and a blue waistcoat.

"If you are coming to ask me what it is all about, don't bother," said Mr. Kraus. "I don't know. I just cannot get over being able to sing in my own spectacles—but I miss the usual operatic costumes to swish round."

You guess

Then Mr. Kraus looked disappointed. He added: "I thought that just for once I would be able to sing an opera"

It's his idea

MICHAEL TIPPETT
"It means what it says"

"I always die . . . I die again in this. I drop dead through some sort of supernatural power. Hoo! Your guess is as good as mine . . . tches ,it comes to this opera."

We met Edith Coates, in a bristly grey wig, three inch platform soles, and a navy blue coat. "What a get-up," said the C.C.O. with awe.

"What an opera," said Miss Coates. "I don't know who I am and that's truth. I am described as an Ancient. Let's content with that."

We met John Lanigan, who supplies operatic interest as a mechanic. His comment: "I can only say that I know no port."

We met Senora Oralia Dominguez, imported regardless of expense from La Scala, Milan, to sing the part of a clairvoyante. Her eyes gazed mournfully out of a face painted bright blue.

In Italian she said: "This music is most interesting, but it is useless to talk to me of anything else. I am not even sure why my face is painted blue"

A kind of . .

Then we met Miss Barbara Hepworth, the sculptress and painter, who has designed the scenery and costumes. She was tripping round the back of the Grand Tier peering from different angles at a set she

ONE of these three dancers in the opera is a tree. You can't guess which? Why—the one holding a bough. The bough is that wooden frame, of course. **(Right)** Edith Coates watches prima donna Oralia Dominguez paint her face blue. Why? Well, it's all part of the opera. No, it's no good asking ... know either

Working and relaxing
with friends: (*Above*)
Christopher Fry and a harp
in 1960, (*Left*) Vaughan
Williams (extreme right)
and Sir John Minchinton
in 1958 and (*Below*)
Yehudi Menuhin in 1964

(*Left*) The first page of the score
of *The Midsummer Marriage*
hailed by *The Daily Express*
after its 1955 Covent Garden
debut as 'the worst libretto in
the 350-year-old history of
music'. *The News Chronicle* was
scarcely less confused, despite
interviewing both Joan
Sutherland and Barbara
Hepworth.

At home in Wiltshire

Through Hugo I met Walter Bergmann, who was working in Schott at the time. Hugo had suggested that I should bring *A Child of Our Time* (by then completed) to Schott and play it over to Walter Goehr. Bergmann came to listen; Goehr later made some useful suggestions concerning the notation of its recitatives. Bergmann was a lawyer who had been imprisoned by the Nazis for defending Jews in court (he was not a Jew himself): typically, when in gaol, he had decided that in case he didn't survive, he would set about writing an authoritative monograph on the figured bass. I persuaded him to come to Morley and teach recorders, then a novelty; his expertise in Baroque music proved indispensable and he supervised entire concerts of Telemann and other such figures. The appointment of foreigners like Bergmann and Goehr at Morley drew a disapproving letter from Vaughan Williams to Eva Hubback, but she stood firmly behind me, and the reputation of Morley's music grew apace.

Our concerts gained widespread attention. They took place in the Holst Room, which could only hold about 150 people and so filled up quickly. Thus I sometimes took the choir elsewhere, to perform in the National Gallery, Friends' House and even the Wigmore Hall. Our repertoire was daringly off-beat, but this attracted keen support from audiences and the press. Pre-classical music was a speciality. Fresca had previously introduced me to Purcell, but it was only when I found some of the large volumes of the Purcell Society complete edition in the rubble after the Morley bombing that it suddenly dawned on me what an extraordinarily rich corpus of music he had produced in his short life-span. Early on, in 1940, we mounted a performance of his hitherto neglected 1692 *St Cecilia Ode*.

The Sunday evening chamber concerts in the Holst Room featured Bach cantatas and Purcell verse anthems, and for these I needed an accomplished small orchestra, mostly of strings. The players readily at hand were medical rejects from the armed services, also women and young refugees who were studying music and who did factory work instead of being conscripted. Amongst the refugees were three teenagers, Norbert Brainin, Peter Schidlof and Siegmund Nissel, who were later to team up with Martin Lovett to form the Amadeus Quartet; one of our violinists, Suzanne Rozsa, became Martin Lovett's wife. Norbert often played Bach's solo Chaconne in D minor as his special party piece in our concerts. At this time he was working in a factory, but often arrived there late, having overslept: we had to pull strings to prevent him from being punished. We sometimes went as a group to do lunchtime concerts outside London, and once in Leicester we had to change the order of the programme, as Norbert had missed the train! The strings were led by Olive Zorian, leader of the Zorian Quartet (all women); Olive later married John Amis (a medical reject who sang in the Morley Choir, and a lively presence on the London musical scene, working for the London Philharmonic Orchestra).

Another prominent member of the group was the pianist and composer Antony Hopkins, and it was he who invited a young viola-player, Michael Tillett, to join the orchestra. Thereafter, Michael appeared regularly at Morley – playing both viola and piano (he performed some of Bartók's *Mikrokosmos* in one concert) and singing in the choir. I recall coaching a performance of Milhaud's *La Création du Monde* (in the composer's own arrangement for piano and string quintet), with Michael playing viola, Antony Hopkins on the piano, and another composer, Leonard Salzedo, as lead violinist.

Soon after Michael left to teach music at Rugby School in 1946, I sent him the first scene of *The Midsummer Marriage* in full score and asked him if he would have a shot at making a vocal score of it. He executed this with such accuracy and discernment that he soon became my right-hand man for all tasks of this sort. For decades, now, Michael has continued to check my manuscripts before they go to the publisher, and to proof-read the materials. But he is more than an amanuensis: he has an acute ear, is a mine of information on the practicalities of music-making, and gives very good first assessments of each episode in a work as it emerges. Occasionally he will suggest that something I've written isn't the best I could do: invariably, I take him seriously and rethink the passage in question. If he rings up and says *alpha plus plus*, I am over the moon!

It was at Morley that I first met Benjamin Britten and Peter Pears. I wanted a tenor to take part in a performance in November 1942 of Gibbons's verse anthem *My Beloved Spake*. Walter Bergmann suggested Peter, who had recently returned from America with Ben. They came together to the rehearsals and performance. (Michael Tillett has told me that a puzzled looking German girl playing the cello afterwards asked him, 'What exactly *is* a "spake"?'). Ben and Peter participated a lot in my Morley concerts: once I conducted Ben's *Hymn to St Cecilia*, with the composer in the choir and Peter singing the solo tenor part!

I quickly became close to them both. Out of our common interest in

Purcell and Monteverdi came my cantata, *Boyhood's End*, which Ben and Peter performed for the first time at Morley College in June 1943. As pacifists, and as artists with a genuine concern for human beings generally, and especially for children, we became close. They visited me quite often, then, in Oxted. Once, Peter had to go off to London to sing and Ben remained behind. He thought it would be nice if we slept together, which we did, though I drew back from sexual relations; Peter was nevertheless quite disturbed at our intimacy on that occasion. At Oxted, Ben wanted to see what I had written and I produced *A Child of Our Time* from a drawer. He was very excited and said it must be performed. With typical generosity, when he received a commission to write *Rejoice in the Lamb*, for Northampton Parish Church, he gave me a small portion of his commission fee so that I could write an opening fanfare – performed as we processed up the aisle of the church (it was the only time I've appeared in a surplice!).

Ben was, quite simply, the most musical person I have ever met. His technical mastery was incredible. On one occasion just after the war, I went into the darkened Sadler's Wells Theatre, and there was Ben conducting with full authority a rehearsal of the first Interlude from *Peter Grimes*. That great opera marked the turning-point in his career, and from then on he was less accessible, less ready to accept jokes or irreverence in relation to himself, his work or Peter; but he never betrayed his sense of vocation or his artistic integrity. Many close friends fell foul of Ben and Peter at Aldeburgh, which was sad. I realised what was going on and stayed apart from it all: if I went, subsequently, to the Aldeburgh Festival, I would send him a postcard saying I'd be there, but since no doubt he was busy, I wouldn't expect to see him. After his death, I was once invited to stay with Peter at the Red House, but found the reverent, mausoleum atmosphere oppressive.

Considering the obstacles, it was amazing how much musical enterprise there was during the war. Wilfred van Wyck, who owned a record shop near Leicester Square, decided to start a private record company and arranged to make use of Decca's studios for small-scale recording projects, such as Oda Slobodskaya singing Mussorgsky songs and Phyllis Sellick playing Debussy piano music. I already felt that my own works might become better known if there were recordings, and approached him to see if a collaboration might be possible with Schott. The idea didn't get very far, but Phyllis recorded my First Piano Sonata in 1941. For this she was paid £10 (probably by Fresca); the production costs were supposed to have been covered partly by Aubrey Russ, but he failed to honour his commitment. Van Wyck sent copies to various critics – amongst them William Glock, who wrote about it for *The Observer*, Edward Sackville-West who reviewed it for the *New Statesman* and Wilfrid Mellers who wrote an article in the Leavisite literary journal, *Scrutiny*. The success of the Sonata recording led Hugo Strecker to publish the work from Schott London. Later, van Wyck and Schott collaborated in publishing and recording the Double Concerto, which was also well reviewed. (This was Max Steffens's way of finding expenditures to set against excess profits tax.) Having had only one professional performance – the première of String Quartet No. 1 at one of the Macnaghten-Lemare concerts in 1935 – I was now, in spite of wartime conditions, just starting to become known and my circle of friends in the world of professional music was widening.

William Glock was one of the most significant of them. I met his father first – he was a secondary school teacher in south-west London and his children's choir was involved in the RACS [Royal Arsenal Co-operative Society]. He had acquired a set of Gill Sans type and as an exercise his pupils printed the text of *A Child of Our Time*, a few copies of which were privately circulated. William himself first came to my attention when I heard him play a Mozart piano concerto before the war. By the time I met him, he was music critic on *The Observer*. At a lunch with William and his first wife, Clement, I met the South-African born composer Priaulx Rainier, and struck up a friendship that lasted right until her death a few years ago. William was in the RAF during the war, so I didn't see him all that often. But we always kept in touch and I came to know him particularly well later, when, under his astute direction, BBC music blossomed in every way in the 1960s: we were both then on the BBC Music Advisory Panel and his catholic sympathies and general intellectual sophistication were invariably a tonic. He was always so independent of factions and coteries, and always on the look-out for new talent. I remain deeply indebted to him.

After my first meeting with Priaulx, we saw a lot of each other. She was then living in a self-contained flat in London with a woman dancer, but this relationship broke down when the dancer went to the USA. Priaulx returned to her own place in Notting Hill, in which she often accommodated conscientious objectors and others needing help.

After the war, we became particularly close. Morley College commissioned a piece from her, which we put on in a series of concerts at Central Hall, Westminster (Walton attended and said afterwards, 'I really think Miss Rainier must have barbed-wire underwear!'); and I managed to persuade Schott to publish her music. At this time Priaulx became intimate with Barbara Hepworth, Ben Nicholson and Bernard Leach and led a double existence, living half in London and half in lodgings in St Ives. Priaulx often bemoaned the lack of performances of her music and her inability to find a suitable work situation. Barbara tried to help by letting her compose in the summerhouse amidst the sculptures in her garden, with no living expenses. But she lacked the necessary obsessive single-mindedness and every time a telephone or doorbell rang, she rushed out to answer it on Barbara's behalf. The cultural attaché at the French Embassy, Tony Mayer, offered her the use of his incomplete house at Menerbes, east of Avignon, so that she could compose a large-scale setting of Rilke sonnets, but she came back in a depressed state with the work unfinished. She had a habit of making things difficult for herself – in this particular instance, she wanted to construct a vocal line such that it could be sung equally well in German or English, without adaptations; almost predictably, she became stuck as a result.

Priaulx's many quirks tended to divide people. I myself loved her vagueness – for instance, her directions to where she was staying: 'Take the second exit on the roundabout before the last one.' But publishers and performers were often irritated. Her driving was incomparably erratic. And when she and Barbara tried to organise a festival at St Ives, in 1953, the administration was hilarious. I was asked for a fanfare, to be played from the four corners of the church tower, and had to rewrite it three times, to match the changing talents of the successive brass groups appointed to play it. Best of all, madrigals were to be sung from a boat in the harbour, but Priaulx and Barbara forgot to check the tides: in the event, the tide went out, taking with it the boatful of inaudible singers!

Back in 1935, I had been one of the 100,000 or so people who responded to the letter sent to the press by the Revd Dick Sheppard – a pacifist in the First World War – inviting anyone who was opposed to war to sent him a postcard, with the pledge, 'I renounce war and never again, directly or indirectly, will I support or sanction another.' Out of that came the Peace Pledge Union, in which I was an active member, and its newspaper, *Peace News*. The PPU had developed from the no-conscription movement, based on the fact that there had never been military conscription in England, nor should there be. There were other peace movements – e.g. the Christian Fellowship for Reconciliation – but the PPU was the umbrella body.

When I was called up to the Army, I followed the usual procedures. I applied for exemption on grounds of conscience and awaited a call to attend a tribunal, which eventually took place in 1942. Sitting on the tribunal were representatives of the Army and trade unions, and a lawyer. I read out a defence statement I had prepared myself, but this was rejected and I was assigned non-combatant military duties. I appealed against this, and had to attend a further Appellate Tribunal the following May, this time in Chelsea. Much the same happened: I was given conditional registration – I had either to do full-time work with Air Raid Precautions, the Fire Service or on the land. The alternative was some kind of approved cultural activity. I consulted with a number of close friends. Walter Bergmann, for instance, advised me to 'bend with the wind', which I thought odd, coming from someone who himself had endured unjust imprisonment. Ben and Peter, who were exempted from military service on account of their work as performers for ENSA, were terrified that I might be sent to prison, but that didn't worry me.

Most curious was going to stay with David Ayerst (by then a colonel), who was billeted with three fellow-officers in a boarding-house at 31, Stanhope Gardens, South Kensington, where there were some spare rooms. With this military group, I discussed the pros and cons of my situation in detail. Like many of my friends, David was all for compromise. Amongst the culturally acceptable jobs that were offered me were Music Organiser for ENSA in Northern Ireland, librarian for the RAF orchestra, and choir-training with the National Fire Service. Instead of working at Morley College I could have done educational work across the road for the ARP shelters, but I didn't see the point.

Apart from the fact that I could never shoot or commit deliberate acts of violence against other individual human beings, let alone groups, there were simply two issues that mattered. One of them might, in a way, be deemed selfish – I would brook no interference with my compositional work, which I felt was the most valuable thing I could do; the other was a matter of principle – why should I be privileged and evade imprisonment by doing officially approved cultural or educational work, while other pacifists, particularly the younger ones, were defenceless? The leader of the South London Orchestra, Fred May, was sent to prison for six months; I visited him there. At one of the tribunals I saw one young man, who was quite illiterate, have his plea rejected on the basis of a statement which was manifestly not his own. I went to him afterwards and told him he must appeal, and helped him through the process.

Refusing to comply with the conditions laid down by the tribunal, I was summoned the following year (1943) to appear at Oxted Police Court. At that time I enlisted the services of a Quaker lawyer, Robert Pollard, who had defended a number of conscientious objectors; he thought it would also be worth engaging a barrister, and recommended Gerald Gardiner (who later became Lord Chancellor in the Wilson government of the 1960s). David (in his colonel's uniform), Eva Hubback and Vaughan Williams all testified on my behalf, even though they disagreed with my position.

The magistrate asked me, 'Are you really trying to say that you are worth so much that you shouldn't go to prison?' I felt unable to answer. His only option was to sentence me to imprisonment for the minimum period, three months. I didn't think I was necessarily better than a colleague like, for instance, Alan Rawsthorne who fought in the war with just as high a sense of morality: he thought he was defending civilisation against the evils of Nazism. But though I agreed that Nazism was evil, I thought war was the wrong means for defeating it. I couldn't accept that Hitler's evil acts justified the gratuitous slaughter unleashed by Stalin, Churchill or the Allies. After all, it is the innocents who suffer most on either side – the mothers and children of Dresden, of Coventry or wherever.

Fresca was frightened by the war and wanted to be out of London as much as possible. At this time she tried to help some of the conscientious objectors by buying a plot of land near East Grinstead, large enough to run as a smallholding. Conchies given land work as an alternative to military service could come to stay on the farm and work there; Fresca herself lived in a flat in the town, though sometimes she came to stay with me when she was really worried by the bombing. Amongst the conchies who worked on the smallholding were Larema Ayerst's brother, Bryan Fisher, and a youngster called Edric Maynard, who had both met at Toc H. Edric was known as the Book Boy, because the only job he had ever had was in a bookshop.

Early on, Edric developed psychological problems, arising out of the obsessive passion he had conceived for Bryan, which was not reciprocated. By this time I had finished with my own self-analysis, and I thought I might be able to help him. On the evening of Good Friday during the first Easter of the war, when I was well advanced in the writing of *A Child of Our Time*, there came a knock at the door. I had an instinct at once who it might be and when I opened the door, there was Edric, leaning his bicycle against the side of the house. I went to him, took his hands and said, 'Have the demons got you?' He replied, 'Yes.' I took him in and talked at length, trying to help him wrestle his way through his problems. On that occasion he uttered a gnomic remark that stuck in my mind – 'It'll all come. These are the laughing children'; I used this (in a modified form) later, for the final lines of Act 1 of *The Midsummer Marriage*.

At bedtime I realised he wanted to sleep with me. I let him do whatever he wanted, but afterwards made him sleep in the spare bedroom. Lying awake, I could hear him singing to the full moon shining outside and became desperately worried. Matters had gone too far and he really needed professional assistance. In the morning I sent him back to Fresca's flat and telephoned to warn her that he was on his way, and to expect trouble. When he arrived, he thumped her dining-room table and demanded Bryan's presence. Fresca contacted his sister, who turned up and showed all the toughness necessary to deal with him. He later had psychiatric treatment, for which a number of us found the money.

Fresca's commune disintegrated partly because she was having an affair with an older man – a conchie in the First World War. At first she returned to her London house but fell so ill (probably as a result of leaving the goitre operation so late) that she had to go and stay as a half-invalid with her brother Cyril Allinson and sister-in-law, near Streetly End in Cambridgeshire; Cyril had a farm there but used to commute each day to the Allinson flour mill in East London. The farms in this region had been poorly cultivated, and they were taken over by the War Agricultural Committee, who brought in lorry-loads of conchies to do the work properly. The chief product was sugar-beet – no corn was grown. Amongst the conchies was the writer, Douglas Newton (known to us all as Den) and a young painter, Karl Hawker, whom I had met earlier when Aubrey Russ brought him to Oxted. I was rarely able to visit Fresca but I wrote many letters to her, and this sustained our relationship to some extent: though the letters also reveal many of the competing pulls of creative and public involvements.

[1940]

Fri.

Fresca dear – it's certainly a trifle uncanny – after writing you, in the aft[ernoon] I went to Oxted to shop, to the accompaniment of an air warning – after tea at home I got down to work feeling as I thought a little oppressed by the heat & by an urge to get some music done & eventually sat down at the table to sketch out the first 4 fugal entries of the pogrom [episode in *A Child of Our Time*] – as I did this I heard the sound of German planes & firing. I had the oddest of feelings as I deliberately completed the 24 bars & then the restlessness was too much & I went to chat to Ben [next door] – the warning then went & Bron suddenly cried 'Look out at those things dropping from a plane over there' & to the sound of gun-firing a fight began over Oxted & over our heads, as it seemed.

Mercifully, I have a feeling that this of last night has slightly broken the charm & that I can (& must) go ahead as fast as I am able.

I have written off to order Grove today & paid £7.10 down for the most of it. I feel it will give me plenty of reading matter on my own art – a thing I'm much in need of every now & then – & at the moment especially.

In case of accident I might say, all the 4 early scores that matter (Symphony, Quartet, Blake, Piano Sonata, Str[ing] Concerto) are also to be found in the vaults of Mainz. The only new score is the oratorio. Freddy May's father has the clean score up to no. 16. (I have a pencil score here, pretty accurate, & a piano reduction to no. 8). The numbers I am writing from 16 onwards now are of course only in pencil on my desk. If anything horrid *should* happen, I think the first 16 numbers are still worth preserving . . . & as far as English music is concerned, for the hint of modern English recitative. But I am not anticipating such trouble, nor have any premonitions forced themselves to my notice.

I shall come over again some time when I get too restless & life too ominous. Den is on holiday here for a week – who is friendly, tho a little war-minded. The main job is to get the pogrom done

& the [spiritual] 'Go Down Moses' – by then of course, London classes will begin again.
Love,

M.

[1940–1]

Fresca dear,

. . . There were two big bonks here last night wh turn out to be bombs beside the Hurst Green factory – unloading, I fancy. Sooner or later I feel we shall at least be shot out of our beds! And I want by the way to farm out various copies of the oratorio music. I shld think that praps your cellar is the best place for the ink full-score if I keep the pencil one here. The pencil one is accurate except for some details of bowing etc. & some notes. I shall have to show someone how it cld be copied from – there are one or two shorthand devices. Not that these bonks affect me very much, having got very fatalistic & re-believing in my star & that of my nearest & dearest. They woke me up, but I was too sleepy to consider their implication – & they were not so near as the [Madame] Tussaud bang was to [Hugo] Strecker.

I think I've got the better method for re-doing the 'Go Down Moses' – so that'll be done today & tomorrow – & then I'm putting the 4 new numbers thus completed on to the ink-score – partly not to have all the ink-copying at the end & partly to have a double copy. There may have to be minor, or even major alterations afterwards. As soon as I've copied in ink these new numbers I shall move on to the final 4 of Part II.

I may come over to see you in t'week if I don't go to town. I am not going to town if the stations are being bombed because it'll be such a nuisance getting back, & also soon I suppose I shall *have* to go to town for & with Edric – & Den [Newton]'s first tribunal can't be long delayed at Fulham . . .

I was sorry to see Fred [May] in such disarray. He needs a different sort of help from the other boys because he's caught up in it so much more . . .

Please will you keep this week's *Times Lit Supp* wh I left on the piano – it has a devastating review of Eliot's *East Coker* wh I brought up for Den to see, but I haven't read the other contents, so please don't throw away if you can find it still.

Much love
Michael

[1941]

Fresca dear,

If you can get Den to bring apples, bacon, & if possible some eggs. There are one or two unforeseen expenses which I am incurring – apart from the records & some more ones if I can find what I am looking for, there is the extra score of the Oratorio & two books which I feel I need v. badly for the slowly maturing conception of the 'Masque' [the earliest idea for *The Midsummer Marriage*]. If you can manage to spare a £10 that would be wonderful – or half that if you can't. I am going to finish the clothes problem on Friday when I got to town – & 2 towels I need . . .

I've had a letter from Anthony Sedgwick [*a former pupil of David Ayerst's at Blundells School in the army*] & in the depths of gloom – but he will probably come through somehow. [*In fact, he was drowned later in action in the Mediterranean.*] It does get some of them badly especially out of that class of home & upbringing. I'm deep in the technical problems of the music [for *A Child of Our Time*] to the 4 numbers & so it's much better with me. And I know quite well that the experiences dealt with in Part III are not particularised of the war at all & that it will be wrong if I get them tied up. Part II finished the 'journalistic' music, even if the journalistic events continue.

I've written David to see if I can go there for a break after completion of Part III & where there is quiet!

Love,
M.

[1941]
Oxted Sat.

Fresca darling

Your letter & enclosures came this morning & all is well. Rimingtons are doing fine with the records & I shall send you a set from myself next week. I shall perhaps bring it on Mon week – for the Mon. is the day – I thank Veronica for offering hospitality for the night – that wld be lovely – & I'll pop home by the early Tues train – also I may bring you a very early Christmas gift in case I don't see you later. I think I must give you 'The Waves' because it's so much our own book in some curious intimate way. I'll try to get it in London on Thursday. Another nice story: I was getting on a bus to Morley at Westminster on Thurs. & a man, a commercial traveller I am pretty certain by his manner & case, hovered round then said, you are Mr. T. – I've just come down on my job from Birmingham & have just bought a set of yr records. He'd recognised me from the photo! He was excited at the meeting he cldn't take his eyes off me & I was v. gauche. He'd had it recommended by a pianist friend in Brum. He was so exactly Eliot's new lower-middle class culture! & a very nice chap into the bargain. This makes the publication even more hopeful on the sales side, but there is no paper for it – Hugo [Strecker] rang up yesterday – his call-up papers had arrived & he told me the news of the sonata when settling the various things at issue before he went. (He's gone into the Pioneers of necessity). I want to talk to you abt the possibility of engraving via America. I'm going to explore the price of photographing a few copies here. As I am putting up the dibs, I may as well go ahead if sensible. Hugo won't mind.

. . . The man [Walter] Bergmann who played the thorough-bass at Morley for the Purcell is quite a find to me. He knows the period in and out. He's also one of those careful Germans who spot any missing dot a mile off. He's doing the piano reduction of the new work for Hugo & me. He's so good, that I am giving all the oratorio parts & scores to him to collate etc. as a private job. (He's an out-of-work refugee & an unusually nice one.) I'll post you the Times stuff on Mon. We appeared again [in concert reviews] ([H.C.] Colles it is) [the music critic of *The Times*] yesterday drawing the moral. But I want to show them both to Goehr tomorrow when I see him again in the middle of BBC broadcasts from Maida Vale.

Glad the doctor thinks better of it – all such nonsense as ulcers must be put firmly aside . . .

Love,
M.

[1941]
Oxted Tues.

Fresca dear

. . . I had a marvellous scribble from Vaughan Williams this morning saying he'd ordered the records, but animadverts against the use of 'piano' for 'pianoforte' – hopes I'll have it deleted. Alas, too late.

If you look at p.8 of the Scholes 'Listeners' History of Music', you will see a marvellous example of Sharp ¾ nonsense, wh sings itself as ⁴⁄₄ without so much as alteration: & there is Scholes as far up the garden path as everyone – further in fact. The page is a classic & probably one of the easiest to use as an example. I picked up the book by accident when looking for something for a beginner. I have it here.

The Dufy [print] looks v. gay on top of the bookshelves. Adrian [Allinson's painting] looks too imposing on the big wall, but is nicer for the room than the Bellini . . .

Love,
Michael

PS: To amuse you after that, the variation in the Handel [*Fantasia*] I've just finished . . . I cldn't help singing [to it]: 'Ah – whoopee'; wh makes it gloriously comic. Phyllis won't find it so because it precedes a filthily difficult cadenza-break. I'm going to play her the ½ of the work next Wed in between classes, & talk over how best to approach [Henry] Wood, Boult, Sargent, [Leslie] Heward. I've got hold of plenty of leaflets now – so shld you want any later you must think out – Is that Adrian worth one?

PPS: I've cut the envelope to add after getting yr letter. No – I don't think it's any use yr wandering after concert-giving that has to be beaten up, so to speak. It gives me personally nausea – thinking of years of nonsense of that order.

No. I'm thinking that what you are on in your job [*i.e. studying folk-songs*] – that there's masses of work to do & I don't think it's all certainly in the British Museum. Also, I think the sorting out & composition of all this material out of [Cecil] Sharp & the B[*eggar's*] O[*pera*] is not to be done in a day. One thing will lead to another. To establish our contention to use the B.O. as *one* of the prime standards of English text, we shall have to go into so much surrounding it all. If you have, for instance, now got 'town' & 'country' groups, then it's good to see how it works out elsewhere & then on to other articulations, such as dance rhythmical tunes – wh will tend to appear in the gay 'town' section, then coming bang out of *country* dancing! I'm sure the question of time-signature is a fruitful one. Because we shall probably eventually get a sort of ladder – the roots in romantic, immediate expression – what Sharp went to find – & the heaven of the ladder will be the classical, artistic, turned, articulated stuff. And what we shall seek to show is the elements wh were at work to form it: such as the necessary formulation of dancing, the influence of poetic forms, the artistic feeling in the composer. The B.O. is a good English work of art because it faces both ways – it protests against the excessive influence of the foreigner & the romantic inchoate expressiveness of the Sharp 'natural' peasant. Hence again we erect it (& it doesn't matter altogether how factual all this is) as a standard for our day. There *must* be cross-currents in art & tension – & again now there are 2 ways to face (if not 3!) – against the German *Schwermut*, against the jazz-nostalgia, against the Celtic Twilight. Positively, on the other hand, for roots in the 'town' & 'country' streams of English tradition, for balance between them, for full artistic integrity – & a historical immediate sense of the good models.

This sounds like a text book, but so much can hang on one essay – *vide* Eliot. The real thrill will be the writing – when every phrase must tell & concur to bring out the attitude. It is not the 'country', as such, that we define against the 'town'. It is the nostalgic, vague hovering with the excellent quality of folk-expressiveness, as opposed to the *consciously* artistic articulation of it. Sharp was probably stymied before it. It got him on his weak, undeveloped side – so he either toned it up with jokey fortes, or tried to present it under the guise of the irrational peasant. We show, if we can, that in an articulated mastered form, it is just good, English, & highly presentable, differing in no necessary inferiority, or superiority, from the gay stuff. What we refuse is inchoate subjectiveness (except as folklore) & Sharp's subterfuges & lack of integrity, let alone maturity.

M.

[1941]
Tues.

Fresca dear
I think it's going to work out v. well the break because I am only
a few bars, but many hours, off the ½ way pause before the fugue
[in the Handel *Fantasia*] – I shall come a Sun evening till early
train Wed morning & will card [?] you from train tomorrow as to
the train down; but shld I need Sun evening to finish I'll wire you
Sat & come Mon. morning v. early. But I expect it'll be Sun.

The enclosed is what I've been trying to plan out – feeling our
way to limits for our book. You'll see that I've shifted the ground
at the end. I see much more clearly now where our 'Little
England' attitude won't carry sufficiently. That's again in the
Sharp past. I thought you'd better see it before I come.

The music might amuse you. It's a condensed portion of the
score, showing conventional tonal patterns, but some rhythmical oddities, so much clearer under the hand – where the fall of the
one part thrusts on the fall of the other. Harmonically it may be
too conventional, but it comes at a point where the music will
stand that. Felt you'd like to see the sort of thing that occasionally
comes out.
All love till Sun.

Michael

[1941]
Sat. even.

Fresca darling
I too have been conked-out, tho not as completely. I played
[Edward] Lockspeiser the 'Child' under a growing 'flu & went to
bed at Layard's & then home here instead of Wed's classes. I went
to town Thursday – Friday was OK – but today have been in bed
till now, am up & sitting in complete lethargy by the fire. And
the new pf & orch work is still not ink-copied. However I ought
to be able to begin again tomorrow . . .

Edward is v. much under the weather & the analysis is sucking
him to perdition. His woman on the contrary, went to John
Layard for her curious trick of missing bars & beats in singing, &
John helped her in 12 sittings to a most lovely set of Jungian
religious dreams – the last one a real miracle. John showed me the
analysis & has the permission to publish. As Jung said some-

129

where, whatever the dream meant to the dreamer 'Es sagte mir unendlich viel' [it told me an endless amount]. I'll tell it you when I see you.

I think the broadcast date to USA is Dec 11; but so far I'm too lethargic to write to New York to anyone. I shall write eventually to Sari Dienes. I've refound Paul & will tell you about him when we meet.

I'm afraid letters will be scratchy – & then we must arrange some visit when you're about again.

I've just finished 'To the Lighthouse' – such exquisite & mature art. I am not surprised the price was what it was for her. Will write again more fully later.

Love, Michael.

Yes, I thought V.W. [Vaughan Williams' work] v. poor.

[November 1941]
Tues.

Fresca darling –

I hope at last you're better. I've begun to pull out of 'flu & colds & feel more normal. There's some idea of my going down to Cambridge to see all the boys on Dec 6–7 – staying with Karl Hawker. But principally I'd like to see you. There's so much accumulation of news.

I'm now more vegetable like again & am trying to finish off the letters due over the records. I'm writing to [the pianists] Solomon, Harriet Cohen – who was the pianist you thought to send to? was it Clifford Curzon? He seems to me v. close to our humanitarian views as he has signed a national petition abt night bombing. Are you in a state to deal with it later – also can you get hold of an address for me which wld reach Arthur Waley, whom I met thro Phyl & who is v. keen on new music.

I had a card from N[ew] Y[ork] from Peggy, & it seems as tho the score [of the Double Concerto] did at last reach N.Y. But I don't hold much hopes for it. I'm thinking that the polyphonic attitude from wh it was written is not an easy matter to get from a score when looked at with our usual eyes. The rhythms look innocent & even ineffective – the play & tensions between them is not felt from the score without an instinct for it. I'm reluctantly being driven to realise this.

The new pfte [pianoforte] & orch work [Handel *Fantasia*] is completed & is quite 'tough' – that may make a breakthrough, &

I sincerely hope it does. There is not any overdose of polyrhythm in it, but some nice bits wh will p'raps whet the appetite or stimulate curiosity. I've felt rather isolated lately, & see that that's a usual effect of having an individual point of view. As you remark – or simply – I need good friends v. badly.

Meanwhile I am trying to temper myself to face a showdown with the authorities soon. If am so wound up in music that the struggle on the special plane gets me a-feared, then I shan't fight it well & be much more hurt if it comes to real sacrifice. There's the threat now of a total conscription into the Home Guard because the firewatching has proved ineffective. Willy nilly that means a collision, because the H.G. has to shoot etc. It has this advantage, that the fight is absolutely clear cut – but I suspect that the penalties for refusal will be clear-cut too – so I'm trying to face up to it & to make the best of it. For instance, if I had to go away for a bit to be entertained by H[is]. Maj[esty]: in a quod – wld you officially reside in the cottage & keep it warm for my return & out of the billeting hands etc? It'll be most likely a matter of time &/or so many months. On the other hand so many of the lads on the land will be up against it too that the nonsense may be too general to pursue too far. I haven't found out the facts of all this yet – so far it's press rumour, but pretty correct.

Write me a card saying how you are & what yr plans are. You seem far too far away.

Love
M.

[1942]
Oxted Sun.

Fresca darling,
I'm sure you're wise not to come to London in this weather – but I shall be thankful when you're properly well & I want to see you about it all badly.

For myself I have felt better again because some minutes before you rang thro I had managed to get going again on sketches for the 2nd madrigal – appropriately enough the first one, the light one, was finished 2 days before Tribunal & the dark one comes now. I feel inside much like I used to do in the Wilf period – something at the pit of the stomach – but it's easier to sustain & many of the soldiers must have it about leaving wife & kiddies. What has principally happened is that the shock, aided by a long cross-examination at David's, produced the most unequivocal series of visions & dreams I have had – I realised that the old shame & fear was hiding behind the pacifism, just as it has hid behind physical cowardice of adolescence & homosexuality of later years – & this time I seem to have accepted it more fully – so that I feel I have the strength to walk towards or backwards to live in the light or the shadow, to be the respectable member of society or the conchie-scapegoat. If the division is forced because of the general situation then I sit down among my own, while knowing to myself that the others are my 'arm' too. I have run with the hare & the hounds all along – but if covered it appears a cowardice within before the *facts* of division in the great world. What David [Ayerst] wants me to do – to compromise – is somehow an attempt to bridge over the gap again.

I seem to be driven towards a cutting-through – tolerance is a great virtue, but not all kinds. Germany went down before the *furor Teutonicus* partly because all the middle people hid in safety in compromise. In England we're a bit tougher. Also, whatever serenity, even gaiety I possess is not an escape just because I have always been linked to the outcast & the scapegoats. However morbid it may appear it is for me a vital link – if I don't accept it when it comes I would cease to be what I am.

Thirdly there is a feeling that I might really be able to do something to break the anonymity of the 700 or so young ones who are in gaol already – for they are the future too. At least in my choral circles & my own profession the issue will be inescapable because I shall publicly explain what I am doing. It was hinted that if I went to O'Donnell I could don the blue uniform & be librarian or some such for the RAF orchestra. That is the usual way out for my colleagues. David does not want me to take that but to go back into London social work, thinking I would have some spare time to write in, & might find myself conducting choirs in shelters & clubs. Do you see the unreality of all this? I can't help feeling I have done my whack of social nursing & that if there is to be a new life it will be a different experience altogether.

For pacifism really is something to me – not for what it is now, but for its future, in an England becoming more insidiously *führer* ridden every week. Heroism at all costs, as [Eric] Kennington paints – & what is to prevent the political powers fighting over the body of the heroicised RAF to make it their S.S., their Communist Party? If Kennington could but once paint the young C.O. sitting in the 'glasshouse' (the military prison & pretty grim) among his blue boys, I should feel England were safer – because of the generosity & the recognition of the double necessity, the healthy tension. Everyone hopes I will compromise, because the other thought [prison] is troublesome & horrid. David even accused me of wanting to go to prison merely to spite the State or myself. That is partly his defence against the intolerable nature of this monstrous world-conscription. Naturally, the authorities hope I will compromise too, for there will be a certain moral difficulty in committing me to quod – while there is hardly any difficulty in sentencing the anonymous youngsters – poor kids. I only wish I had a name like Walton to play around with!

An odd business – but this inner situation is foretold in Eliot's horoscope! Isn't that queer?

I may write to Layard abt Ruth – all my love.

Michael

[1942] [to Fresca]

To talk practical politics: the hope that returns so easily is probably necessary for me to write, but it's deceptive. Until the decision I have to be able at any moment to put the music voluntarily aside. Also I might v. much rather have the matter decided at once now, but the weeks' grace are probably essential. First of all I have to finish the 2nd madrigal, sell the copyright to Stainer & Bell, & perform them at Morley if possible & launch them thus. Secondly the concert Mar 7th. must be gone through & the new work with Goehr's help sent on its travels – this means printing a leaflet of criticism etc. & hawking it around.

If I am taken away before this is completed, I think it's something you could manage for me. It may mean visiting Manchester & such places to interview the Hallé & so on. It can only be done successfully at the start in person.

Next I must prepare the String Concerto for Goehr to produce
– either by helping his losses on the expenses of a big string band
– and/or rescoring the work so that it can be played temporarily
with few strings & double woodwind.

Goehr thinks to offer Boosey & Hawkes our 'arrangement' of
the 4 Gibbon fantasies. The editing might even be done in gaol,
on my side. What I have got Goehr to see in the Gibbons is the
modernity of the music & the need for a different notation from
Fellowes. You will hear on Mar 7th Goehr is broadcasting them
as a try-out, to the continent next Wed morning after the 9 a.m.
news on the *continental wave* (as George Walter & the Orchestre
Raymonde). I think his times are always 9.20–10 a.m. every
Wed. and the programmes are great fun. I go up Tuesday to
BBC for the rehearsal.

Finally I want to see you about the songs etc., because that can
be meditated on if necessary in quod – & I believe that thro V.W.
& Eliot you could even get material in to me, & stuff wh I can
hear without piano. So get well as soon as you can. There's a
further problem of Morley. A lively little choir dead nuts on the
English stuff – & Bergmann to fall back on for donkey-work &
rehearsal if you were unable – might well be yr cup-of-tea – &
you would be the nearest to myself I cld find for them!

Mar 7th is only settled to the extent that after the concert [there
will be] tea at David's – when the party clears away – you, I,
David, Layard & [David's officer colleague] John Campbell
probably go to dinner together at leisure – we've decided to send
the boys off to flicks, because it's difficult to take Den & not
Bryan etc. & the dinner will be rather older. OK? Den tells me
you think to come in trousers – I'd rather you didn't. I want to be
able to take you to meet Goehr in the artist's room & his wife, &
Phyllis & the orchestra etc., & it'll look a touch of masquerade, &
in your proper dress you always look essentially feminine &
good. Change at David's if you like after. On this occasion it is
for the boys to wear their corduroys, Wilf to wear his beard & his
green trousers & Meg her peculiar make-up – but I shall be in a
suit & you will be virtually wife – that's to say something besides
our joint selves, something public & professional. I've got Goehr
to give me two seats not too close, but just nice – Row M!

Adrian (Francesca's painter-brother) was at the Solomon
concert & rushed up to me most friendly – he is coming to Mar

134

7th – p'raps I'd better ask him to the party – in fact, I will. I've asked Alan & Nancy [Bush] – but Alan is in army, tho Nancy will come.

Uncle Tom Eliot might conceivably be there – & if so, I want to introduce you to him.

I've taken the burden of expense of the tea-party off D[avid]'s hands – because he's been so good to me, putting me up each week at his expense (wish you had a room in town again) – It'll be £3–4 – so probably we can share it. I've given all the boys tickets & even by a wangle Ruth & John Campbell, at David's, the dearest person, will do the catering & I shall give him money enough ahead.

M.

[March 1941]
Oxted Fri.

Fresca darling,
I had an idea from yr letter today that you expected me this Friday – not next week – however the telegram will have told you by now. I can't catch the early train from here, where I will have to be. So I'll try & take some nourishment before I catch the train & p'raps Mill House could give summat when I get there – possible? If not, let me have a card, & I'll take sandwiches – only I have the half-difficulty of not getting back till 10.15 Thurs, & then leaving by 9.30 Friday, with two days' correspondence to do after getting supper, & packing to do before getting breakfast.

The criticisms of the Fantasia centre round the two first variations (you & Jeff Mark) & the bit in the middle wh worried Edwin Evans & Sackville-West. I think their point is only really a matter of orchestration & due also to Goehr's sudden stoppage of the movement at a wrong point, wh he felt he had to do to keep the orchestra clear. What you & Jeff felt abt the start is more difficult, because in fact, the first variation was acoustically not there, owing to some trick at the performance – tho Jeff gives other factual criticisms from the copy itself. But I can't decide till I hear it again. We are angling for a broadcast. I've also an idea to try Goehr at a concert in Cambridge &/or Oxford. Your feeling that the work was continual is my feeling too – And I think it's come for good. It's a sort of growing-up inside. And it goes hand in hand with my increasing knowledge of the English tradition! I think the oratorio will sound even more continental too. The point is that the temper is of that order, irrespective of myself. I am quite happy about this, & indeed welcome it. Not but what the English ancestry is really there all the time – it's the technical equipment that is growing intellectually maturer & consequently un-English, as per Bax – V.W. & Ireland etc. See you Friday.

Love, Michael.

[1942]
Oxted Tues.

Fresca darling

I had a lovely & dream-like time in Cornwall & have left my heart there. P'raps I shall get back later on this year, further west. Lamorna way. We might even go there together. There is no one about & no soldiers & such heavenly colouring & things just as they ever were.

Today I start the new string 4tet, a gracious work, I think. It's always an exciting moment. The laborious days come later.

There is no chance of central heating. It needs a Government Order for National Importance. But [next door] Miriam & Ben's lavatory pan has gone the way of Jack's (wh I have already paid to replace). & I have suggested that Miriam has her larder & lavatory changed over (at my expense – £6, I think) just the same as Jack & Bronwen did to theirs at their expense (I supplied the lavatory pan at 30/-). This makes for a great deal more amenity to the two cottages & seems worth it. It is done cheaply because Jack &/or Ben help the artisan with labour. It enhances the value of the property, of course.

I've also O.K.'d Den's quotation for re-printing the Oratorio (£10 or thereabouts). I don't know if this is wise but I need some more copies, & tho this means 500 (to be economical) it means that there is a nice printing we can use on sale at any performance & I can hand over the surplus to Schotts when that time comes. I suddenly had a feeling that the thing to do was to print while one can (Schotts wouldn't spare paper for such a thing just now). So on the whole I am rather going it – & I don't think it can be done entirely off my own bat. I don't believe it is really extravagance tho because it is material value which will become ever scarcer & rather now or never. (The debt to Rimington, [for production costs related to the recording of Piano Sonata 1] which Aubrey failed to pay is a debt of honour & has got to be solved – & I will do that as soon as I know the exact amount).

[1942]
Oxted Sat.

Fresca darling,
I thought of ringing you last night, but I realise I don't know the geography of Cyril's phone & whether a call wld get you. I came back from town yesterday, & after all this constant palaver of seeing people & strange beds & winter & the need to get W. Goehr's new score finished for him so that I can start my *a capella* motets, I cldn't face any more travelling, nor Karl [Hawker] & the boys – I'm growing middle-aged! So I sent him a wire – then had a telephone call to go today, Sat., to take the Goldsmith's Choral union rehearsal of the Beethoven Mass, for 2 guineas. Reluctantly, thinking of the oratorio, I accepted – it will be odd to handle 100 voices – wh they get on average at rehearsal. I think I shall prefer Morley & its 30.

Hugo [Strecker] is gone & so I came right up to old [Max] Steffens the head of the firm in England. He says that Hugo has left an inextricable mess almost. For months I cld never get any word abt music, but only troubles abt his latest girl. I had an idea that Steffens was OK really – so talked to him frankly & he on his side was in the same mood & there & then made out terms of contracts for the 3 MS rather than the oratorio. I get £10.10. on account I believe. Anyhow it's v. satisfactory. Steffens also is sending me with his recommendation to Stainer & Bell when the a capella work is finished – wh is generous – because they will be the only possible money making sort of things in England at first.

I seem to have become Goehr's admirer at times. Also I have for the moment persuaded him to open 'my' concert with Gibbons string fantasias – 4 of them. He also does one Purcell 3-part sonata in another program. He hopes to get BBC interested in recitals of unusual 17th & 18th cent. stuff that refugees have brought over & thro me (& so you) to include English stuff – wh is the right way to do it. He wants the English stuff in order to temper the German with the specific English quality . . . & that's I think where I come in myself & my own music with him – he does sincerely like it. So after the new work I shall show him the String Concerto & try & help him do a concert with enough strings – because he hopes to go on concert-giving of an adventurous order, but without the colossal fees to 'draws' wh he has had to do for the first lot in order to get away with it.

To stand behind a conductor like this is what I always hoped for & is like the Vienna of the old days – the composers & conductors & players approximating to a unified professional society. I expect it happens here each generation, but also there is something a bit more to it this time, because the whole standard of taste is wider & based on better scholarship & the BBC & others have taken the burden of the endless production of the hackneyed off our shoulders & left us free to collect up the audiences for the more discriminated stuff, without wh no real high level of taste can obtain, & no good native music either.

I miss you v. much and it's the Monday visit that I wanted most. What chance is there to see you elsewhere, nearer I mean? If there isn't, I think I shall have to come down just to see you – but if you cld trust yourself to Miriam's & my tender care for a while, you'd be most truly welcome & that wld be the ideal.

I see I shall be de-reserved in Jan or Feb & so will come naturally to Tribunal in the end. That doesn't worry me. Counting on an Appeal, shld I get into difficulties, I shall still be at large on Mar.21. Also, it is really fairly well on the cards that I shall get the exemption I want & all serene.

I shall order your records – for the moment to yr account because they've got mine in a mess & tell me I owe £22 when I've paid everything in the mail. It's I think Aubrey's share in the recording fees & a muddle of my £15 cheque for my share.

Love M.

[1942]
Oxted. Tues.

Fresca dear,

Would you see if you could get for me from the Times the autobiography of a fighter pilot called *The Last Enemy* by Richard Hillary. Macmillan. I have an idea it is the thing that is missing – the attempt at a spiritual understanding of the indifferent attitude of one inside the racket. I want to see it very much.

I have been reading the Everyman copy of Gilchrist's Life of Blake, wh I got a little while ago. You would enjoy it. Gilchrist was a raconteur & brings the man himself to life & late 19th-cent London & its arty crowds too. Quite fascinating. Makes Blake v. human & substantial, as well as being a real mystical genius. A very great figure.

Work has gone well & the 4tet moves. But the prison walls worry me & sometimes dry everything up. I am frightened in my body tho unafraid in my mind. Evelyn seems to think it may finally come to grips with all the long traditions of fear, from childhood up.

Was glad to hear [Fresca's friend] Jude [Wogan's] voice on the 'phone & what she said. Hope it all comes out alright & a love based on the great quiet after the storm & not with admixture of hysteria any more.

Yesterday & today am hampered by an inner chill. V horrid. Blake always got such whenever he went to N. London – Hampstead countryside etc. He didn't believe in 'discipline' for this ailment because he didn't think the Lily should learn of the Rose.

Much love, Michael.

[1943]

Fresca dear,

. . . I've been much moved by the *Journal d'un Curé de Campagne* – that sort of sensibility can make all English & German art seem suddenly crude & adolescent – but it's dangerous too for me to read such books. I begin to move insensibly into that half-world where I can't distinguish reality from fantasy – my greatest temptation (& by the way, what a reality was expressed for me by his temptation; *manque de l'espérance* – how one can cling to a memory, a self-description, a vice, as to a lover.) I rang up & got on to Vicky – that makes for sanity – because just before I foolishly played 'Wise old Horsey' & it has an incomprehensible effect on me – as tho it came from the world, years & years ago before the moderns were thought of, & as tho the Americanisms just covered up this eternal source as tho to disguise it deliberately, or hide it from themselves. I suppose it's got changed by me with sort of overflow of subjective emotion & feeling. I wonder if you will think so – it will be amusing to see. While this half-world persists I can't compose, I'm too restless – this mood often precedes work – so I have to write & I can't write to Wilf who seems to be going dead in me. I shall be in at abt 10 on Wed – have a lot to tell you here & there. M.

[9 March 1943]
Tues.

Life is fearful – composition hopeless. Morley concert on Sat. Bedford Wed evening next week –interval talk with Peter Pears on *Fidelio* – 8 p.m. National Gallery with Morley on the Thursday after!! Two local choir concerts Sat–Sund[ay] – so – so. Still thank God it's all at one go. Don't forget the new 4tet is Sat fortnight – Mar 27 – but will be broadcast Ap[ril] 8. My father hit in the raid of Exmouth – slowly getting better – head & knee wounds healing – but blast has shaken him badly – & the whole business upset my poor mother – if you feel to write – it's 12 Louisa Terrace, Exmouth. (24 killed) horrible business. 170 suffocated themselves in a shelter in London last week thro panic – actually no planes over London itself at all. Shows the danger of crowds.

Am v. tired – but gay. Have done first section of new piece [*Boyhood's End*] – Peter finds it a bit wild I think. Shall *have* to take fortnight off from writing to do all the shows. Main news that is.

Love, M.

[Late March/early April 1943]
Wed.

Fresca darling
Sorry to hear you're off to Addenbrooks [hospital in Cambridge] – but I suppose it'll be alright – let me know the moment you come to London.

Thank you for the enclosure – just in time!

4tet was a success – smashing notice in *The Times* – all going well.

Lots & lots of love,
Michael.

[1943]

Fresca darling,

All what you want will be sent you.

Was good to see you & I enjoyed the weekend with Den – am mentally fallow & fairly relaxed, but the eyes betray me – am absurdly tired & 'shortsighted'.

. . . Meanwhile, I've actually started doing the new movement for the first 4tet. Haven't heard Britten's yet but expect I shall feel as you do abt it. He's been talking to me a lot abt himself & his music. [They?] both seem to like the cantata – & so does Goehr – it's quite a serious work & in one place v. moving. I've been down to see Goehr & got the Double Concerto in train for July 17. Thank you so much for the book, comb, oatmeal etc. I did enjoy the lovely sunshine in the Mill House Garden. It's a dope I'm given now to play for me tomorrow on the radio. You'll hear if you listen.

Hope to see you soon again.

Love,
Michael.

[1943]

Darling –

. . . I shan't write a lot of dope abt the case at Oxted etc. because I'll meet you off the first bus next Friday. Once in the lawyers' hands it is v. difficult to remain a human personality. The 'counsel' by the way costs 25 gns. for Oxted – & I've just said yes & realise I can't v. well say no. I expect between the lot of us we'll manage it. I definitely want a small sentence (to appease the Ministry's legal claim) & keep in contact with the 'boys' (Billy [a young conchie] is in now) – & a moral win or approval for the cultural v. total war stand. The lawyers want a headline case & V[aughan] W[illiams] in court & what not.

There – will tell you how it goes when I see you.

Love,
M.

[June 1943]
Sat.

Fresca darling,
In some ways I've got an intense wish to be there – & the central point is the Quaker Meeting – & the value of it all a feeling of dropping off all the ties wh have been so much accumulated the last year or two as the price of success – & thus to reach an area of peace & meditation from wh something deeper can be created. I shall try & get a 'Cloud of Unknowing' into my cell or a 'St John of the Cross'.

A book you would like – or the temper thereof – Henry Miller: 'Colossus of Marroussi'. I'm reading Den's copy wh I cld send you. Also you shld read Gill's autobiography sometime. Let the Cornford [*The Origins of Attic Comedy*] be – Miller on Greece is more passionate.

It's best on Monday to ring John Amis. Langham 2270 & 1937 – he gets news. Peter Pears will go into the LPO on return from the court case. I haven't got yr phone no. Please ring it to John. And will you thro him get & choose a new professional photograph.

Yr dreams are v. good – am so glad . . .
See you when it's all over.

Love, M.

THE PRICE OF PACIFISM

On 21 June 1943, I was the first to arrive and be sentenced at Oxted Crown Court and afterwards had to remain in a police cell until the proceedings had finished. When I was taken out, I was handcuffed – to my surprise – to a young soldier who had killed someone with his army vehicle and been given a Borstal sentence. We were led to the back of a police van and then driven to Wormwood Scrubs (principally an adult prison, with a Borstal wing). It was a beautiful summer evening and, as we drove up over the North Downs, I couldn't but think it ironic that I was going to prison chained to a soldier. We parted on arrival and I was taken for the usual physical examination and placed in a temporary cell for the night; I was given my proper cell the following day. Locked up finally the following evening, after supper (bread and cocoa), I felt almost safe, but to my distress I heard the cell door being unlocked. Instead of a warder (or 'screw'),

142

however, it was a Quaker minister. The Society of Friends allowed prisoners of conscience to be members for the period of their stay. The minister's opening words took me aback: 'You got a very short sentence – there's a lot of work to be done here, you know!' This was a very Quaker attitude. He himself had been in the prison twenty-five years earlier as a conchie.

The daily routines – slopping out, washing all together, breakfast (tea, porridge and a small loaf of bread) – took their course. In my ignorance, I thought it would be advantageous to keep half a loaf to add to my later meal (tea). Little did I know that the cells were left open when I was working, and the bread was stolen! One of the conchies told me that if I wanted to keep anything, I should wear it under my shirt. A prison 'prefect' (or so-called 'red band') had gone into the kitchens and had stolen a complete tin of corned beef: but its size meant that he couldn't conceal it under his shirt for long without being found out. I was one of those who received a chunk of his corned beef, which I found quite unappetising!

The Scrubs was really a first offenders' prison, but because of the war many were brought here who should probably have been elsewhere. The prisoner in the cell to the left of mine had raped his young daughter. At the furthest end of my section was a man who had been a director of Beezie Bee Honey and who was serving a sentence for black-market activities. Since he was wealthy he paid an impecunious prisoner by cheque to do his workshop tasks. Somehow his mailbag was taken out of the workshop by a prisoner into a cell: and by morning, when we awakened at 6.30 a.m., the work had already been done and the mailbag returned into the workshop – how, was anybody's guess – via a bent screw, no doubt!

Since we would not do war work, we conchies had to sew mail bags. I was hopeless at this: we weren't allowed thimbles and I couldn't get the needle through the canvas. The workshops were supposed to be silent, but as conchies were not real criminals, we were free to behave normally. One prisoner came to me and asked if I had anything to read. As I hadn't, he said he would bring me some reading. The next day he arrived with two serious books under his shirt. 'Floaters' [i.e. unofficially circulated books] had also come into the prison: you could either find them in the library, or they would be given to someone else to keep away from the screws – they were never openly visible. The prisoners looking after the library were an odd group: one of their privileges was to be allowed to wear red socks!

They filled baskets with books just as they came off the shelves and brought them around the cells for distribution. Most of those handed out to me were children's books intended for illiterates. After waiting a month, I was allowed to have a book of my choice sent in. I decided to improve my score-reading and asked for Bach's *Art of Fugue* (which I had just been given by Walter Goehr).

To the screws, we conchies were the lowest of the low. Our crime was despicable. However, they were very understaffed and after a while, realising that we weren't criminals and wouldn't try and escape, they let us move around largely unattended. One evening, my cell door was unlocked and a screw came in to consult on the musical education of his daughter. Naturally, I gave him the best advice I could. What I thought ludicrous about the system was that you couldn't ever survive unless you told lies and behaved like a child.

Not everyone accepted the situation as I did. There was one young man called Arnold Machen, a sculptor or designer who worked for Wedgwood china, who was intensely frightened by it all. When, after six weeks, he should have been moved to another wing and allowed to associate more with others in the recreation room, he couldn't bear to go and asked to be locked up instead: this the authorities allowed. He spent his days decorating the recreation room and I was very drawn to him. Strangely, the largest single body in prison were the soldiers – mainly deserters and those who had committed offences whilst training. They knew that – unlike ourselves – when they left they would immediately be rearrested by the military police at the door of the prison. Consequently, they used to try to lose all their remission by banging on the doors, ringing the cell emergency bells etc. The result was that if you were ill, it was almost impossible to win anyone's attention: you just had to avoid being ill.

Wanting to do something to widen the prisoners' education, the authorities thought a prison orchestra would be worth trying out. As they knew of my work at Morley College, I was naturally asked to do something about it. The standards, of course, were low, but I did what I could. I already knew that whichever religion was put down on your forms, you were allowed to attend the Anglican morning service in the big chapel; if not, you remained in your cell. I always went because the sound of massed men's voices singing hymns was so moving. Special services in worktime were held for such sectarians as Catholics, Jews and Quakers. I contrived to be called out of the workshop on Fridays for a Quaker meeting. Needless to say, although the service was essentially a silent one, I didn't succeed in keeping quiet for long. I was moved by this form of service also.

In the recreation room there was a piano. This was once moved to the chapel for a concert by Ben and Peter, which had been arranged long before I arrived at the Scrubs. Desperate to try out some musical ideas, I slipped along and sat once more in contact with musical sounds. Unfortunately, the Prison Governor appeared with some visitors and asked what I was doing: I immediately bent low over the instrument and started banging specific notes – 'Tuning the piano, sir', I replied. Ben and Peter brought along with them John Amis to act as page-turner, but I had protested to the authorities that the music was so complicated that the recital would be impossible unless I also turned pages for the pianist. This was allowed, though it was touch and go: at the last moment I stepped out of the ranks of prisoners and sat down unexpectedly on the platform beside Ben. It was a strange moment for us both.

My chief visual memory of prison is of climbing up on the landing and looking out northwards: there I could see the crudely built yards of the Great Western Railway near Paddington. My sense of being in a community disrelated from the rest of society was acute. I wrote of my experiences to Evelyn.

[12 June 1943]

Evelyn dear – no letters allowed except an answer to each one I send out – every fortnight. Write to V.W. if you will & thank him from me. If the Surrey Mirror has a write-up of his evidence let John have a copy to show Schotts, Boult etc. Ring Sellick & wish her luck for Sat July 4. Tell John to wish Tony luck for his Prom July 7. Cis Bennett will contribute to the case if you write. Tell John to get the message about Eric Mason's Appellate from Peter to tell him & Ben to give their recital to us as soon as possible. Send a message of encouragement to the good Rose [Turnbull]. Visitors will be in a month. Would like to see John Amis. I suppose Ben and Tony would talk same language. If not, David, Fresca, Ben, you? As to holiday it seems I shall be out Aug 21st all being well – early morning. If John can wait I suppose it would be nice to have a week in Cornwall with the 'children', & possibly some time with David after. Otherwise shall be rampaging to get back to work. It'll be a desire to be with one's own again & praps a need for fresh air. Please send me in

145

books – Art of Fugue (on the piano), War & Peace – any good work on Astrology – the Cornford etc. – 2 or so at a time, the sooner the better. I think I can have up to four at once – but I'll let you know how it goes next letter.

They remain in the prison library. Shall want if possible 3 or 4 more Gillette shape razor-blades. My father would spare some I think. Came from Oxted chained to the young soldier whose case we heard first, with one of the lads who stole the rabbits. Wasn't that curious? It's rather like the first days of term before the days begin to move. In the good mood it's rejoicing, it is – as you can tell everyone – comradeship, peace & a full heart. On the recoil it's somewhat of a waste, negative & like being unwell in a foreign hotel.

On second thoughts tell John as to the various plans suggested at Eric Mason's Appellate etc. that they're better left – & in general not to worry about me – this includes the visit of Mrs Mason. John will understand, & tell him straight away. It is only gradually that one takes on the new life. Write straight away if you can. I'll get it quickly then.

Tomorrow is Quaker meeting which I look forward to. There's also a baby orchestra I hope to be allowed some time to help on its way.

Love Michael.

[5 July 1943]

Evelyn dear

Yr letter was a great pleasure to get. I will reply to its contents first. Books – I got the 2 Devotional books, but haven't read them. In fact I read little. Cell task occupies a lot of time & there is a baby prisoners' orchestra here wh I conduct & try to improve – & that takes 2 hours out of possible reading time. It's a sort of light café orchestra, & with instruments all of different pitch – in fact throw-outs. But we manage – & I hope to get in better music. On Sunday we are to play in chapel, in the middle of a recital by Peters Pears and Ben Britten – all v. amusing. So don't worry to chase after books. But there is a text-book I'd like (I've got the Bach) – will you ring Alec Robertson [at the BBC Music Dept] & ask him from me if he cld spare me a copy of his book: *The Problem of Plainsong* – on the art of wh he is an authority. If &

when you get it, take it to Friends House as you did the Bach. I shldn't send the Cornford just yet.

Tell mother if you're writing any time, not to wonder at the letters about me to her – I'm sort of a general favourite. As to getting down there, I might manage after the proper holiday on way back from Cornwall if it's to be there – otherwise I think to write the long delayed 1st movement of the old 4tet & then take another break away, at Exmouth p'raps, & then start the Symphony – wh will be a big thing.

I agree with you completely abt press hoo-ha – no interested party shld write at all.

Holiday – I'm quite as ready to go with David first. The point is anyhow that I come out Sat. 21st Aug. & will make the 4tet performance at Wigmore the public meeting ground for all & sundry. Rhse choirs etc. – then come home & get things together etc. Sunday.

The question of my getting something from people, like books, is difficult. I don't know for instance how much I really get from David – sometimes I'm rather repressed by him. I get a great deal from you – but that is a more subtle business, & in this case must wait till I'm properly home & at work again.

Keep the Hölderlin, Maritain etc. they're for my library & the autumn.

Haven't read any Paul yet. It hasn't worked out quite as I expected. One gets not only fallow but sluggish. We're all the same. You can't manufacture the proper conditions & there's a lot of interval & strain – a great deal of dreaming & inner adjustment – & the weeks inside seem monstrously lengthy and disproportionate, so that you fail to realise how easily they pass to those outside or how little one might oneself get done outside.

As far as I know there is nothing against length in letters in. Write on thin paper perhaps. You might send some 18 or 20 stave score – a few sheets – with the Robertson book. I shall probably get permission to use it. But 12 stave will do, if the other is too big.

And now messages, a special one this time to Ben & Miriam, who use after all my home & my own. Tell Miriam to use the tin of sugar in the larder wh Den gave me for jam. I shall have forgotten the taste by the time I come out. I have already. Is anyone in the cottage yet?

A message of greeting to the [amateur] choirs p.o. Tolworth (book under T.): hope they're managing. Write if you will to the deputy [conductor] Tanner & say he must choose music to suit himself & that I shall probably take at least September clear away for my own work – (if not give the choir up altogether). Ask to pay for those times he deputised for wh I signed the register – & generally to try & solve the payments, claims soon, p.o. Tooting (under T.) Just send them greetings, either via Tony or the Sec. Will see them again next term of course.

Morley. Give them best wishes for the concert on the 17th & hope they do well. Will be thinking of them. You can let them know sometime that I shall make my first reappearance on 21st Aug. at Wigmore.

Fresca. Give her my love – tell her I'm managing fine – that I came across a typical Irish ABBA tune in *Songs of Praise* masquerading as English Traditional Melody. If she thinks to come to the 4tet on the 21st, would like to lunch with her beforehand & go with [her].

If this gets you in time ring Peter & Ben, Primrose 5826 & wish Ben well for his Prom on Sat evening – & tell them not to be distressed by the [prison] 'orchestra' in Handel's 'Largo' & Bach's Chorale on Sunday. It's for the sake of social progressiveness not to rival their artistry. If they're still at home on the 21st would like to breakfast with them & bath!

John Amis: Not to forget 6 tickets for Tooting choir via Tony [Hopkins] for 17th – & if to spare send a couple to Wilf Franks c/o 45 Holmesdale Rd. N.6. To send my love to the two Walters: to Goehr, not to worry abt the 17th, but that he'll probably gain by all the publicity – & good luck to him & it. To Bergmann my love – & next season. I think [the Schulz anthem] 'Absalom, my son', or some such title, a v. fine one. To Schotts in general. Cheminant & Steffens my regards & good wishes. John can do all that. As to visit, the order is due on Mon 19th, but it probably won't reach John till 21st or 22nd. It will have 3 names on it: his, Tony [Hopkins]'s & Britten's (?) – is that O.K.? Otherwise we must invent. All the 3 come together – 2.30 at the prison is a good time. You take no. 7 from Oxford Circus to the door (½ an hour) or central London to Wood Lane, 1½d. Trolley Bus a minute or two to Du Cane Avenue & Walk down 2 or 300 yds. Quite quick. Ring the bell & ask to see me & show the order. Sld like to see read to me any press notices etc.

As to the 4tet movement (please keep these notes): I think the 2nd subject needs a longish bit (B) & the repeat of A to lead straight to the constricted portion; probably using some of the old material [to] reach the same chord before cello up-going cadenza as before – then a possibly contrapuntal development of wh the reprise of the opening themes will form the climax – & a recapitulation as varied as the material allows & leading by the same coda material to the down-going cello cadenza.

So far I've only had this one 'thought' about my music, as above; I don't think it's any good trying to make things move when the circumstances forbid any real output or creation. Prison is not a creative experience at any point – except perhaps in human contacts. I dare say it will seem less wasteful when one looks back – p'raps it may be a real holiday mentally. It's difficult inside not to give exaggerated importance to its actual length of days – & to brood on them so that they go slower. In fact I am pretty active & the time passes somehow.

Razor blades – we are allowed to change the permitted one each week. I have 4 only in 'properly' if you post some more to me, they'll just be put with the rest & I can either use them or bring them home. I like to keep shaven & as clean as may be. It's better for one's self-respect. Any blades that fit a Gillette 3-hole type – or slots.

I've experienced a lucky chance with eye exercises that may be helpful afterwards. It's v. hard on the eyes here. Sewing etc. & bad light in the cell & little time to exercise at all. I shall just about manage to keep them no worse than they are.

One has moments of nostalgia, but not too many. I shall come through. It's boring of course. It *is* good to know things happen outside. Much love to all friends & especially to you.

Michael

I dreamed of a green flowering olive tree in spring last night. Good.

[19 July 1943]

Evelyn dearest

Have been hurrying up my cell task so as to be able to write at leisure. I sent off the visiting order with the one envelope, so this may be delayed while I get hold of another. I'd better answer your letter first. Tell Morley if still going that I got their messages & thought of them hard at 6 p.m. last Saturday. And will you ask Miss Cowles there what the date of next term is because it may curtail the holiday away to 10 days. I'll come back on this. Please write [A.L.] Rowse – say I am so glad to hear he's written, I will look forward to reading the letter when I come out. Sorry he's been ill again. Tell him plans to be at Portloe & shall I look him up on way back. Does he know off-hand a pub, hotel, that wld breakfast the 5 of us on Sunday 22nd at St Austell. When I come to holiday you'll understand why. Betty Hamilton leave. Ditto the Greenwoods & others, but tell John Allen if you think fit where I am obtainable when I'm out.

Holiday: I'll write it you, tho I intend to ask John to do the trains etc. on visit. But you can never be sure of anything in prison! If the Sat. night train is O.K., we shall go to St. Austell & bus to Mevagissey – John must check the Sunday buses. We need to be at Mevagissey by lunchtime (I believe it gets in at 1.30 or so) & therefore take food for Sun: & walk along coast to Portloe getting in to tea: tho it's a good step. If this won't work we must go to Truro & walk over Malpas ferry & Lamorran woods. J. needs to get £10 out of Britten (?) in cash for me: get tickets for Den & myself & let me have the change. The Ration book etc. I wld have to get you to do & send after me. It may be rather rash to plan so hasty a departure: but it feels good. I'm hoping that a day's good food will recover me: I'm as weak as a kitten & we shall have to carry packs. If John has no pack he can share mine: or have you a rucksack of Evan's [Evelyn's son]? I don't see how I can be away more than 2 weeks at the most because of the fanfare for the church [at Northampton]. If Morley first do is Thurs 2nd Sept, then I'd better be back for it & so home. You'd better settle this and warn David.

I suggest you advise Mother of the fanfare commission & that I will come 1 night to Exmouth to see them, or 2 if possible: & put off the real visit to October. It wld be advisable therefore for D & Larema to be away already so that I can go there on Monday the 30th, but it won't be for long if Morley is open. Otherwise I wld like to get home by Sat. 4th for certain.

If Rowse suggests that we all breakfast with him, then I cld cut a visit there on the return & travel to David on the Sunday. But if

Morley is not opening till the 6th Sept, then I'd enjoy a night at Rowse's, Sun 29, some days with D[avid] & L[arema] & 2 nights at Exmouth & travel home morning train Sat. I'll write you next time the clothes I wld want in the pack – apart from a pair of flannels & a jacket to replace the suit I've got here & will wear at the Wigmore. I think, by the way, it might be worth putting a nicely worded advert in P[eace] N[ews] for the Aug 14th issue, that I am coming out all being well, & hope to be present at W[igmore] H[all] at the perf of the 2nd 4tet in order to do Cooper a possible fillip for his concert. Or is this too publicity like? I think actually the BBC Orchestra would put it in under their notes. I'm hoping, in any case, to make it an occasion of public return, so that the more it's broadcast around the better. Tell mother also that I'm so pleased to hear of my nephew John's successful operations. Cornford was a book I meant to buy so don't worry. Will be glad of the Robertson [book on plainsong] I think. Ring him & thank him if you will & give him a cheerful message from me: he's a very nice chap. If you have time write a note to Emily Borner, Fred May's sister, give her a kind message & say I'm so glad to hear Fred is joining the hospital staff. Hope to see her at W.H. on 21st. When writing to mother tell her I wrote Phyl before I came in but no reply. What you wrote abt 'endless patches of Time' was extraordinarily helpful. I do believe in it & it gives strength to endure the apparent wastage.

(Incidentally, the Symphony is gestating alright, almost consciously. I shall have the whole form mapped out in my mind by the time I come out. It's going to be a big thing.) I am only really close to you, B.B. & John Amis – no one else. And while John is simply a projection of my musical self and therefore often in my mind, Ben is v. near just because he is himself, I sense, so moved by my imprisonment. (You of course are something almost eternal: the closeness is more to be expected. Every one else is nowhere.) The concert here was a terrific success, & to be next him at the piano was absurdly deep-going. The orchestra did not function. I'll tell you all the story sometime. I haven't been to practice this week either. It matters not, except where I can be of service. The 'library' is musical comedy selections & v. tiring. Later this week I go on 'association' as it is called & have meals at tables in community & move to another cell – the Upper School! & that marks my exact half-way wh will seem better afterwards I think. Cld you get me a fresh tin of Calverts tooth-powder & send in for me. I have my specs in fact but the truth is that the strain of the eyes is v. great & I shall have to do exercises in all seriousness this autumn to try & undo the damage. You might suggest to Fresca, if she is still at Mill House, that she bottles a few things, extra, for me. I shall be sorely in need of that sort of food, at suppers & so on & generally the Allinsons have quantities. I want to try & get a better supper arrangement for a bit anyhow to try and feed myself up – I'm v. thin & long – if not haggard! Fresca has the Irish Folk-Song Journals.

Wld like you to cheer Steffens up if you see a way. I can't help feeling that wrongly or rightly the publicity has done good not only to the cause but to the music – he need have no fear. And please write Hugo – 2nd lt. H. Strecker c/o Schotts – & give him my love & good wishes & tell him I'm gay & surviving brooding on a smashing symphony, & give him news of the various nice things said by V.W. etc. Wld like you to ask Rose if she managed to get any of Cooper's handbills for 7th & 21st to send out & to get them via John if not. You will let me know, of course, abt [Evelyn's daughter] Pam's new babe, when & what sex; name. V. pleased abt [Evelyn's daughter] Gillian. You know the thought of yr being whisked to Oxford is somewhat shattering. I can't quite imagine what becomes of the cottage without you nearby. I am not in the least ready for such an eventuality – oh dear. But we won't cross the bridge before we reach it. Wish I cld have seen the ceanothus & the jasmine. But will next year. What they want if I can manage is good earth fetched to them from elsewhere because they are really bedded on the clay foundations of the house & with no proper soil except what is brought them. I'm sure she'd do it if you explain. The [manuscript] has come but I haven't applied to have it yet. I just brood mentally on the Symphony & have the plan for the fanfare. Wld like to know the exact date required if you cld ask Ben. If I apply to get my next visit (due in my last week) put ahead, wld it amuse you to come & see me in my prison clothes & I'll send the letter to mother, say?? (This must not interfere with meeting me at 7.30 on the day. You'd better come and breakfast at Ben's too.) It won't be worth seeing the others really as I should see them all a day or two later in freedom. Please get the watch, & bring for the holiday.

All in all, my dear, I am V. close to you & your letter is a great excitement when it comes. It's all v. dream-like, indeed freedom often is to me. But here it's stronger. I, actually in prison, sense something so natural & yet so like a dream existence. That's enhanced, you see, by not feeling or being a criminal. I got terribly excited on Sat the 17th thinking of the music outside. And there are whole days of impatience – days also of boredom. Wonderful moments like the hundreds of men's voices singing the Old Hundredth – & that brings tears. One is rather emotional naturally, & fearfully self-conscious. We all are. That takes a bit of time to go afterwards I believe. Quaker meeting means a lot. One is also closer to the spirit here, by the act of cutting off. I've never felt it more strongly tho I can't as yet go the violent ascetic way. But I have a sense of clearing the grossness by means of wh the spirit shines clearer thru one – it may affect the music, I think, gradually. And I think the Symphony may gain by this enforced rest. I'm pretty certain of it itself anyhow & think I shall pull it off. But I've decided to get the 4tet movement done first. Give my love to all & at this moment I am at peace – god bless you. Michael.

[15 August 1943]
Sun.

Evelyn dearest,
At last the final letter & few days to go. Am ever so sorry to hear of yr pneumonia & hope indeed it is as slight as you suggest & that it was in the nature of a rest & that you're back now at home. John on visit last Thursday told me you were still in hospital then. Shall be delighted if you're at the gate on Sat, but I don't know how sensible an early rise will be for you. If you can't come will you let Britten know – if you still feel I ought to be met by someone – failing B.B., John wld be preferable. For you to get here you go from Chiswick by train or bus to Hammersmith or Shepherd's Bush & get on the north going trolley buses, wh go from the former to the latter & on to Wood Lane Und. Stn. at the White City & the next stop or so is Du Cane Avenue – you ask for that – straight along the road abt ½ of a mile. I believe it's 7.30 to 7.45 or so, release – but will wait for you. If Ben B. is to come his quickest way, other than cross-going taxi, is tube via Oxford Circus and Wood Lane, Trolley bus to Du Cane (2 stops?)

Hope John gave you message to add my leather belt to the clothes list – & the watch. Now about my final & proper home coming. I'm so impatient for the cottage and work that I am not staying away longer than I planned, but will definitely travel up from Taunton (& David) on Thurs Sept 2nd & try & get the 2.30 train from Victoria. Praps you cld meet at the Halt 3.35 or so & come over to tea. And bring some margarine if you cld as I may not have much rations after sharing between Mother & David's Mother – & the week-end to go. And ask Miriam if she cld keep me some eggs for the week-end for suppers & then we can start normally the following week. Give my love to Miriam & say I'm dying to be home & that even Cornwall is only necessity & good sense. And let us all pray that I shall be left in peace now because I'm so full of music. Also, Felix Aprahamian, who came with John and Benjamin on visit, wanted to pencil the L.P.O. for the first perf. of the Symphony subject to publishers' approval – & for the spring! Well they will have to wait. Yet it's great fun to have offers thru the glass window of visiting box! & shows how the publicity & performances are beginning to tell.

John told me the Morley choir, who will earn 20gns from BBC for the Seiber recording, want me to have the balance after singers' expenses etc. for my holiday. Isn't that a nice gesture? So we can all have a good time – Excursions across the Fal by ferry & such cheerful holidayish items.

I've written Mother about Rose – just to tell her that of course I'll go to Exmouth whichever way it goes but that in fact it will prevent any real family intimacy, put me on edge – & after 9 weeks' imprisonment quite the worst thing for Rose or me. She had better face up to the fact that she will just spoil my (& her) homecoming – for the old usual motherish moral reasons wh spoilt so much of childhood. I had a fearsome but illuminating dream on that a night past. It must have been quite the most decisive emotional influence of my upbringing. It's as well to attempt to assimilate it now that the possibility has arrived of looking at it dispassionately as far as the personalities are concerned.

I don't think I've quite reached the point of being ready for memories & their refreshment – except occasionally. But I anticipate it. As yet, it's still plans & the future – only not in so youthful a manner or matter. The music particularly is fairly concrete & serious – tho apparently much more ahead to be done than already created. That won't be other for a year or more – & a fair number of good launchings, like the oratorio. Bergmann told me by the way that he's nearly completed the first reading of the proofs. So that goes forward & will be out in the autumn – a good time. Meanwhile I hope to get Steffens to print the 'Boyhood's End' which had good reviews & unexpected ones.

Sept. 11th at Morley is a Bergmann concert – choir is not till Oct. 16th (Weelkes) tho that means a lot of work already. Mrs Hubback rather jockeyed me (or I did myself) into giving Wed evenings to a Morley orchestra – but since then I've given a message to John at visit to try & keep it at bay – at least for the beginning of term. I just must write & everything else must & will have to wait. The November concert B.B. refers to is a proper Britten-Tippett do, financed by London Philharmonic Orchestra lot. Clifford Curzon to play my Sonata, a 2 pf. work of Britten's with him – P.P. to sing [Britten's] Michelangelo [song-cycle] & 'Boyhood's End' – praps also something else of Britten's. A nice show? I gather that Kalmus is toying with letting Goehr repeat the Double Concerto at a Boosey & Hawkes concert – I do hope it comes off. Sellick is down to play the Sonata at Nat. Gallery on Sept 21 or 22: forgotten which. So things are not too bad – and John decided to begin negotiations with [Arthur] Bliss [at the BBC] to redeem his promise & do the Fantasia broadcast after the prom. season.

Yes, praps it's better I breakfast with Peter & Ben *à trois*. And lunch? It looks like a crowd & not really yr crowd. I fancy if you can but make the early morning that's nicer & then tea on Thurs. Sept 2nd in our proper surroundings. Oh, that will be a good day.

As I feel now, I'll go to Mother's on Sunday 29th – move to David at Taunton on Tuesday afternoon 31st & leave the same on the Thursday morning – two nights at each of them – & the Wed. David can plan an expedition. He will think I ought to take more holiday as I can, but he can't have it. I know that after 10 days of holiday & differing company, decent clean food & fresh air, I shall be champing to get back & let out the damned up stream of sound. First the fanfare for Brass –then the 4tet movement – then a short break & re-visit Exmouth probably. *Höffentlich* all this by mid-October – & then the real thing – the new Symphony wh is very much getting up steam.

As this letter tells you, I'm already living outside the prison – I try not to get in a fever, but occasionally I do, tho not for long or seriously. By the time this gets to you, if it does in time, the thing will be virtually over – & I have little wish to repeat it – but of course will do so if driven.

Have made some very good friends & seen a great slice of life so to speak. Extraordinarily childlike, if not frankly childish. But all of a piece with the army, factory-life & all other mass phenomena. We are indeed 'such stuff as dreams are made on' – I become more drawn to Shakespeare & his viewpoint – only in another age's setting.

Love to you, my dear, & praps will see you Sat.

Michael.

On leaving prison (21 August 1943) I had breakfast with Peter and Ben and then went in the afternoon to hear the Zorians play my String Quartet No. 2 at the Wigmore Hall. The occasion was also an emotional reunion with all my friends. With John Amis, Antony Hopkins and Alison Purves (who later became Tony's wife), I took the night train to Cornwall, arriving at St Austell in time to have breakfast with A.L. Rowse, staying thereafter at a café with rooms at Mevagissey. A few days later, I nearly ended back in gaol, as the four of us were apprehended by a coastguard for nude bathing. Fortunately Rowse was able to get us off a charge.

By this time, Walter Goehr was doing his best to arrange for professional performances of my music. He was gradually building a reputation as a conductor and although Sargent and others regarded him as a dilettante, he was able to obtain work: he was active and successful also as a film composer, writing major scores like that for *Great Expectations*. He was closely involved with the Overseas Service of the BBC, for which he directed music programmes under the pseudonym of George Walter. When Ben became enthusiastic about putting on *A Child of Our Time,* Walter was the obvious person to conduct it. Ben was already involved with Sadler's Wells opera and, in addition to Peter, was able to persuade two other Wells singers, Joan Cross and Roderick Lloyd, to participate. I thought of using Morley College forces, but Goehr felt that professionals were really necessary. Somehow or other the money was scraped together to engage the

London Philharmonic Orchestra, and Morley Choir joined forces with the London Region Civil Defence Choir. The event had some mixed reviews: the main objections were to the use of Negro spirituals in the work. But the important thing was the breadth of response to it.

[1944]

Fresca darling,

Got yr letter this morning, which pleased me a lot. It's fearfully good news about yrself (not the present flu but in general – and the London orbit) – & all you say abt the 'Child'. It's got over not only to the ordinary [listeners] but even to the intellectuals like Seiber, who has written to me of the 'lovely texture of some of the numbers' & the use of a 'motivic idea' – & the absorption of 'the true choral tradition of our musical heritage'. But the 'Star', according to Tony [Hopkins] on the phone, thinks the script the best part of it – the music lacking in passion – & had I written it now of course, it would have been tougher – as it is, the music is of the level of Coleridge-Taylor's 'Hiawatha'!! So now you know. Of course, for that critic, 'Hiawatha' *may* be meant as a compliment – but I don't think so all the same.

'Times' was very nice – will show it you sometime. We have yet to have Eddy [Sackville-West] in the N.[ew] S.[Statesman] & most serious of all, Glock in 'Observer' – he's a pet that man. You must get to know him – only don't make Clement, his woman, jealous. We'll go together there one day & that will be alright.

If there were a morning bus to Streetly End on Monday, I might come & have lunch with you & go home by a later train. Ben Britt. comes down to Oxted by the 9.20 p.m. that night. The raids make him sick – so I've arranged for him to sleep here over the next week he has to be in town.

. . . I'm gradually waking up – but still fearfully washed out emotionally, & so unable to start proper work on the Symphony – wh *will* be tough I imagine. But I doubt it will please the 'Star' all the same. Sounds to me as if the Star chap is a political [journalist] & making a judgment backwards.

Love,

M.

Efforts were then made to organise a BBC broadcast, and when this came about there was a lot of publicity, notably in *Picture Post* magazine, which placed the oratorio within a full account of the Grynspan case. Two years later, I myself conducted a further performance at the Royal Albert Hall, in aid of the Polish children affected by the war. Kokoschka, whom I had met through Feliks Topolski, designed the cover for the programme.

THE SHADOW OF DEATH

Morley College's musical reputation grew considerably after the war, constantly drawing praise from the press, and also interesting the BBC and the recording industry. We repeated our performance of Stravinsky's *Les Noces* for the BBC; HMV recorded Thomas Tallis's wonderful 40-part motet, *Spem in alium*. Morley's concert programmes were still distinctive on account of their many novelties. For instance, we gave the first performance of Seiber's cantata, *Ulysses*; Frank Martin came over from Switzerland for the British première of his opera *Le vin herbé*; and, having long ago acquired those wonderful discs which Nadia Boulanger made of Monteverdi's madrigals, I was delighted when Walter Goehr proposed we should do the 1610 *Vespers* – the first complete performance in modern times. Goehr was friendly with the Monteverdi scholar, Hans Redlich, and made his own edition, which included two keyboard continuo-players – Redlich at the harpsichord and Geraint Jones on the organ. Since it was difficult for the choir to start straight off in the very first bar of the work, I wrote a tiny *Preludio* for organ which landed finally on D major, thus enabling the choir to get their notes. Writing the piece, I spent some time at Geraint's house, discussing the appropriate organ registration. One evening, when I came into Morley before one of the concerts, there were two American GIs who had arrived early and were sitting in the auditorium reading the programme. I overheard one say to the other, 'Monteverdi! Attaboy, Attaboy!'

On the other hand, my activities at Morley were now increasingly becoming a strain and a distraction from composition, especially since I had embarked on the writing of *The Midsummer Marriage*, which was to take me six years in all. When Eva Hubback died in 1949, I interpreted this as a signal to begin withdrawing from my involvements at Morley. I finally resigned after a special appearance with Morley College Choir at the newly opened Royal Festival Hall in

1951. I was making a small income from BBC talks by this time; and since I had made many new friends and contacts, I knew that I wouldn't be isolated from professional music-making. The big boss of HMV Records, Walter Legge, invited me to dinner one evening and after a splendid meal discussing everything at large, he took me to the station in a taxi, and only then told me the purpose of our meeting: he wanted me to become the chorus-master for the new choir he was founding alongside his recently formed Philharmonia Orchestra. Realising that this would mean I had to train them in all the standard choral repertory, irrespective of whether such music was of interest to me as a composer, I turned down his offer and returned to my poverty.

Schott was at last in a position to publish and promote my music and I got to know everyone there – befriending even the dragon-like Miss Lucca, Max Steffen's secretary. I had a natural instinct to liven up the Dickensian atmosphere of the Schott building and tended to become involved there in ridiculous antics, such as dancing on the saleroom counter. Francis Poulenc, coming up the stairs one day to the office where I was engaged in some tomfoolery, called out, 'I know that laugh!' A younger French composer, Henri Dutilleux, appeared there one day and, at his request, I took him to the East End of London to buy trousers on the black market.

Just after the war, I encountered Howard Hartog. He was still a soldier in occupied Germany and had been given the task of re-establishing music on Hamburg Radio. He had heard *A Child of Our Time* over the air and decided to mount a performance in Hamburg. Walter Goehr went to conduct, but I was not allowed to attend because, as a pacifist, I wouldn't wear uniform. Howard, meanwhile, had typically gone in search of the conductor, Hans Schmidt-Isserstedt, then in hiding, and invited him to build up the Hamburg Radio Orchestra: I was later to benefit greatly from this, for Schmidt-Isserstedt subsequently conducted some of my pieces in Germany and London. When Howard returned to England I helped him obtain a job at Schott. From that point onwards, he became one of the most idiosyncratic figures on the musical scene – finally, indeed, an institution. When he moved from Schott to the concert agency Ingpen and Williams (which he later bought up), I was one of his artists.

On his return to England, Howard found that his wife had left him with their son. This made him for a while an embittered misogynist.

At a performance of *A Child of Our Time* in Lausanne, however, I met the pianist Margaret Kitchin for the first time, and was delighted when she and Howard married soon afterwards. In the early days of this marriage, Howard was often insecure, but Margaret always stood by him and they became totally devoted to each other. Right to the end of Howard's life, he and Margaret were assiduous in attending concerts featuring new music or the artists Ingpen represented. Hard work that could be: but then Willy Strecker once told him that the best sleep was *Der Konzertschlaf!*

Already at Schott, Howard's eccentricities had become the stuff of legend. He couldn't be bothered to change his socks and, having bought a new pair during his lunch break, he threw the dirty ones out of the window. A deputation of younger composers in Schott once came to me and asked if I would approach Margaret and suggest that she should persuade Howard to put on a clean shirt once a week. Max Steffens believed that everyone in Schott should start at the bottom of the firm, in the packing department: Howard was not very good at packing and was soon moved elsewhere. He was not in sympathy with recorders and early music, and thus never saw eye to eye with Walter Bergmann. Once day Howard so enraged Walter that the latter threw a telephone directory at him – and then collapsed with a burst appendix. Howard had the loudest laugh in London and at some stage at a concert, either beforehand or during the interval, he would erupt and the entire hall would fall silent.

Established at Schott, Howard began to build up the catalogue. He once said to me, 'My job, Michael, is not to promote you – you are already through. I must look after the younger ones' – he meant Peter Maxwell Davies, Harrison Birtwistle and Alexander Goehr. At Ingpen, he was one of the few agents with the widest knowledge of the repertoire, able to advise young string quartets on which Haydn they should next tackle. As time went on, his tastes became more attuned to the continent. Howard and Margaret's closest friend, musically, in later years, was Pierre Boulez, who was like an adopted son to them. Howard partly enjoyed caricaturing himself, posing as the great concert agent seated in a large leather armchair, with a telephone in one hand and a cigar in the other.

During the Depression, in 1930, my parents had returned to England and bought a house in Timsbury near Bath, where they did their best to alleviate the local unemployment problems. They also later took in

Jewish refugees from Germany. At the outset of the war they moved to Exmouth. My contact with them was minimal. They had by now become reconciled to my activities as a composer, but we got into such arguments that eventually I declared my intention of leaving them for good. I refused the £50 a year offered by my father on the grounds that I did not give anything acceptable in return; he sent it anyway, and I reconciled myself to this. But when eventually I went to see them again, I never stayed very long, so as not to get up against my mother. My relations with my father were quite good, though he found it difficult to understand what I was up to. While my mother was a pacifist and declared it her proudest moment when I went to prison, my father supported the war. He remained a lively person in his old age, still (as he once told me) sexually active, or at least potentially so. Peter also rarely visited them: he had the same sense of not being loved. Once he was married and had his home, he would occasionally come with the children, and sometimes I was there too. But it was an uneasy family gathering, not one which I liked to stay in for long.

A pencilled note reached me from my mother one day in 1943:

Homeless!!

Well beloved – here we are safe after a perfectly good raid which blew out the windows (not all, thank goodness) & dropped a most destructive bomb at the back of us & very, very lucky are we for some were killed & 2 not yet found. So we were told to get out of the house quickly & off we packed 3 children & 4 grown-ups to the Y.M.C.A. where they received us with the greatest kindness, cups of tea & packets of biscuits, chocolates for the children & so forth. And before nightfall they had found us lodgings, such good kindly folk who took us in at a moment's notice & have made us most welcome. All this happened last Thursday & this morning Sunday the police said that we might go back. So off we packed, I lit fires, swept up glass etc. etc. When down came a second policeman & told us it was all a mistake & the unexploded bomb was still within striking distance & back we must all pack!!! What a game. Well I found myself very calm under the circumstances.

M.

The Germans that year had begun day time raids to bomb southern cathedrals in revenge for the bombing of German cultural monuments. They tried for Exeter Cathedral, not far from where my parents lived in Exmouth. My father was digging in the garden one day when a plane came over and unloaded a lot of bombs. He looked up, fascinated by the sight of them coming down. One bomb landed near him and blasted him to the ground. He received severe internal injuries from which he never recovered: he died a year later. When he was dying, my mother wrote to me, asking if I would come to Exmouth. By the time I arrived my father had already decided that he would finish the matter off as soon as possible – he believed individuals had that right – and had obtained a large quantity of sleeping tablets for the purpose.

On reaching the bed, I instinctively took his hands in mine: for the only sense of immortality he had would be through his children – even if I would not continue the line by having children myself. He had asked my mother to bring him his pills and she had refused. Now he asked me to go to the chemist and obtain some more. I said no, not wishing to be implicated along with my mother. I told him that if he so wished, he should have taken the pills himself. He made a deathbed confession, mainly about his own father's court case. Within the family it had been put about that my grandfather had served a prison sentence for bigamy: in fact, it had been a fraud charge. Both he and my father were brought to court. But whereas my grandfather had died in prison, my father went free.

After this confession, he lasted out quietly another twenty-four hours.

My mother and I meanwhile had an almighty row. She accused me of never behaving properly towards her and I replied by saying exactly the same about her behaviour towards me. She took no interest in the funeral, and my brother excused himself on grounds of Admiralty appointments or other business. My father's wish was to be cremated and it was left to me to accompany the coffin with the body on a train to Plymouth. I took it to the crematorium and afterwards was given the ashes in a small container. Since I was on the borders of Devon and Cornwall, I decided to throw the ashes into my father's native Cornwall. But when I tried to do this, a strong wind blew them back into Devon.

In the early years of the War, David [Ayerst] had sent his wife Larema to the safety of Canada. This made communication between them

csimile of the first page of the
re of the Concerto for Orchestra,
dicated to Benjamin Britten for his
tieth birthday in 1963; and the two
us celebrating my sixtieth birthday
January 1965

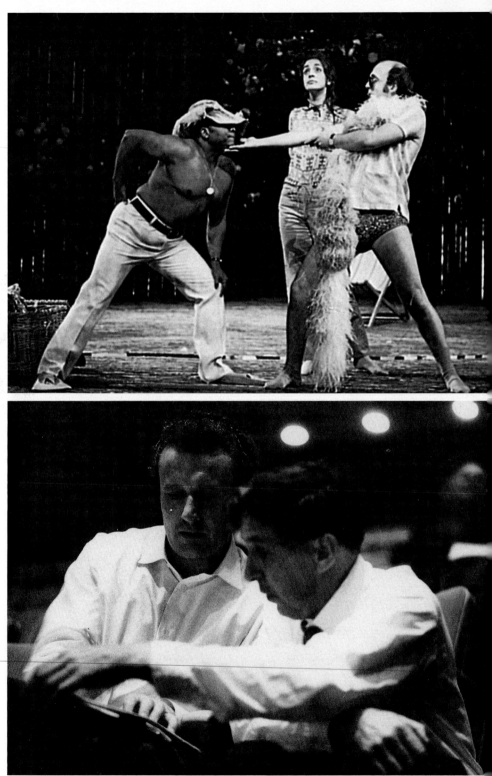

(*Top*) Peter Hall's 1970 Royal Opera House production of *The Knot Garden*, with Bob Tear as Dov, Thomas Carey as Mel and Jill Gomez as Flora and conducted by Colin Davis

(*Above*) Working with Colin on one of many occasions

(*Left*) With Sam and
David Koltai, who
designed the scenery and
costumes

(Below) The revival of
Sam Wanamaker's
production of *The Ice
Break* in 1979, with
Elizabeth Vaughan as
Gail and David Atherton
conducting

(*Below*) Taking a break in Zambia from rehearsing *A Child of Our Time* with the choir of native Zambians and ex-pats

(*Right*) With Jessye Norman, rehearsing for the 1979 Prom performance of *Child*

(*Foot*) The memorial to the victims of Hiroshima, where I laid a wreath during my world tour of 1984

Two *King Priams*, Nicholas Hytner's
wonderful production with Kent Opera in
1984, where Rodney Macann was Priam and
watching rehearsals with Meirion Bowen of
the Royal Opera House production at the
Herod Atticus Odean, Athens, in July 1985

Receiving and handing out awards, mine in 1981 for *King Priam* and Leonard Bernstein's Royal Philharmonic Society Gold Medal in 1987

The BBC TV production of *New Year*, co-directed by Dennis Marks and Bill T. James and conducted by Andrew Davis, was premiered on 21 September 1991 with James Maddalena as Merlin, Richetta Manager as Regan and Kim Begley as Pelegrin

(*Left*) With Oliver Messiaen and Bath Festival Director Amelia Freedman, 1986

Back to my roots in 1986 and with
my old friend David Ayerst on
holiday in Italy in 1990

difficult, and after a while Larema returned. This was just as I was about to go into prison and in my absence they took over my cottage for their reunion. I had earlier been able to take a few brief holidays with David, exploring the countryside of England and Wales. One of the most memorable hikes was along Hadrian's Wall to Wall's End. We pitched tent by the wall itself and I still retain a memory of staring out north to Scotland, just as the legionaries must have done in Roman times. We also went on a couple of trips with John Campbell – ex-Professor of Architecture at the University of Munich, who was billeted with David at Stanhope Gardens – to Cornwall (where Campbell had built some houses; John Layard lived nearby), and to Abergavenny.

During the war period, Fresca and I shared each other's troubles, ambitions and dreams.

[6 September, 1943]

Fresca darling,

. . . Den's decided to refuse Civil Defence training & to take the consequences – wh unfortunately landed him in Bedford not the Scrubs. But I sympathise with him. He needs to feel the toughness, tautness somewhere in the conscientious experience & he must regret it. Next, he's going to take his holiday come what may in a fortnight's time. Coming up to the first Morley concert on Sept 18 & staying up the week – sleeping here & a season ticket. I'll pay his whack for his holiday as I wld have done in Cornwall. In that week on the 21st there is this 50th ann. festival in Northampton at St Matthew's Church wh Ben has written an anthem for (just finished) & I am writing (after Ben's extraordinary kind & persisting effort on my behalf when I was in) a fanfare for brass – wh is gay & serious & rather good. So I suppose I shall have to go to Northampton & will take Den of course. There's also a commissioned Madonna from Henry Moore! Then on the 21st & 22nd, 2 of the nicest chaps to come out of the Scrubs – both of whom we shall all get to know – one a serious, gentle sculptor called Arnold Machen (my age or approaching) – the other a young 'anarchist' of the Johnny [Amis], Den age & ideas – a natural member of the young family. And on the 24th the Sonata 1 is done by Sellick at the National Gallery. So all in all Den's visiting week coincides nicely with a rush around.

October is less wild. The 16th is a Morley do – Weelkes, Kodaly, Hindemith – & on the weekend after, 23rd, Peter & Ben hope for a stay here at the cottage, with a concert to do at Haywards Heath on the Sat! It's first free weekend for them. After that I had hoped to have cleared off: oratorio proofs – fanfare – possibly song for Peter – new 1st movement for 4 tet I – & so to be able to take another short holiday – probably Exmouth (or with you by the sea somewhere?) – & come back for the Britten-Tippett do at Friends' House, Nov. 6 – where Clifford is to play the Sonata – & then to shut myself up, mentally, at any rate, to begin & carry thro the new symphony. I tell you all this so you can have an idea of my plans & do what you like when you think good.

I've decided the time is ripe to float the oratorio willy nilly. The first idea was a Britten–Tippett do again – to have his *Sinfonia da Requiem* (20 mins) as 1st half. To get a special choir, hire the New London Orchestra etc. etc. A guaranteed fund of £300! – & the little Alison, Tony's girl, offered us £50 on the spot – wh. Tony agreed to! Ben would fork out. Ben thinks I could throw away one of Schott's advances of £100 – or rather the whole lot nearly after this sudden Income Tax nonsense. Then Johnny put the proposal up to LPO – who are discussing it – but refuse Britten in the same programme – something classical – & Boult to conduct – to be in their London series at one of the theatres. Ben thinks this a bit unfriendly – but if they will place it & don't need a lot of guarantees I think it probably better.

Meanwhile, I have driven Morley to agree to a flat rate – only £125 p.a. on average for 2 classes a week & my director's work – but it means [?] their type of work, all under one roof – & that with occasionally outside jobs (deputising for Tony!) & the £60 that comes into the bank from yr bank, I shall live. It's OK at present because of the money from Schott's, because I'm fairly decided to use up any savings in what is really a capitalisation: concert performances to establish one's name & reputation. Sound?

I have agreed to do up the other cottage at £20 for Miriam etc. if I have the money . . .

When on holiday – saw A.L. Rowse again – v. jolly – made it all up with John Layard & parted on the warmest terms with him & Doris.

Mother & father well – tho ageing – & v. nice time there – nice time with David & La & children at Mother Ayerst's – lovely kids & D. is quite sweet with them – another on the way – to be called 'Scrubs'!! They loved being in the cottage & La spring-cleaned it – but the problem of sheets is becoming acute. D. wanted to repay by buying a pair – the shopman said: 'You'd better have a couple of aspirins before I tell you the price' . . . 14 guineas the cheapest pair! Have you any getatable anywhere? for when you come.

That seems all the news . . . it was just heaven to be in the home again. It *is* a lovely place really & one is damned lucky.

All my love,
Michael.

[16 September 1943]
Wed.

Fresca darling – it *was* good to see you. Soon I feel you'll be about in town & that will be grand. I need to talk to you ever such a lot – get a bit musically frightened; being now as it were 'launched'. I am afeared of getting off my proper balance by a lack of true humility – wh up to date I think I've had – at any rate patience! And also these seem queer dream-like days within this war – 'gay & grim' – that spruch of Yeats, that's kept by me.

. . . I gave Evelyn a £20 cheque to cover expenses before I went in. But I'm not worrying so much – & just don't care.

And the dream. I can't keep feeling that there's a somewhat special psychological balance for people like ourselves – perhaps it says that we can't force a union of our 2 sides – masculine & feminine – that they may have contrary, if complementary, functions. I'm beginning to doubt the absolute claims of what is called normal psychology. Life is just a bit more mysterious – & can't be contained in formulas.

I've finished my blessed Fanfare for Northampton (Mon & Tues next) – & feel terribly tired. I'm a silly Billy – & must quieten down to a sedater & more regular life – music to order just *not* my meat, even for a continental Marie Rambert! However, it means now finishing one song for Peter (he's going to sing a 10-year-old baby song of mine already) – & then to proper work – the new 1st movement to 4tet no. 1.

Eric Blom [critic] fell for 4tet 2 with a crash (Leamington on Sat) – I'll show you the B[irmingham] Post-cutting. Goes a little too far – something like 'breathtakingly beautiful' – but other than that, just the right crit: Schott's are doing a min. score & parts alright.

I live in *such* dream world, half the time. I hope it won't mean a fearful crash when peace comes – because in some ways it's a defence against the horror. So that p'raps prison was a good thing – to come closer to something.

D[en] will be here for a week's holiday as from Sat. I'll find out if his prison is really likely or imminent – & get him to phone you at Mill House. But see him in Cambridge, on his own ground – not with I & V.

My love to them – & to you
Michael

[1941]
[Sunday]
Fresca dear,
. . . I've long wanted to try an experimental hand at an opera with recitative & all & have just spent the morning on a fantastic plot to be called: 'The Man with the Seven Daughters'. [This was *The Midsummer Marriage* at the earliest stage of its conception.] He's a widower, the daughters are called Gert & Daisy & Doris & various names & they all go to work of sorts except the littlest – who goes to the Secondary School

The first scene is breakfast during wh all the daughters get ready to go to work & eventually the littlest goes to school & the man's left to wash up – but he's more likely to read the morning paper till the pub opens. (Of course you realise at once that having seven daughters he is the most unconscious man in creation) – the next scene is probably in the pub, because the man's only crony is the barman & the barman's wife – a deep-bass I expect & a shrill mezzo – & here the man relates his woes & plays darts possibly with members of the chorus, one of whom is probably Jeffrey Mark – but the scene comes to an inglorious end when it's fetched away by the littlest daughter who wants her dinner & he leaves amid the scandalised exclamation of the bar in general. One realises he is a wastrel & refuses to carry out his duties.

It is probably Saturday & all the daughters have their half-day – & in any case the real event is the arrival of the handsome cousin from the North. He is a lyrical tenor & is v. attractive *of course*. There ensues the most terrible complications among all the daughters as you can perceive, & I haven't thought them out yet, but in the end to all their chagrin he takes the littlest daughter to the cinema! At this the other six daughters turn & rend the father & to such a degree that they do him in – (He becomes completely unconsious, sinking into the great [?mother] – naturally, tho none had suspected it, the Man is really the only centre of the household & once dead, all the daughters 'fly apart' – they may fetch a doctor & th girls fly around & the barman comes to grief & various strangers from the bar, & when the chorus is assembled they are *very* shocked at the heartless ways the daughters are going on, who are preparing to leave in their various ways – but beer & chips fetched from the fish shop lead to an outsize Mozartian or perhaps Verdian finale, in wh they all go out & leaving the sozzled barman sentimentalising over his dead friend.

I feel this is a suitable offset to the 'Child of Our Time' & ought to go a long way to restoring the balance. 'Take a boozy short leave of your girls on the shore' as the Chorus says in *Dido*. All in that spirit – & think of seven-voice female recitative!!!!!!!

Much love to you both,
Michael.

[March 1944]

Fresca darling – . . . I'm asking John [Amis] to send you the masque [another early draft for *The Midsummer Marriage*], wh he got in London. He thought it a private joke on 5th form psychology & opines that it'll be a waste of possibly good music. So I want you to consider that point in all seriousness. It's certainly off the run of romantic-realist opera-drama, & bang in the fantasy world of *Zauberflöte*. I think this the right move at the present juncture in opera history, but it wd be fearfully misunderstood. John anyhow can't visualize it as a stage do, because he thinks it wld make a good story – wh is precisely what it wouldn't do. It isn't a story at all, but a mime – an allegory in modern technique. However, I shall go rather to what you feel. I have no fear of its getting musically clothed properly once I begin – but it's sensible to begin on the right thing!

Could you make a copy of the enclosed on a typewriter – as you won't find the German a problem. It's such a nice bit – meant for *Die Zeitung*.

Let me know later when you come up again. Love M.

[1944]

[to Fresca]

Enjoyed the [Edmund] Wilson very much & it's off back to the Times. What a subject for an opera *The Wound & the Bow* would make. Dickens' preoccupation with prison is most interesting. I suppose it's a deep-going affair, through Dostoevsky & the rest & whose reverberations we still feel. I found that in myself it's becoming resolved, tho is appears as a significant symbol in the oratorio. But I have only just woken up to the realisation that in the proposed masque [there's] another shooting – only a magical one. That is a profound dream symbol for me, wh. I have not resolved at all, except that it is the magic weapon, as in Philoctetes & Arthur & all the rest, & I suppose it's a sexual weapon & many other things (modern war & revolution). The masque is nearly imagined in structure, but there's a hiatus yet wh hasn't clicked to. But I can re-tell you the story as it now runs. There's a hell of a lot of rubbishy mythology in it that gives David the creeps. But one can't manufacture a speculum for the deep things except out of indefiniteness. The art this time is to do all this in a gay & sun-lit frame.

Please get well soon,
Michael.

April 24, 44

Fresca darling,

Sorry to see you poorly again – hope it soon passes over. Let me know how things go. I've had a lovely weekend, both in the June-like weather & writing – which as usual meanders along. I never seem to be able to take advantage of such times to write quickly. I just waste hours of time looking around. It's an odd sound that's happening – warmer in some ways & tougher – not perhaps less adaptable material, at times very impure. It's what I would call typical 'middle-period music' when one seems to reach out in all directions under the impulse of new-found strength & so get at exuberance rather than refinement. But I dare say you can't reach a better music of a 3rd period till you've gone thro this mill. Nevertheless this symphony will be a step forward as far as non-existent good English symphonic works go; it's got drive & it's highly wrought & never gets bogged in vacuity or hatched up into an orgasmic emotional discharge wh is the weakness of the Walton symphony.

See you again soon.

Love,
Michael

Oxted Mon. May 4
Fresca dear –
Relieved to hear you're getting better again? I think you'd better see if you can get over here for a bit if the spring is going to be so lovely & warm. I seem to have kept fairly good hold over dates away – & a long one to include Leicester & Stamford again has been postponed to autumn – wh is probably lucky in all ways.

Went Friday to see the Shaxsons at Elsted, who asked after you. It is a lovely spot that underneath the Downs.

Den was here (& John) after a Morley concert. He's such a nice lad & growing now at such a pace. I fancy that he's taken a sudden jerk on again that the need for physical warmth wh he had of me is passing. He probably begins to feel surer of himself, as he gets so much easier now & with new folk he happens to meet.

Luckily for me I haven't become seriously entangled in this manner & have always known that the pace of the friendship has to be set by the younger person, & that in his case in the long run it's the intellectual stimulus he really wants. All this brings up the old question of the impermanence of some particular forms of relationship, & that the matter seems to have to be resolved into music in the good old-fashioned way. But now, at this age, the music of course has the real pull over all & the matter resolves itself very quickly.

[The music critic] William Glock is getting married to his [first wife] Clement in a week or so. I think they are folk we shall like very much when we can re-make our circle more permanently after the war; & that always seems to turn out in my mind as after your weakness passes. There's also Peter Watson of 'Horizon' who is a sweet gentle chap of our own life – & with an encyclopedic knowledge of art in the widest & best sense.

I guess it may be the coming storm, but following on some considerable nausea as to the war & all things of it, I have got emotionally fast-centred in the cottage house & the symphony & am abstracted from London & Morley. It's also partly the spring wh I've wanted so much. I hope to have managed a 6-week stretch in July–August. But it seems too good to hope for in the world as it now is.

I've agreed to write a 3,000 word pamphlet for [Peace Pledge Union] PPU – 1d price & 10,000 sale. I'll probably send you the MS to vet before it goes to press. It's a very forthright & clear-stated exposé of what I think to be something of the underlying processes in the relationship now of artistic creation & the mass society. That's why I've agreed to do it for PPU – because I want to talk to the youngsters who however unconsciously have contracted out of something & who must build from the new position consequent on that shift. Also I want to make public again my stand against the mass-state at a time when they would like to gloss over the past indiscretions & 'try out' the new name. *[This pamphlet was later revised and republished in* Moving into Aquarius.*]*

Don't fear as to the masque – I shall come to it instinctively at the right time, I'm pretty sure. It has the same accumulation & inevitability as 'The Child' had. I expect I shall get a whole mass of stuff 'digested' out by the symphony.

Love
Michael

Tuesday, May 11, 44
Fresca darling,

. . . I've been exercising my eyes on my own, seriously & there's already an improvement. It really is rather miraculous at the time. The trouble as yet is that the better condition doesn't remain. However if I persevere when I'm here all the summer, I ought to get somewhere. I'll tell you all about it when I see you –

it's too much to write about just when I am short of time. I may go later on to see the woman whose name & address you sent.

David & La have another daughter. D. was here last night on his own [on his way] to the Crowborough hospital – & will be here tonight again. I find I am continually so up against his war affairs that I am quite ungenerous to him – & had a dream last night which sharply corrected this. I feel so bitterly about the whole disillusion of the war that I can't always keep the 'state' & the 'person' separate.

I'll sent Plotinus in a day or so. I'm just reading it. Wld like to have the Turgenev if you can send it.

Much love,
Michael

[25 May, 1944]

Please read this [draft for PPU pamphlet] & comment – as soon as maybe. It worries me that it's too indefinite & subjective. All I really hoped to do is to stand people on their feet & so give them confidence to go forward re-creating values that war & usury have smashed. Even if they only are drawn to read the books mentioned, it will be good. I do not believe in the solution of problems – only in wrestling with them. I have been writing it such a time that I am too close to see it now. How then does it read 'out of the blue'?

The Symphony goes well – will post you yr book soon. Forgive rush – am off to town.
herzlich,
M.

Oxted Monday
(June 1944)

Fresca darling – I've been reading Virginia Woolf, & as usual becoming so overcome by the atmosphere as to lose sense of the here & now. It's extraordinarily powerfully associated stuff & feminine to a degree – in the best sense that is. Sometimes the artistry is almost uncanny.

I have rather a thick month of concerts etc. – but 'the season' ends for me then, & the summer break begins on July 1st. I expect to go for holiday June 8th. The symphony progresses slowly. It's a 'big' work, for me – rather on the oratorio scale – so will take the rest of the year anyhow, & will be followed by smaller things for a year at least, I suppose, before the Masque. But I am probably happiest in these productive periods – it feels to be like a good year of one's life – last year, with prison & what not, being not so good a year. But in those productive periods one seems to withdraw from the outside matters of one's *renommé*, performances & so forth – not caring so much while the new works are written. But last year when so little was done in that line was a very good year from the outer success point of view: all of wh seems to work out very well.

Glad to hear you are getting your strength back gradually. You needn't make any fixed plan for the autumn or wherever. I shall always be around & you will always be welcome. Sometime in the summer break, I shall probably go once to Cambridge & will come out to Streetly End for a day or so. If you get hold of any more of this utility paper – yellow, pink, grey or what, please keep some for me. I am nearly at the end of the yellow lot you gave me in the winter sometime.

Love,
M.

[Letter from Francesca Allinson]
Invasion Day [1944]

Michael Darling – Ah – ah – ah –I had a waking dream last night which I must tell you before it fades at all. I was lying in bed thinking what scum I was and wondering if I couldn't even begin to be good & why I didn't know how to approach God, when I saw a number of fair-haired young women all pressed up against something that looked like a tomb or pedestal. I was behind them. My thoughts rambled off but every time I thought of God the same picture appeared so I decided to attend to it. I very much wanted to join these young women who were dressed in late Victorian blouses & skirts. I even tried to get into a pew among them but it was no good – So I had to take myself off – and I know that I had no place among them because they were young & beautiful & innocent & I wasn't. Now two nuns appeared in black & white habit. They were in a bare semicircular chapel. One was oldish and stood in the middle – the other was small & young & stood behind her to my left. After a while I went to the older nun. She was willing to help me and asked me what I wanted. I expected to hear myself wish for health, but instead heard myself say – I want to fulfil the object for which I have been put in this world. She was pleased at this –and motioned me forward. Then the scene shifted a little. The young nun came forward & I knelt opposite her & the young fair-haired women were in the nave of the church. So:

YM   Old Nun
Women   Me

I knew that the old nun was wise and controlled things. But she knew that the young nun was greater than herself though humble & serving – The young nun did not know that she herself was that which she was adoring. I was to look at the young nun opposite me, but couldn't open my eyes. I was arguing with myself & accused myself of cowardice. But gradually although my eyes were closed I knew that in place of her was a golden flickering vision, that she was transfigured. Sometimes I looked at the old nun and saw the vision out of the tail of my eye. I knew that there was something to be done – but didn't know what. I wondered whether I should join the young women but knew that that would spoil the symmetry – then I wondered whether they should join me – but then the gold vision faded. She became a young nun again and everybody left the church & I felt sad and decided I would kneel at the very back of the church. When I was there I couldn't look at the altar (which wasn't there I think or never was) but only at this arch by the altar. Upon it were painted apocalyptic animals. I tried to look at them all but could only see this at this left side of the altar. It was the lamb of St John with its thin little cross. And I knew them. I too was a lamb, bore only a very small cross and was one of the innocents after all.

Sat. [10 June 1944]

Fresca darling – it's a joyous dream & ought to satisfy you a long while. It'll bear a lot of pondering on & savouring. Invasion Day is a sort of symbol too – *Einbruch* [a collapse, invasion] – of the two sides coming to grips after years of preparation. Only in the dream sense, there has to be no defeat & capitulation, but tension of forces & balance. All the feminine figures show that it's at its most conscious – never likely to be more explicit. It reminds one

173

of a dream of marriage between 2 long lines of young men in a church headed by Wilf & myself – refreshing contrition & forgiveness. [see p. 109] In your dream the various symbols have their proper place. The crowd of young women are a symbol that recedes if you try to force your way into it but returns when you are ready to stay in your place for the sake of symmetry. The black & white nuns seem to show that the deep-seated moral problem is beginning also to be assimilated & to have its place – in fact to be the basis of transfiguration. I have always known somehow that we can't throw away this terrific deposit of moral value (the black & white habit), but like you, I spend my hankerings on the beautiful young crowd – tho for me it's usually Greek & not late Victorian. While the transfiguration of the moral into the divine would seem so extraordinary that I would close my eyes & prefer to retire to the back of the church & contemplate somethime less aweful & transcendent.

I suppose the young crowd do belong in the nave of the church & don't personify so sharply as the other elements. I found the dream wonderfully cheering. It's a general, 'big' dream & means a lot to me as well as to you.

Really the dream is already one step beyond this: the general problem (that's why it's so exciting) –

> Nur wer die Leier schon hob
> auch unter Schatten,
> darf das unendliche Lob
> ahnend erstatten.
>
> Nur wer mit Toten vom Mohn
> ass, von dem ihren,
> wird nicht den leisesten Ton
> wieder verlieren.
>
> Mag auch die Spieglung im Teich
> oft uns verschwimmen:
> Wisse das Bild.
>
> Erst in dem Doppelbereich
> Werden die Stimmen
> ewig & mild.
>
> Who alone has already lifted
> the lyre among the dead

174

dare, divining sound
the infinite praise.

Who alone has with the dead eaten
of the poppy that is theirs
will never again lose
the most delicate tone.

Though the reflection in the pool
swims often before our eyes:
Know the image.

Only in the dual realm
do voices become
eternal and mild.

[Rilke, *Sonnets to Orpheus*, No. 9]

[June 1944]

We have had little aeroplane armada effects over us. Little to remind one of the battle. I came down in the train with 4 soldiers due off the next day. It was not pleasant. One was shattered & clearly felt he was going to his death. Tho Evelyn tells me that the losses are much less than expected. I hope with one half that Germany collapses & that it stops – & with the other half that we reach stalemate & so force a much deeper adjustment on us all. I imagine it's going to be the former, & it's a tragedy. Germany will be the scapegoat & will be dismembered & reduced to a colony of big business, with labour gangs snatched into Russia.

The Symphony goes along slowly, but good. I must send you the Canterbury anthem – classicising tho it probably is.

herzlichkeit
Michael

[1944]

There is a balloon barrage on the Limpsfield Common to catch the monstrosities on one of their routes. The whole thing has been v. uncanny & no one has liked it.

However down here I feel fairly at peace despite the things going over & the London guns that have moved down. (Poor little Ted Armstrong of along Sevenoaks way has been blown out of his house – but both alive.) But I expect I need a holiday now – & hope the plan to go to the Welsh coast will really happen.

My father is gradually passing away. V. slowly & mother seems to be adjusting herself to the matter marvellously.

That was the last sheet of yellow paper!

Sorry you are still weak. But you are better where you are until things become more normal again.

Love,
M.

[8 July 1944]
Exmouth Sat.

Fresca darling,

Father died on Thursday as peacefully as can be imagined. I go to Plymouth on Monday to see to the Cremation. Mother is wonderfully well, considering, & I think will come thro quite alright. Peter comes today for family chitchat. Mother won't expect a letter from you & in any case will hope not to have to write one back. She is snowed under with them.

I am now beginning to be less tired. I shall travel back home Wed, & then off Friday all being well, to St David's, Wales for a week with Den & John. Looking forward to it no end. I shall see when I get home again how the bombing goes & the music in consequence. Also Bron[wen next door] will have had her baby, & Miriam may be still incapacitated by her stroke & fall, so that it may be policy to move to a room with a piano in Cambridge or wherever. However, I'll settle that all later. I think the new plan for Chapter III [of the folk-song book] excellent.

I worry a bit about all these delays to the Symphony: but it's no use. Wars are *not* ideal times for composition, not modern wars, & it's no use crying for the moon. I still hope to get 5 weeks' clear writing, & shall do that at the cottage as long as it's tolerably possible. I may take to sleeping under the piano! I gather Miriam's roof now leaks from shrapnel, but I'm more interested to hear how many bombs are brought down round about while I've been away & what Evelyn thinks to it – who has considerable common sense in such matters.

Much love,
Michael

Sat [mid July 1944]

Fresca darling

I have just bought a book: Survey of Anglo-Saxon Art by [?] Kendnick, wh deals with the question of Celtic movement & Teutonic barbarism meeting Latin humanistic tradition, in the Golden Age of Northumbrian art c. 700 AD. I'd better send it you when I've read it, because it's extremely interesting on an allied theme tho much earlier. Also it will give you confidence too in this way – that the archaeologists & the art people go into great detail as to Celtic provenance & so forth, & it's really nonsense to suppose the same problem hasn't existed in the music.

I have been badly knocked out by the new raids – a typical confusion of emotions because I had a lot of concerts & recordings to do: so that it was like a return to 1940 & a sharp panic. And it all got mixed up with everything else as ever: the realisation that I am caught sensually just where there is never to be a lasting union. & That all the panic & the tangle have sharply bust the symphony, so that I must so to speak try to 'take off' again; & in the middle of the first movement. Such a confusion of sensibilities that it's been grim. If Den had managed to phone last night, as I wired him to, I cld have gone this weekend to Cambridge. But I don't feel like going out of the blue. & holiday D.V, is in a fortnight. So I am still here, but not in much of a composing mood.

My brother Peter was down for the last 4 days at Exmouth. He is a great dear. He['s] really [a] model son. Despite his leg he leaps up for everything & anything, responds to all another's emotional demands in the wisest possible manner. While I remain detached and unmoved & generally lazy. I just can't manage these atmospheres where manners & housework are moral duties. I wither away.

And I don't seem to be able like Peter to disregard it by complying before the event. I'm afraid it's the residue of the age-old quarrel. It never seems entirely to be overcome.

Mother is left quite well off & probably later on v. well off indeed. Whether her almost parsimonious streak will go I don't know – but I doubt it. She then intends to get her Bank to divide up the year's savings on her income equally between her sons. I dare say this will suit Peter, who has to educate a family. It means not so much to me, because its generosity is all deadly tied up in the over-strict economy from which it will spring & will be a sort of emotional lien on the family ties. But finally mother lives for & in the grandchildren, &

Peter clearly likes that too – so all works for the best. If I do get spare money then I am going to prepare to be able to build Bron & Jack an extra bedroom on the back of the cottage there: to lay down a garden path & new gate – & new linen & bedding & crockery & clothes: & then consider small scale provincial concert promotion through Johnny, on the lines I care about.

At our Friends' House concert we cleared £110 for the charity above billing & hall & all expenses. So in Dec the same people will do another such on behalf of Morley music. And these concerts are absolutely uncompromising in programme. We had 1900 folk there in the middle of these bombs.

I am looking forward to the holiday and end, upon end. Will give Denlein [Douglas Newton] yr message. I like his stuff very much: & it augurs terribly well for the masque.

Love to you all.
Michael.

[20 July 1944] Oxted Thursday
Fresca darling
This letter is on the new supply of paper for wh many thanks.

I got to Waterloo yesterday as the siren went & 2 bombs whizzed over the building – so I went straight down here, waiting for the connection in Croydon wh was delayed because they'd hit the line & while the woman out of the speaker announces 'Your attention please! Yr attention please! hostile aircraft approaching' I'm amused at their being called aircraft. It seemed lovely to reach the Halt, altho it is in fact rather more dangerous here than when I went. The AA are getting better shots. 5 have come down in Broadham Green, just behind Hurst Green Church, but only damaging houses everywhere & people cut by glass. Bron has her ceiling down in the front room & lies upstairs in much mental distress clutching the new babe, born on Sunday – a girl. It's a bit difficult to adjust to. Yesterday I just sat staring out of the window when one dropped, until brought to earth by the bang. Evelyn at the other end of the phone had rapidly left her window for a better spot. However, I expect I shall continue here after all. I write better – & I don't quite like leaving Bron & Ian & Sheila [Larema's brother in law & sister] & Miriam in the thick of it.

Canterbury Cathedral want me to go & sing as a lay clerk for the August weeks, when I get back, because their only tenor is a-bed with rheumatism. But tho it's attractive in many ways, it means living in the town, & being respectable etc. through the only clear weeks of the whole year. So I shall probably try to get out of it.

I think we are off to Cornwall not Wales, now the ban is lifted. That's Den's hope. I've sent a wire enquiring of the place where I stopped over last year in Mevagissey. I dare say in any case we'll take pot-luck.

There's one just gone over now. The musical difficulty is to keep an ear open for them, while using one's ears for other more subtle purposes. P'raps the whole war won't be much longer now.

[1944]
Oxted Thurs.
Fresca darling –
When they let off what seems to be a fortnight's savings of bombs, as they appeared to last night, it makes one doubt the wisdom of staying. I can't make out whether the fall of one of those abortive glass shades in this room is a good or a bad omen! The blast from quite distant bombs draws the windows outwards. We leave them on the catch, so they fly open at a touch.

However, I'm extremely happy inside & work goes well: & seem too lazy to move. When a bad night or day is over, you feel like that & while it's going on you can't move, it's too late.

As for V2 wh David & everyone think if it happens, to be the really serious danger, then we shall wait & see. It's no use going away from it now unless for good because it mightn't happen yet awhile & I've got to be back in a fortnight or so, unless V2 has knocked public activities right out.

I'm afraid I regard an early end of the war as still optimistic. They'll make an enormous effort to stick out the summer & autumn. I think & hope the winter will bring slackening of the allied offensives. But of course Russian victories may just end it all by reaching Berlin.

Want to see you frightfully badly. I suppose it'll mean my trying to get over to Mill House some time later on.

Will write better & more fully in a day or so. I must get down to washing-up. Miriam can't do any housework for me. She thanks you for the welcome tea. Do you have any Household tin milk powder to spare? I can't get it here now. I am rather sunk therefore.
All my love.
Michael.

[10 August 1944]

On Tuesday at 5.55 a.m. the thing decided itself. The other cottages destroyed – both children & Miriam & Ben unhurt. Jack in hospital & will recover. Bronwen dead. We are all pretty tearful – a real tragedy. I felt it like my own.

My cottage is not to be lived in at present. Present address will be c/o Shaxson, Elsted Manor, Nr Midhurst, Sussex (tel. Harting 92). Will be there from Friday midday. Short stay for Bron's funeral wh is Sat. Will send a wreath from you, or us both.

Love, M.

[1944]
Oxted Fri.

Fresca darling

. . . I've just got back from a trip to Leicester (rehearsal for the 'Child') & Eric (Karl Hawker's brother) has turned up from Cambridge & is going to help me sort out the remaining habitable rooms – i.e. bedroom, bathroom & kitchen & so get the cottage back to the condition where a char can take over. Tomorrow also I hope to have a visit from another nice glazier who will finish off all the windows (except your bedroom, wh got it most & is unusable as yet, full of their junk & salvage). This new glazier is a builder & carpenter & v. ready to do all he can to put the place back. So don't worry overmuch. If the Council people don't come soon to put ceilings in the bedroom & part of this room, I'll get hold of the material & get him to do it. The problem will be a bit more difficult when the full winter comes – but we shall wait & see. The real point is that at present I'm so glad to be here, I don't grudge the housekeeping difficulties etc.

Yes – you'd better go straight to Alexander technique training if there's any sign of a continuous set-back. Just ring me up if & when you get to town. & failing an answer Johnny has a London number (obtainable mornings up to 10 a.m.) Primrose 3370 if you note it down. He would probably know where I had got to. The week of Oct 9–14 I'm rushing about in the Midlands roughly:

Sun Oct 8	Concert at Morley (evening)
Mon Oct 9	rehearsal at Morley (evening)
Tues Oct 10	go to Lincoln
Wed Oct 11	probably return London for a rehearsal

Thurs Oct 12   Go afternoon to Leicester
Fri Oct 13   Go on to Stamford
Sat Oct 14   Return home

. . . All love, Michael

P.S. I think the caravan might well be a help here – because it might be used to house any young couple even, who might like to 'farm' the land temporarily – keep the gardens going. I have an idea that conchies will get thrown out & may be glad of a tide-over. In any case it would do one proud as an extra room. But if Jude [Wogan] is in need of the £50, then she'd better sell. Do what you feel to be best.

I gather *Boyhood's End* was a wow at Wigmore [Hall] on Thursday – & a terrific bit of virtuoso singing & playing [by Peter Pears and Benjamin Britten]. A distinguished audience, beginning with Sargent . . . & they could have sold out twice over. 'Child' broadcast is postponed to January, thro muddled dates on Joan Cross's part. I've decided to risk a London performance on my own account – even if I lose a bit on it – as I am pretty much bound to. I think it worth it to clinch the work, so to speak: & prepare the way for the Symphony. 'Plebs Angelica' as sung by Morley sounds quite lovely – strong & pure.

[1944]

Fresca darling –

Here I am undergoing a fresh-air cure. I've got hold of some glass & am awaiting a friendly glazier before the open window. It's a frightful mess but it's terrific to be back.

Before I forget, wld you thank P. &. V[eronica] for me all over again. I shan't get round to a letter because I'm snowed under & too busy putting up Cyril's white windowlite wh is excellent. I expect you've guessed about the laundry I need as soon as may be. And has anyone found my nice red tie wh seems to have disappeared in the move?

Next. Could you once more order me that nice oatmeal, I'd opened the second little bag of 14 lbs, but I found yesterday it was full of glass: & afraid to risk it.

Now if & when you come up after & Veronica had any spare cheese or margarine at any time, I would be more than grateful –

or any sort of cooking fat – dripping or what not. It means suppers & pudding occasionally & something to fall back on, in an otherwise empty larder. Without the other cottage I feel I must get in a little stock of some sort. Is there any spare tea?

I find that sheets is my worst danger now. For whatever reason, I don't know but there don't seem to be even the pairs I got from my mother. Nevertheless, I think there are 3½ pairs in all – tho not all v. strong. Have you in the Red House any sort of curtains wh could do for 2 interior doors? i.e. to hang down to keep the draught out? I have nothing of any use.

The glazier (– a v. nice old chap) has come & says it will need a partial re-building eventually & can't be patched up. So I'll have I expect to manage then either at Evelyn's or perhaps at Dorothy [Shaxson's] again – or Red House or London. I expect a mixture of all the lot. I shall have to be on the spot then to see it's done properly, otherwise it will be hopeless. However, I have no idea yet just when it will happen – it may be weeks, maybe months.

Anyhow, I am ever so happy to be home even tho there are inconveniences. Somehow I shall have to procure at least a bit of ceiling in this big room to cover the big hole. It'll get too hopelessly cold – & later take to sleeping here . . .

Love,
M.

[1944]
Tues.

Fresca darling
The curtains came today & will be of great use: many thanks: & for the tea. Shirts came: Oatmeal came this morning. Mother has sent me up a Deed Box (to keep my contracts in), filled with apples, jam & what not. So that's not bad also. I think it's going to be alright. As soon as I can get the carpenter to get round to some ceiling boarding: then I am set for the winter. At present I've got semi-permanent muscular cold in the left shoulder.

So good that you aren't off on a relapse again. The *Boyhood's End* show [which I didn't get to] seems to have pleased all round. Glock again is being an absolute stalwart on my behalf. I'll tell you details when we meet. I've finished the 1st movement of the

Symphony & will start in on the Sitwell [setting of 'The Weeping Babe' for the BBC] – probably for mixed voices after all. I've seen a background.

Paradoxically 'Child' is postponed to January. Schade! I might be able to slip down to Mill House sometime – but at present [the diary] it's rather thick & I feel I need to keep down to work, being rather behind hand. Also I've got to make several trips to Leicester & Liverpool à propos performances. So I may have to make those trips my sort of holiday treks.

Lots of love,
M.

Oxted. Tues. [2 January 1945]

Dearest beloved,
Everything has come safely – many, many thanks. The cottage is still a muddle mostly because the spare room hasn't been put back, so that there's an accumulation everywhere else. The good Mrs Brown is busy now scrubbing my bedroom, & every fresh scrub brings the floors back to a bit nearer their proper colour. But it'll be a wonder if the white mortar ever really comes off entirely. The walls go successively whiter & have nearly dried out. The next job I think is to try & get curtain-rodding put up by a carpenter. I hitched up that dark red material you left & it's lovely in colour.

The pipes did not freeze, to my surprise, & tho the cottage still strikes colder than it ought, we shall probably overcome that as it's lived in continuously & the weather slowly warms.

Our Bach–Purcell concert at Friends' House on Sunday last sold out! Despite rather a 'crab' from the Times, it was really a great success, & I enjoyed every moment of doing it. I do *not* enjoy trying to get a tolerable performance of the 'Child'. I shall have to get thru the ordeal again, end of February at Albert Hall.

Hope now to get back to the Symphony & get at least another movement done. Your piano is a problem I must tackle too. The blast has in reality lifted all the 'ivory' off the keys wh gradually comes off key by key till one will play on wood only soon. Also,

I hadn't realised there's glass inside too, so I'll consult Chappell's about it first, & then if no go my own local people. Will write more later. Am 40 today,

Love from all,
Michael

Oxted Tues. Jan 9 '45
Fresca darling, Just a tiny note to try & tell you news. My new char – Mrs Brown – is wife to a would-be smallholder: he has got the use of the hill field behind here (for next year I think) from Parsons, & will take over my plot, as well: for hens. Cows on the hill-field & a small dairy etc. So I propose to try & get the family as tenants of the re-built cottage & then I shall be in the centre of a baby farm. Isn't that grand? The Browns are applying to the War Ag. Council to try & get the rebuilding on priority. The only problem to solve is the Lewises (humanly) & the actual size etc. of the re-built cottage (administratively). But it's rather like a dream that just may come true. Could you spare *me* a portion of tea? Am down to zero & Miss Pratt up the lane is in pawn, so to speak. I need a bit for background. I use it sparingly of course myself. The men are hanging a new front door in the teeth of a north wind – v. cold in the house!! Should they cut a glassed portion out, as before? Den says 'no'. And I've left it that they leave out the glass to have it done if I like later. The whole wood door looks better – but darker in the room. A [Alec Robertson] is in the Music Mag[azine] programme on the air on Sunday at 11. Child [BBC radio broadcast] on Wed at 7.35. Had photo in Radio Times too.

All goes well.
Love M.

The last years of the war were also Fresca's last years. We could not really live together: I could not support her financially and when she came to stay, she managed a fortnight and then left again – for my obsession with musical composition kept getting in the way. Depressed by ill-health and the war, Fresca had indicated to her family that she might commit suicide, and they then watched over her very carefully. But she managed to evade them one spring day, took a taxi out to the village of Clare (in Suffolk) and threw herself from a bridge into the River Stour, in imitation of Virginia Woolf. She was wearing a tiny silver cross which Evelyn had originally given to me, but which (insensitively) I had given to Fresca. She left two letters – one for Judy Wogan, the other for me: also a tiny photograph, taken during our 1930 tour of Germany and Czechoslovakia, of myself with a little child; and a copy of Shakespeare's sonnets open at No. LVII:

Being your slave, what should I do but tend
Upon the hours and times of your desire?
I have no precious time at all to spend,
Nor services to do, till you require.
Nor dare I chide the world-without-end hour,
Whilst I, my sovereign, watch the clock for you,
Nor think the bitterness of absence sour,
When you have bid your servant once adieu.
Nor dare I question with my jealous thought
Where you may be, or your affairs suppose,
But, like a sad slave, stay and think of nought,
Save, where you are, how happy you make those:
    So true a fool is love, that in your will
    (Though you do anything) he thinks no ill.

[Letter from Francesca Allinson]
Darling – it's no good – I can't hold on any longer. One has to be a better and a stronger character than me to be able to face a life of invalidism. The monograph has kept me going these years – and now I am too exhausted to give it the finishing touches & see it into print. Will you & Den do so for me. You don't know how long & ardently I have longed to die. I should love to have talked it over with you –but that would have involved you in responsibility for my suicide and so it could be. I have thought endlessly about whether it is wrong – and perhaps it is. But one would have to feel very sure of its wrongness to go on existing as a helpless unhelping unit in the terrible post-war years that are to come. I am to be going during Germany's agony and don't want to survive it. If we have to live many lives, may I live near those I now love again and make a better job of living. And may I love a bit better. I can't live without the warm enfolding love of another person – and in this life I have smashed up my chance of that (in my love too). Darling, forgive me. I am so tired and have been for so many years.
All my love,
Fresc.

In my grief, I wrote bitterly to David:

[8 April 1945]
Oxted, Sun.
My dear David,
I am too out of my mind to be very coherent just yet. Fresca seems to have reached zero point & felt herself unable to go further & drowned herself in the Cam [actually, as I later found out, the Stour]. I can't adjust to it easily. Her gaiety & gentleness & even her waywardness & her love of pretty things all seem irreplaceable values. I loved her more deeply than I knew when she was there. The memory is extremely sweet & fragrant. Her going out has turned everything topsy-turvy. I got myself into one of those black moods of *Weltschmerz* on Friday & wrote you as a whipping boy – but naturally later destroyed the letter. The nightmarish quality that hangs so easily over or just behind our present life. It isn't her going that seems wrong or unexpected, it's that the manner seems to enter with me this nightmarish world. If she were cold & afraid I would or should have been there.

We were both marked as so many of our generation have been – but perhaps my career especially got in the way & she is part of the price. We never learn about real loss till it is there in our persons. Her going is less perhaps than the maiming & death of so many young folk, children, mothers in this lunatic power-driven world. But I know it sharper. She was a lovely, lovely creature as I feel, & lived her birthright out with courage – poor lamb.
Love,
M.

[*added on envelope:*] One is exclusively selfish whether over life or death. We can't accept anything or venture anything with grace. So it seems to me.

[10 April 1945]
Oxted, Tues.
My dear David,
Thanks for your letter & its pertinent remarks. I have come to my own senses again now.

As I guessed, her letter shows that she was tied up with Germany's agony, did not want to survive it, or into the post-war years without a constitution to take her there (as she felt necessarily practical & energetic) in the healing.

My letter to you about all that & general agony of mind on the Friday seems to have corresponded with her own – poor sweetheart. She would have liked to have talked it out with me, but that was impossible to prevent my responsibility. But I am sorry she didn't do so. I would not have wanted to prevent her, but to express the love felt & the help I might have offered . . .

Michael

It was nearly five years before I wrote a commemorative work for her. When I did, finally, with the encouragement of Peter and Ben, I widened it to commemorate all those who lost their lives and loves in the brutality of battle. Prompted by Howard Hartog, I set to music verse by two poets – Sidney Keyes and Alun Lewis – who themselves had died, aged 19 and 20, respectively, in the Second World War: I thought of the song-cycle as having a subtitle, 'Love under the shadow of death'. The title itself I took from the second song – *The Heart's Assurance*: and I am still unutterably moved when I hear it performed.

CHAPTER EIGHT

THE ARTISTIC MILIEU

LITERARY EXCURSIONS

As someone seeking to fertilise creative projects with intellectual ideas and perceptions, I was running very much against the grain of English musical life. Not surprisingly, I found in the 1940s and 1950s that literary figures were far less patronising towards me than musicians and critics. Eliot was the most rewarding of them – a true artistic and spiritual mentor. He guided my reading to some extent: through him, for instance, I developed a profound love of Yeats. The Sitwells also accepted me though they were much closer to Walton. I had no illusions about this tiny group of upper-middle-class dilettantes: Edith was the only one who seemed to me to be producing work that would hold.

I first met Edith through Edward Sackville-West, who was then working for the BBC and had conceived of a collaborative project on a programme to be called *Poets' Christmas*. Sackville-West paired off various poets and composers and it was obvious that some were natural alliances – for instance, Ben Britten and Wystan Auden. Why he thought I should be paired with Edith I don't know. I didn't really know her work well. I agreed, as it seemed a chance to do something of quality with others of my generation. It didn't turn out that way. Working with Christopher Fry, on past and future projects, I was able to engage in a creative dialogue with him. Edith merely sent me a poem, and that was that. I set it to music as *The Weeping Babe*. Oddly enough, Edith never kept a copy of the poem, mine is lost, and since in setting it I shifted her lines around, it no longer exists in its original format.

Edith came to hear a performance of the motet, presented by John Amis in his LPO Club events after the war. I introduced it, discussing how I had gone about setting the words to music, unaware that she was there. I explained how I had noticed that in her poem, some words like 'bitter' were softened into others like 'bower', and talked about her use of trochees and iambs. Apparently, she commented to Amis, 'I shall never write another iamb in my life!' I suppose she had never thought of it that way herself.

Edith then decided that I should belong to her entourage when she came to London. The main figure with her was always Stephen Spender, though her brother Osbert and Walton were often there also. I enjoyed myself enormously in this circle, partly because I didn't have to talk all the time about music. Our meetings took the form of lunch parties at the Sesame, a women's club in London. Edith usually invited about five or six people to join her at a round table, and the discussion varied according to who was there. I was always the subversive, partly because of my leftist politics, which they nevertheless tolerated. After lunch, she and any other women in the party would retire upstairs; she expected the men to follow in due course, and continue conversing with her until teatime. Walton, at one such lunch, asked me if I had seen the latest Britten opera, *The Rape of Lucretia*, at Glyndebourne. As I had not, he telephoned to Glyndebourne immediately for tickets that afternoon and took me off with him. Edith was very annoyed.

I talked with her once about Eliot's poetry: the opinion she expressed was that his early poems were the best; the later ones she found strained in language and imagery. At one memorable lunch, all the Sitwells were present, along with Spender and Eliot and his friend John Hayward. Eliot had just returned from collecting the Nobel Prize in Sweden. Drily, he told of his discomfiture when, just before dinner with the King, he had received back his only spare woollen underwear from the laundry, in an impossibly shrunken state. On his return to England he had to buy replacements and parted with an appalling number of clothing coupons! The discussion turned to religious faith and I teased Eliot by telling him about the absurdly naive missionary film I had seen in prison; it was quite provocative, in such company. I don't remember how long I obeyed Edith's royal summons, but I never went back to her for any future texts for musical settings.

My creative aims were never such that collaboration with writers and dramatists could be simple or straightforward. Guided by Eliot – who drew my attention to the writings on art and aesthetics of Suzanne Langer – I took the view that whatever words I had, the music I wrote would swallow up their intrinsic poetry: if I took the words of a fully-fledged poet or dramatist, there would be conflict. Interestingly, when in 1952 I contributed a madrigal to *A Garland for the Queen* (a group of pieces commissioned from a number of composers to celebrate the coronation the following year of Queen Elizabeth II), I turned again to Christopher Fry. But he had rather lost his way as far as writing poetry was concerned. My inclination, in any case, was to guide him quite firmly as to my needs as a composer. I said I wanted real madrigal verse, beginning with a 'call to attention'. He produced the line, 'Dance, clarion air', which was perfect. Christopher wanted to incorporate something from the Coronation service, to which I grudgingly agreed. The outcome was odd, and when I showed it to David Ayerst, he said he didn't think it was good poetry. Nevertheless, it seemed to me just right for a musical setting. I went back to Christopher again, many years later, for a text for a cantata, *Crown of the Year*.

Just after the war I began to earn a small amount of income doing talks for BBC Radio. Already in 1943, I had produced a portrait of Stravinsky; then from 1946 onwards, with the creation of the Third Programme, the opportunities burgeoned. The first real break came in 1945 when I was asked to do a talk after the nine o'clock news on the BBC Home Service – which was peak listening time, and before the age of TV would have drawn a large audience: it was called *The Composer's Point of View*, had to be direct, lucid, simple and it thus took a great effort to realise. Further broadcasts soon followed, on the BBC World Service (I recall a discussion on corporal punishment in which I thumped the table so hard, the microphone almost fell down through the hole in the middle!) and on the Third Programme. The most important was a series of seven talks on Purcell, with musical illustrations performed by Morley College Choir and instrumentalists, and one on Stravinsky's *Les Noces*, in connection with a broadcast of the Morley College performance of the piece; and a number followed on the general problems of art, aesthetics and society. One of the programme producers I had to deal with was Alec Robertson, who was inclined to water things down, but I argued and would not give way on the quality and depth of what was being said.

My most stimulating partnership was with Anna Kallin, a producer who was then working in the BBC World Service. Niuta (as she was called) had left Russia as a student before the Revolution and had gone to Dresden, where she studied to be a concert pianist and became a girlfriend of Kokoschka (whom I met through her). In London she was living with Salomea Nikolaevna Andronikova, a Russian princess who belonged to the group of acmeist poets before the Revolution: her youthful beauty was celebrated in a poem by Anna Ahkmatova. Salomea escaped from St Petersburg during the Revolution, through Yalta to Paris, where she married a writer named Halpern. When I first met Niuta and Salomea, they had a small house in Chelsea and I visited them regularly, right until their deaths in the 1980s. They had a wide circle of artistic and intellectual friends, including Isaiah Berlin and Sviatoslav Richter who, whenever he gave piano recitals in London, came to them for chocolate truffles.

When Schoenberg died in 1951, the Third Programme first asked the Music Department to produce a series of commemorative programmes. They turned out to be a rather dull series, put together by Leonard Isaacs, in which pieces of the same date were juxtaposed. This added up to nothing in particular. The Third Programme then decided to ask me, as an outsider, to do a series of programmes as a kind of extended obituary: there was opposition from some of the Schoenberg pupils and acolytes – figures like Erwin Stein and Hans Keller, who in my view were not good broadcasters, anyway – but the plan to use me prevailed. Anna Kallin was the producer for these, and together we were able to widen the scope of the programmes to show Schoenberg's life as symbolic of the artistic problems central to the first fifty years of the twentieth century.

For myself, as someone committed to singing those twentieth-century blues, it was an absorbing task, following the story of the general emigration of top-ranking artists and intellectuals from the Europe of 1900 to the California of 1950. The programmes extended over three months and ended with a consideration of Schoenberg's unfinished opera, *Moses und Aron*, to the complete libretto of which I was given access by the composer's widow. These talks and many others I was able to collect together for publication in 1958, as *Moving into Aquarius*: I took six months off composition to do this, and dedicated it finally to Niuta.

Although Eliot had told me that we each had a 'second art' – his was music and mine was literature – I never regarded myself as a true literary artist and (to my financial disadvantage) I have tended to resist any regular obligation in that domain. Once, in the 1950s, I was asked by the editor of the *Observer*, Michael Astor, to a staff lunch in the

Waldorf hotel. All the paper's critics were there and a lively, wide-ranging discussion ensued. After lunch, Astor leant back in his chair with his jacket off, pulled out his startlingly scarlet braces and made me an offer to write a regular weekly column.

Although I could have earned a lot of money from this, I turned it down, partly because I thought there was no real context in England for high-level intellectual debate on musical matters. As a regular reader of the *Times Literary Supplement*, I was aware that such a context existed in discussion of literary and philosophical ideas: but the main musical journals were concerned, as far as I knew, only with specialist matters of musical scholarship. The average literary-minded person reading articles in the *Observer* would have known where he stood; the average musician would have been all at sea: maybe this was condescending, but that is what I felt. Besides, such a regular commitment to writing would have distracted me from composition; so that was that.

VOYAGES MUSICALES

After the war, an awareness of my music seeped through to Europe and I began to receive invitations to conduct and adjudicate in competitions of various kinds. The first invitation of all came from the Head of Belgian Radio, Paul Collaer, to attend a performance of *A Child of Our Time* in Brussels. He had heard the BBC broadcast and came to Schott London to obtain the music. The performance took place in the big Radio Hall in Brussels, before an invited audience. Afterwards so many of the audience crowded round me, wanting to express gratitude for a work which, they said, portrayed exactly their wartime situation, that I had to be rescued.

The composer Mátyás Seiber, despite his central European background, was open and sympathetic to all kinds of music and after hearing the première of *A Child of Our Time* he had commented, 'This is a drama of its time.' Subsequently, he persuaded Hungarian Radio to present the work and in 1947 I went to Budapest to conduct it. The original intention was that it should be sung in English and some not-so-good singers from the State Opera who knew English were engaged: but because of difficulties with the chorus, it was sung in Hungarian instead – which I found a very odd experience, as composer-conductor.

Flying direct to Hungary was impossible at that time: you had to change planes in Prague. As I disliked air travel (which was far less comfortable than it can be now), I decided I would catch a night train from Prague to Budapest. No money could be taken out of England at that time: and since I had to spend a day in Prague I wrote to a musical colleague whom I had helped when he was a refugee in England. He met me at the air terminal and took me to the Wilson railway station where I left my luggage. We then walked to a small park in the town and he led me round behind some bushes, changing now from broken English into German. He wanted to leave Czechoslovakia and asked if I would take a letter with me to post to the USA, where he had a brother who would provide the necessary job invitation.

I was uneasy about this, since I was an official guest and if such a letter were found on me there would be a great deal of trouble. I asked him to tell me his brother's address: I would memorise it and write to him from London. When I returned from Budapest via Prague, he met me again. Now he was very concerned that I might forget the name and address. He implored me to take his letter, and wrote on a piece of paper in the air terminal that his getting out was 'um der Hals' (a matter of your neck). I could hardly refuse. Mercifully, when I reached Customs that night, the place was empty save for one guard who said, 'Sprechen Sie Deutsch? – Gott sei Dank!'

During rehearsals for the oratorio, the soprano soloist's husband suggested that on the Sunday, when I was free from other commitments, he should drive me up alongside the Danube in his motor car, to see the cathedral at Esztergom. He arrived an hour late and said, 'Don't worry about late – this car go very fast.' Nervously, I responded, 'Not *too* fast, I hope?' We set off, with his wife, the alto soloist and her husband in the back of the car, and myself in the front nursing the soprano's baby. At one point we took a short cut down a country road, which turned into a muddy farm track. I kept wishing the driver would slow down: anyway the inevitable happened – we skidded and plunged into a ditch. Fortunately none of us was hurt, but we had to wait an age before a peasant cart turned up, which was loaded with turnips. The two husbands wanted to bring the car back, so the two ladies, the baby and I climbed on top of the turnips and set off with the peasant to the nearest town to get help. I had to ring the British Council man in Budapest and explain I would be late for a reception that evening: 'Thank God, you're alive!' he exclaimed. 'There could have been a serious diplomatic incident!'

The following year I was invited to be on the composition jury for the International Bartók competition in Budapest, but refused, as it was all done from score-reading, not from performances, and I felt inadequate to such a task. I suggested instead that I might help them judge string quartets, each of whom would be playing quartets by Bartók and one other of their own choice. They agreed to this and asked me to accompany the very distinguished President of the International Society for Contemporary Music, Edward J. Dent.

Dent was a great friend of the Intendant of the Budapest Opera, Aloda Todt, and through him we were able to attend a number of performances during their festival – most notably, a stunning triple bill of Bartók stage-works, *The Wooden Prince*, *The Miraculous Mandarin* and *Duke Bluebeard's Castle*. We also went to a Hungarian production of *Peter Grimes*: afterwards Todt's chief query to Dent was 'Did it really look like English seafaring life?' – which amused me.

The jury were put up in a hotel on the same side of the city as our meetings – Buda, I think. We were taken to the first meeting in a bus, but Dent said he would prefer to walk, as he knew the way. But he didn't appear, and, after a considerable period, we telephoned the hotel. When he arrived, he explained that he had jay-walked across an intersection in the city and had been reprimanded for this by a formidable lady police-officer. Dent had politely taken off his hat and said in the only Hungarian he knew, 'I am very sorry': but she fined him such a large number of florins, he had returned crestfallen to his hotel, to await rescue.

A very nice double-bass player who had played in the orchestra for *A Child of Our Time*, asked me to arrange a session for him with Dent to discuss early Italian opera, for which he had an enormous passion: I did so and they conversed in Italian. He then invited me to his home where we talked German. 'Why we like your conducting,' he remarked, 'is that when you say play B flat not B natural, *ist keine politische Frage* (it is not a political issue).' I told this later to my cousin Phyl – who had reappeared that year, married to an Indian called Aschraf – and they refused to accept the implications of the remark at all. (A Hungarian refugee I met later told me that below the pavement of a particular street I often walked in Budapest was the room where she had been interrogated by the secret police.) At the quartet adjudications I suggested that, to avoid political bias, the competitors ought to play behind a curtain or screen, and mischievously added, in French, 'Ce n'est pas un rideau de fer' (it's not an iron curtain). Dead silence. The curtain was supplied: but the winning quartet was still Hungarian – the wonderful Tatrai team.

For a few years, the conductor (and founder) of the Basle Chamber Orchestra, Paul Sacher, invited me to be present at various performances of my music which he was conducting: these included the first performance of *Ritual Dances* from *The Midsummer Marriage* in 1953, before the opera itself was first produced, and the Divertimento on 'Sellinger's Round', which Sacher commissioned and premièred in 1954. Sacher, of course, is probably the greatest individual patron of living composers in the twentieth century: for decades, he and his wife Maya (who is one of the owners of the Hoffmann-LaRoche pharmaceutical company) have used their wealth and artistic discernment to support every major figure from Bartók and Stravinsky onwards. Paul invited me to stay at his house, Schönenberg, outside Basle, and here I met a number of leading Swiss composers, such as Arthur Honegger and Frank Martin. Maya also showed me her immense collection of major twentieth-century artworks.

I, of course, was impecunious, but the Sachers quite understood and were extremely kind. On the first evening, we sat in the drawing-room before dinner. The double-doors at the other end were suddenly opened and Werner, the major-domo, appeared in white gloves to announce dinner. This was served at a specially constructed round table with extra circular components enabling it to be expanded or contracted according to the number of people present. After a few days, I felt obliged to enquire of Maya whether I should tip Werner and how much. The next morning I found that Paul had slipped a large Swiss banknote into my pocket for the purpose. The last time I was there, Richard Hawkins, then promotion representative for Schott London, was also present. Richard talks excellent French and German and is a wine expert. Maya recommended the fish, as it came fresh from the lake in the mountains and asked Richard what he thought of the wine. Richard began to make compliments and speak of his interest in wine, but Maya interrupted to say that the Sacher claret was shipped from Bordeaux to a port in Holland where, to keep it at the right temperature, it was buried in sand; after which it was brought up the Rhine in a boat. Richard was deliciously upstaged!

Paul told me a delightful story about the occasion when Boult came to conduct the Basle Orchestra and was invited to Schönenberg for lunch. The Sachers were at first surprised to find that he preferred to drink milk rather than wine. When it was time for him to return in the early evening, they offered him a choice of the Rolls or the Mercedes. Boult replied, 'I think I would prefer to walk' – and set off on foot along the ten miles or so of an industrial road that took him into the heart of Basle.

When I was invited to conduct a small choir at Radio Lugano, I asked Paul which language I should speak at rehearsals. He told me, 'Begin in Italian, which will please them – then go into French or German!' I went to Lugano two or three years running, conducting not only *A Child of Our Time* but Purcell's *Dido and Aeneas* – both in Italian. I grew to love the little impoverished Canton Ticino, south of the Alps.

In the 1950s, I was invited to attend a performance of *A Child of Our Time* in Vienna, conducted by Michael Gielen. I had agreed to go just beforehand to Poland, to serve on the jury for violin pieces to be written for the Wieniawski competition (I thought I could just about assimilate scores of solo violin works, without a piano to play them on); so I decided that after Poland, I could take a night train from there to Vienna. I had one enormous Swiss banknote, which had previously been given to me by Sacher, and which I intended to use in Vienna. When I flew into Warsaw, a group of musicians came to meet me with flowers and expedited my passage through Customs. I realised afterwards that the undeclared Swiss banknote was illegal and made enquiries as to how to take it out. The advice I received was to hang on to it and hope for the best. My Warsaw fee was in zlotys and of no use to me, so when I was seen off on a night train, I decided to distribute this local currency to anyone on the platform who needed it. The conductor of the train told me that the train was packed with Jewish refugees going to Israel and I would have to share a sleeping compartment with an Austrian diplomat, who turned out to be pleasant enough. As we reached the Czechoslovak frontier, I became apprehensive. The passport officer came along, looked in and having seen that the man in the berth above mine was a diplomat, assumed I was one too; I heaved a sigh of relief – my precious banknote was safe.

All through Czechoslovakia the train remained locked. When we entered neutral Switzerland, it stopped within a tunnel of barbed wire and I could see the snipers up above it. Jewish refugees were standing motionless and silent in the corridor on the side where the snipers were and I said to one of them, 'Surely you don't want to leave Poland' (which I thought relatively free then) 'for Israel?' (which was in a state of guerrilla war). The woman looked at me and replied, 'Nach Hitler, hat man keine Furcht mehr' (After Hitler, we have no more fear). At that moment, the whistle was blown, the Jews remained silent, and the train sped over the frontier to freedom.

In Warsaw I was invited out by a nice Anglophile woman and her husband (who had been in the English RAF) to see Chopin's birthplace and have lunch in a country house for artists. We set off very late but were nevertheless given lunch in the country house, which was built in an eighteenth-century château style. The manager took me into a small room, where I spotted some period furniture and asked if it was Chippendale. This he confirmed. After lunch, we went upstairs to the library, to meet two men and women in their twenties. The conversation after a while turned quite serious and one of the men became particularly overwrought. He asked me an odd question: 'What are your feelings about Gandhi?' It was clear that he knew I had been a conchie and I could tell their conversation was becoming deeply immersed in the question that has always dogged Stalinist societies – what do you do with the dissidents? The two who had brought me now said it was time to go, and the two women kissed me goodbye. The calmer of the two young men shook hands, but the other held me with his hands and said, with tears in his eyes, 'You won't forget us, will you?' You leave such a person knowing that only by the luck of the draw you are not there in his position.

FÊTES MUSICALES

The prominence I attained in English musical life from the war years onwards led to a number of invitations to sit on this committee and that. From 1949 until 1965 I was on the British Council's Music Advisory Committee. When Vaughan Williams set up a charitable trust, typically he wanted at least one figure who was known to be antipathetic to his nationalist ideas, so he invited me and I attended meetings from 1952 until 1978: I resigned then because I was establishing my own charitable trust through the sale of existing manuscripts. Such trusts are wonderfully free of bureaucratic restrictions and it was a pleasure to see so many lively musical projects receive the financial support they deserve by such means. Whereas some members of the RVW Trust were preoccupied with conserving financial resources, Ursula Vaughan Williams and I preferred to splash out.

Believing deeply in the cultural importance of radio and television, I also sat, between 1966 and 1970, on the BBC Central Music Advisory Council, which in those days had teeth. Admittedly, it contained a few 'passengers': Malcolm Sargent usually came only for the lunch beforehand; and Walton, living on Ischia, attended rarely – and then only asked why there had been so few radio performances of one or other of his compositions! This advisory group was chaired in his characteristically dry manner by Professor Jack Westrup from Oxford. I always liked to liven things up and I was particularly stupefied at the indifference shown by my colleagues towards television (not to mention their ignorance of it). I persuaded them that we all should at least go to the television studios to see what went on.

I felt that TV was still largely unexplored territory from a musical standpoint. I disliked what I called 'gala performance' music programmes of the kind that were then predominant – the stars doing their bits of Puccini or Brahms concertos or whatever. My own TV appearances had blossomed in that period, thanks largely to Huw Wheldon, who sometimes invited me on to his frontier-breaking *Monitor* programmes on the arts – each one rehearsed and televised live in the course of a single hectic day.

As part of a general attempt to see what artistic and creative people could do in terms of TV presentation, Walter Todd once prepared a TV realisation of my Concerto for Double String Orchestra with Colin Davis conducting the London Symphony Orchestra. He then asked me to come and see it, at the rehearsal for the programme, and, watched by a second set of cameras, we discussed what I would have preferred. After lunch they tried out my version, watched by another set of cameras. The first problem was purely technical – knowing how to cope with the proliferation of moving cables and lighting equipment. Secondly, it became clear that all such programmes would need an overall director: for the moment the cameras stopped and Walter and I debated pros and cons of everything, Colin began to rehearse the orchestra and it took ages to get started again. My ideas for showing the structure of the piece, by moving cameras around in different ways, simply didn't work. But Wheldon then rang down to say that the rehearsal of the programme was visually so exciting, why not forget about the performance? They nevertheless went ahead with it all.

In the 1960s, musical life in Britain burgeoned, through increasingly generous Arts Council patronage, championed by Jennie Lee, the

Minister for the Arts in Wilson's new Labour administration, and by Lord Goodman at the Arts Council. Music began to flourish in education as well, and in 1964 I myself became once more involved in such work, when I was invited to be Patron and Director of the Leicester Schools' Symphony Orchestra (LSSO). Eric Pinkett, the County Music Adviser, wanted me to conduct the orchestra at their first annual festival in the De Montfort Hall, in the city of Leicester. I replied that it was difficult for me to go constantly all the way to Leicester to rehearse with the orchestra. But Pinkett said that was no problem: regularly during the school vacations, they held courses based outside the city and he arranged to bring the orchestra for two weeks at Eastertime to stay at secondary schools in Corsham, Wiltshire, where I lived at the time. I was thus able to compose in the morning and rehearse with the orchestra in the afternoon.

From the outset, I made it a condition that I would not do the standard eighteenth or nineteenth century repertoire: I would conduct my own music and that of other twentieth-century composers. Our programmes, straight off, ranged from Holst and Vaughan Williams to a new piece specially written for them by Alan Ridout, and the American music I was just discovering – Copland, Ives, Gershwin etc. Some extraordinarily talented players emerged from the LSSO – including three members of the future Medici String Quartet and the wonderful boy-trumpeter James Watson, who had previously played jazz trumpet, and whose bluesy solos in Copland's *Quiet City* I shall always remember. In 1985, Jimmy was playing in the Covent Garden orchestra, when the company took a version of their production of *King Priam* to the Athens Festival, and it was great fun to meet him again. Teasingly I enquired what had happened to the LSSO cor anglais- player who had been his girlfriend. 'I had to give her up,' he said, 'as she had protruding teeth – and that ruined my lip.'

Twice I conducted the LSSO on tour, in Belgium and Germany, where they astonished all their audiences. There were always escapades, of course. Our final concerts in Belgium were in Ostend, one afternoon, and in Brussels. The night before the Brussels concert there was a reception in the British Embassy. When I met the Ambassador, it was clear that neither he nor his staff realised what state school children could get up to: and indeed, the older children quickly observed where the drinks were coming from and stood by the doors, picking up glasses of gin and whisky as the trays appeared. Soon, Pinkett approached the Ambassador and apologised for making a sudden diplomatic exit with the kids!

Next morning, I arose early to be in time for the rehearsal, but Pinkett telephoned to say that it would have to be delayed as several members of the orchestra had hangovers. Later, I told the children at rehearsal that if they played well, they would get the alcohol out of their system. That final concert was one of their best – including an absolutely stunning performance of Elgar's *Enigma Variations*: afterwards a Belgian composer came to me and said, 'What an extraordinary work – more interesting than Brahms's *St Anthony Variations*!' In Berlin we appeared at a youth festival and played in the newly built Philharmonie. The young Richard Rodney Bennett came for nothing to play *Rhapsody in Blue*: and I was told that the audience – unaccustomed to Gershwin – thought the opening upward slide on the clarinet showed how poorly the orchestra were going to play – but soon changed their minds! We ended with the most cracking account of Hindemith's *Symphonic Metamorphosen* they had ever heard.

Although, over a period of five years, I wrote a work for the LSSO – *The Shires Suite* – I had eventually to discontinue conducting them, such were the pressures of composition; others, notably Norman Del Mar, took over. But I have retained a link ever since: and indeed, conducted them in my *Ritual Dances* in 1985, at a special open-air Bath Festival concert in a disused railway station. I am particularly pleased that the Leicestershire authorities and parents have joined forces to ensure the orchestra's survival, despite the appalling cuts in state education finance and their consequent impact on peripatetic music-making; and I am proud that my own charitable trust regularly enables talented young performers in Leicestershire to receive further professional tuition.

As I lived close to Bath, it was perhaps inevitable that I should have been invited to sit on the Council of Management of the Bath Festival, with which Beecham had been associated in 1955, but which was really put on the map by Yehudi Menuhin. Yehudi was incredibly active through each festival – too much so: at times, we had to tell him he was playing in too many events! He regularly invited Nadia Boulanger, and some of my own pieces took on a new lease of life when Yehudi included them in his Bath Festival Orchestra programmes. Suddenly, when Yehudi's band played my *Fantasia on a Theme of Corelli*, everyone fell for the piece, and we made a recording for HMV which I still cherish. In 1965 Yehudi brought over the

Moscow Chamber Orchestra and planned to combine them with his Bath Festival Orchestra for a performance of my Double Concerto. There were, however, problems. The Russians wanted to stand to play, while the English players wanted to sit. Yehudi could not get them to agree. Nadia Boulanger was sent for, but was equally unsuccessful. In the end, I came along myself and ordered everyone to sit which, amazingly, they did. The performance was wonderful and they decided they would record the work: but because of their schedules, the recording had to be done after a London concert, throughout the night.

Yehudi's new-found enthusiasm for conducting opera led in part to the financial difficulties of the festival and in the end a change of artistic direction had to be negotiated. At first, in 1969, I was invited to join a triumvirate that consisted of Colin Davis, the agent Jack Phipps and myself. The logistics of this soon proved impossible and eventually I was invited to become the sole director, in 1970. Even so, there were shenanigans behind the scenes about my appointment: Phipps was particularly irked at losing an obvious vehicle for the artists under his management; and it seems that a letter of dissuasion on moral grounds also came from Aldeburgh to the Bath Festival Council which seemed to me ironic!

Given that the festival had a deficit of about £12,000 and the bank could not extend further credit, I made it a first objective that all events had to be agreed by the Council, with proper budgetary limits in operation. I had also observed that there was a lot of dead wood on the Council and contrived, in short, to replace the aristocracy with commerce. I manoeuvred to have Mrs Barbara Robertson of the famous Robertson's jam company become the new Deputy Chairman. Barbara was superb. She soon saw to it that anyone on the committee had to justify his or her place by actually doing things, above all raising money to pay off the deficit and ensure the future of the festival. In addition, she and her husband were amongst the most cultivated people on the committee, and it was thus a joy to work with them.

I myself made a rule that restricted the tenure of the artistic director to five years (which was broken, I am delighted to say, by my successor, William Glock). To safeguard my own compositional work, I emphasised also that all the general administration should be undertaken independently – and in 1971 two young men, Luke Rittner and Anthony Tootal, were appointed, who proved more than competent. Council meetings, now, were not held over delicious lunches in stately homes and castles, but over bread and cheese in Bath itself.

One of my aims was to change the festival's eighteenth-century bias to achieve wider appeal: and I said at the opening press conference that I didn't mind if people turned up to concerts wearing jeans, rather than suits and dinner-jackets. The opening concert was usually in Bath Abbey, and for the first I devised an odd programme – a Bach cantata, a Liszt organ work, Charles Ives's *Three Harvest Home Chorales* and *General William Booth Ascends to Heaven*; and after the interval, Purcell's great 1692 St Cecilia Ode. This was the beginning of an association with the Schola Cantorum of Oxford, a brilliant choir then conducted by the young, multi-talented Andrew Parrott. The weather was wonderful and outside the Abbey there were young people everywhere in summer clothes. We wondered whether they would come in for the concert – and indeed, they did: so already we had a new audience. We went on using the Abbey for some time, regularly inviting Neville Marriner and his Academy of St Martin-in-the-Fields. The Abbey authorities weren't always co-operative. After one concert, there was a soprano who needed to get away early to catch a plane. We were all talking away in the vestry (which served as changing-room), but then found that the verger, fed up with the delay, had locked us in. We had to hoist the soprano out of the window so that she could reach her plane, and also find someone to let us out!

I managed to make some deals with the London Symphony Orchestra in order to have major concerts, which we took to the Colston Hall in Bristol (the biggest venue available): thus we were able to feature the Verdi *Requiem* with the young Riccardo Muti conducting, and Beethoven's Choral Symphony with Colin Davis. Joan Sutherland and Richard Bonynge came to do an operatic recital and as ever, Joan proved a lovable, riotously funny character at the reception afterwards. In order to ensure that contemporary works were properly represented, I instigated some Director's Choice concerts of chamber music, whose programmes ranged from neglected figures like David Wynne to Pierre Boulez and up and coming composers such as Robin Holloway.

We also went to the newly created Bath University to try and win the support of students. They, of course, wanted rock music and for two years we tried to provide it. The first such concert, in 1969, was a hugely successful Blues Festival on a Saturday night at a recreation ground within Bath: we were expecting 7,000 but 23,000 people turned up. The following morning, however, the youngsters who had come and camped out after the concert, unable to find milk in the shops, stole if off people's doorsteps! The City Fathers were not amused and told us we could not put on further events of this kind within the city limits. So, next year, we mounted an even bigger event – a two-day festival of blues and progressive rock, featuring artists like Led Zeppelin – on the grounds used outside the city for the Bath & West Agricultural Show. News of this spread around the country. It was before the days of the M5 motorway – there was just the main road from the North of England down to Cornwall: so the traffic that Bank Holiday weekend was jammed solid with rock music fans coming to our concert. Luke and Anthony were bombarded with telephone calls by worried parents and others wanting reassurance about their children's safety. One mother rang and said, 'My daughter is going to your festival. What accommodation can you offer?' When she was told that various-sized tents were on offer – from single to multiple, orgy-sized tents – she asked, 'Can you guarantee her virginity?' The grounds had to be protected by barricades, but unfortunately these were broken down and a good deal of money was stolen. We realised that this kind of event was outside our organisational experience and capacity, and although jazz and other popular music remained a feature of the festival, we had to scale things down somewhat.

The festival now had all the variety it needed – everything from brass band concerts to a hot-air balloon meeting – and to raise money, we even published a festival musicians' cookbook. By the time I completed my stint as artistic director, the festival was financially secure and had a new lease of life: and it is rewarding to see how well it has flourished since then under the direction of William Glock, Bill Mann and Amelia Freedman, in turn.

My meeting with Nadia Boulanger at Bath led to an invitation to become a member of the jury for her annual composers' competition in Monaco, hosted by the Palace there. In this particular year, she thought I might be helpful in the selection of a one-act opera. Since I thought I could gain access to a piano, I agreed to go. The two other composers on the journey were Georges Auric (of the famous group 'Les Six', from the 1920s) and the Danish composer, Vagn Holmboe (who invited me to spend a holiday at his house south of Copenhagen): we all stayed at the Hôtel de Paris and most of the time enjoyed ourselves drinking champagne and chatting together. True to form, it was Mme Boulanger herself who stayed up all night and decided on the winner! We also attended a concert and an opera. The concert was an all-Gershwin programme, played with great exhilaration. The opera was *Tristan und Isolde*, whose scenery and costumes had been borrowed from the Paris Opéra. My main memory of it is of the immensely corpulent tenor who played Tristan. At his death, he lay flat at the front of the stage parallel to the footlights, so that my attention was inevitably focused on his great semicircular mound of stomach, which Isolde gently caressed as she sang her *Liebestod*.

CHAPTER NINE

INTERPRETATION AND ITS DISCONTENTS

Like many other composers, from Berlioz to Gershwin, I have found myself stretching performers in ways they hadn't imagined. Already with the first performance of my String Quartet No. 1 in 1935, the Brosa Quartet were in a state of great agitation over the irregular (so-called 'additive') rhythms which they had to execute. Even in the early performances of *A Child of Our Time*, a work which I deliberately made as direct and as simple as I could, stylistically, there were upheavals. I remember Wilf's father, Dan Franks, who played the violin in the first performance, getting up at one point and banging his chair on the floor in fury: 'This is impossible!' he exclaimed. No one would have guessed that this would become the most frequently performed of all my compositions, nationally and internationally, by amateurs and professionals alike.

Two facets of the work seemed to defeat interpreters in the early days, and even now, are often distorted. The bass recitatives, which are mostly narrative and need a relaxed, rather than melodramatic, delivery; and the style of the spirituals, whose 'lilt' (a word that seems to be peculiar to English, difficult to translate into other tongues) and whose throwaway jazz endings on the last (weak) beat of the bar, are often subverted by pulling back the tempo.

Older-generation conductors were rarely happy with anything I wrote. Sargent and Boult, for instance, treated my music with scepticism. I think they lacked the knowledge of pre-classical music from which I derived so many of my ideas; and they even missed the clear relationships with classical precedent which were equally strong. David Webster, the manager of the Liverpool Philharmonic Orchestra after the war, wanted the first performance of my recently completed Symphony No. 1 and engaged Sargent to conduct it. As ever, Sargent liked to have the composer by the rostrum to answer queries from the players, since he had not really studied the score. During the rehearsal, a trombonist asked about a clash between two notes a semitone apart which seemed to him a possible inaccuracy. 'We will ask the composer,' said Sargent, as usual. Without hesitation I confirmed that the clash was correct and said under my breath to Sargent, 'It's the same as the opening of Monteverdi's *Lasciatemi morire*'; but he had no idea what I was talking about – such music was outside his experience. In the furore that erupted over my Second Symphony, several years later, Boult moaned to me, 'I don't understand this modern music.' I replied, 'There's hardly anything here you wouldn't find in Brahms!'

In December 1952 I had to make the embarrassing choice between attending a London performance of Symphony No. 1 by the BBC Symphony Orchestra with Ernest Ansermet conducting, and a Turin Radio performance of *A Child of Our Time* conducted by Herbert von Karajan. The latter had come about through Walter Legge, of HMV, to whom I had been introduced by Walton. I chose to go to Turin. There were star soloists – Elisabeth Schwarzkopf, Elsa Cavelti, Nicolai Gedda and Mario Petri – and so many chorus rehearsals that there was not very much for Karajan to do, save conduct the performances. The problem was the bass recitatives: Petri couldn't sing them, and after the final rehearsal Karajan called him to the green room, along with myself and an engineer with a tape recorder. Several times over, I played the simple recitative lines and Petri was then recorded trying to sing them. Each time the tape was played back, Karajan indicated what Petri had done wrong and he tried again. This continued for some time; it made little difference – Petri was still at sea in the performance. At the concert, I arrived early and went backstage to wish everyone luck. Karajan had been staying in the same hotel as the soloists and five minutes before the start, a radio engineer asked me, 'Has the maestro left the hotel?' I replied that I hadn't seen him and advised him to ring the hotel to find out. But instead, he took up the telephone and said, 'Get the records.' Karajan was deliberately late. When he arrived, and was about to go on stage, he turned to me and said, 'Would you mind, Michael, if I make an interval half-way through Part 2 of the work; I think it would be more effective.' I replied, 'I would mind very much, but I can't stop you,' and on to the stage he went. His interval was taken without any warning to the radio people or to the performers.

When I returned to London, a letter from Ansermet awaited me, declaring that the slow movement of the symphony was just paper music: there was no harmonic relation between the ground bass and the variations above. I replied, saying that the relations were similar to those you would find in Purcell. My confidence in the quality of the work had been reinforced by Walter Goehr – a musician from right outside the English tradition – who, when he saw the score, had said, 'But this is a *real* symphony'; and he had conducted the first London performance.

Although I had good personal relations with Sargent, he was always patronising, and matters came to a head over the first performance of my *Fantasia on a Theme of Corelli*, which he was due to conduct at the 1953 Edinburgh Festival. When the score was complete, I sent Sargent a copy with a little letter saying that he would find this a warm, lyrical piece which he would enjoy conducting. His response was to ring Howard Hartog at Schott and tell him, 'I intend to get the intellectuals out of music'; he followed it up with dismissive remarks at a press conference. I immediately decided that I had had enough and asked Howard to tell the BBC that I'd prefer to conduct it myself. The problem then was how not to have a confrontation with Paul Beard, the leader of the BBC Symphony Orchestra, who was always very difficult about my music. I was advised that if the rehearsal was on a Friday he would not take part, as he would be out on the golf course: failing that, I should ensure that one of the two solo violinists was a woman, as Beard would then be more relaxed. Thus it came about that the two solo violins chosen were Maria Lidka and John Glickman.

Some time later, Hermann Scherchen was asked to conduct the work for the BBC. He had devised a method of performing string orchestra pieces with fewer players, but amplifying them. Consequently the contrasts between the group of soloists and the two supposedly larger string groups were quite lost. Another perverse idea was applied by Antal Dorati, when he conducted the first performance of my little *Praeludium* for brass, bells and percussion. This was commissioned for the 40th anniversary of the BBC in 1962, and in the same concert were Bartók's *Cantata Profana*, Schoenberg's *Dance Round the Golden Calf* (from *Moses und Aron*) and Stravinsky's *The Rite of Spring*. Dorati decided that each piece must be interpreted from a nationalist standpoint: and since, in his view, English music was pastoral and soothing, he tamed the barbaric splendour of my *Praeludium* by reducing all the forte markings to piano!

By a piece of good fortune, Howard had managed to interest the German conductor Hans Schmidt-Isserstedt in my music: and when this conductor gave the German première of the Double Concerto with the Hamburg Radio Orchestra in 1949 and brought the same piece to London, at last the concert-going public was able to hear a performance truly representative of my intentions. This piece, which had been turned down by the BBC, was then acclaimed by the critics as worthy of anything in the Elgar and Vaughan Williams canon etc. etc.: I roared with laughter. Thirty-five years later, on my first visit to Japan, I heard the NHK Radio Symphony Orchestra play the work with complete stylistic understanding under a guest German conductor, Horst Stein. I asked him afterwards how he came to know the piece and he replied, 'I was trained by Schmidt-Isserstedt.' Thus are the best interpretative traditions sustained from one generation to the next. (Another reassuring instance of this occurred when I was in Cincinnati during my 1990 world tour. The Cincinnati Symphony had played my Second Symphony a few months earlier, under Charles Mackerras, and one of the violinists stopped me, now, in the corridor and said, 'That sure was a difficult first violin part in your symphony – I really had to practise it, so now I'm teaching it to my students!') Schmidt-Isserstedt also took the *Corelli Fantasia* into his repertory, but demurred at my later music: he was supposed to conduct the première of *The Vision of St Augustine* for the BBC, but drew back. I had to take over, and he confined himself to the *Eroica Symphony*; I teased him that I would really have preferred it the other way round!

In general the 1950s was a period of disasters for me, as far as performances in England were concerned. The Australian pianist Noel Mewton-Wood, who had played *The Heart's Assurance* so memorably in many performances with Peter Pears, took his own life at the age of 31. It was for Noel that I had written my Piano Concerto, and the City of Birmingham Symphony Orchestra now invited Julius Katchen to undertake the première. Katchen, after seeing the score, declared it unplayable, and the performance was delayed until October 1956. Now Louis Kentner was engaged and he astonished everyone by committing it immediately to memory. But the rehearsals under Rudolf Schwarz concentrated so much on individual notes (a Teutonic bad habit) that the sense of the music was lost. Unbelievably, when the BBC Symphony presented the work two years later, with Schwarz conducting, Kentner was bypassed and his first wife, Ilona Kabos, was asked to play it; she performed it extremely well, but it was left to me to tell Kentner what had happened. Like so much I had written, the Piano Concerto had to wait for a younger generation of pianists – John Ogdon, Stephen Bishop, Paul Crossley, Emanuel Ax etc. – and conductors like Norman Del Mar, Colin Davis and Andrew Davis – for a properly coherent interpretation.

The most contentious situation arose over the first performance of my Second Symphony in 1958. Paul Beard, who was leading the BBC Symphony, objected to the way the string parts were laid out, with notes grouped across bar-lines; he insisted on having a set of string parts with conventional groupings. I pointed out that this would cause more problems to the players than the procedure I had adopted – and so it turned out. As is well known, the first performance at the Festival Hall broke down about two-thirds of the way through the first movement and Boult, who was conducting, turned to the audience, and said, 'All my fault, ladies and gentlemen'; the horns in fact had come in a bar early at one point, thus producing confusion. The piece had to be restarted. Worse was to follow: Beard slowed down his violin solo in the scherzo, and the string-playing in general became more and more ragged.

The press was not enamoured of all this. Stung by their criticisms, the then Controller of BBC Music, R.J.F. Howgill, wrote to *The Times* defending the orchestra, whose 'comprehensive technique', he said, 'was equal to all reasonable demands'. The implication was that I was in the wrong. Since I was scheduled to conduct the piece at the Proms that year, I wrote to Howgill and asked if he wanted me to withdraw. After a while, it was determined that Boult would take over and it was clear to me that all the technical problems would arise afresh. In due course, I received a telephone call from the BBC asking me to appear at the rehearsal to demonstrate to the players that I was not displeased with them: *but I was not allowed to come within 40 ft of the platform*. I rang Boult and informed him that for the sake of the work and of good relationships I would do as requested; 'But', I told him, 'if you wish to ask me a professional question and want a professional answer, you will have to come all the way back to speak with me.' The rehearsals and performance all went ahead in that way. To my surprise, I received a letter from Schwarz, saying he was on the side of the players. Replying, I didn't mince words: 'If composers of my age' (I was then 53) 'are to be treated in this way, then heaven help the younger ones'. One of the odd things about the whole affair was that

Boult, for all his stature and achievements, was not able to stand up either to the orchestra or the management as anyone might have expected of him.

Not long afterwards there was some plan for the Hallé Orchestra to do the work under Sir John Barbirolli. As he had heard about all the shenanigans with the BBC, he invited me to come and discuss the piece with him. We went through the score together: then and there, he bowed up the first violin part, and although he was a cellist, he was able to work out the fingering straight away. It was a shame his projected performance with the Hallé never came about. Nevertheless, since then, a younger generation of conductors has discovered the piece and done it justice – from Colin Davis in his LSO concerts and recording in the mid-1960s, to David Atherton and Mark Elder in the 1980s. In the Glock era, the BBC Symphony rose to new heights under Dorati, Colin Davis and Boulez and have remained leading exponents of contemporary music. The arrival of the London Sinfonietta in the late sixties and early seventies also set new standards, not merely of virtuosity, but in taking a responsible stance towards new composition: and many new-music ensembles have sought to emulate their example. Life is by no means a bed of roses for the up-and-coming composer, but the situation is now streets ahead of what it used to be.

Intriguingly, individual performers have also become more versatile over the years, mainly because their training has encompassed a broader, more inclusive range of skills, not least those of jazz, rock and pop. When, in the late 1960s and 1970s, I wrote for the electric guitar, in my third and fourth operas, *The Knot Garden* and *The Ice Break*, finding a player who could cope with the part was almost impossible. You either used an acoustic guitarist who could read accurately but had limited knowledge of the special sonorities of the electric instrument; or you engaged a rock musician, whose variable reading ability and inexperience at playing to a conductor's beat placed the security of the ensemble at risk. Indeed, to try and surmount the problem at that time, an electric harpsichord was often substituted; this was unsatisfactory.

In the late 1980s, however, those difficulties have disappeared: players like Steve Smith are at home with any kind of guitar, acoustic or electric, and their musicality and intelligence are an asset. Writing *New Year*, I was able to consult with this particular performer all the way through, and his instructions on which special effects are needed have been incorporated into the published materials. I am not alone in benefiting from such advances in instrumental skills: for instance, I gather that when Pierre Boulez's *Le Marteau sans Maître* was first played in the mid-1950s, it wasn't possible for xylophone and marimba players to deploy two sticks in each hand. Now the level of virtuosity on keyed percussion is astonishing. It is not merely an excuse or a pipe- dream for a composer to say his or her music belongs to the future: in matters of instrumental technique this may, quite literally, be the case.

While many notational traits in my work have long since been accepted, the need to give clear information and directions in the score remains paramount. It used to be part of the house style of Schott publications that all directions should be in Italian. I myself abandoned that in the late 1960s and 1970s. If detailed description of the character of the sound I want is worth while, I will supply it in English. Sometimes I have failed in this respect – notoriously so, in the case of the 'breathing noises' needed for Symphony No. 4. When I wrote the work, I didn't take enough trouble to discover how the sound I wanted could best be produced: I just wrote 'wind-machine' in the score.

Georg Solti, who conducted the première in Chicago, told me, 'We have the best percussionists in the world.' But at the première the old-fashioned wind-machine on hand made such a din when used, it had to be played off-stage: and it was more suitable for *Sinfonia Antartica* anyway. Later, human breathing over a microphone was tried, which was closer, but critics and other listeners read into this some kind of sexual innuendo. I went to the BBC radiophonic workshop and a tape of breathing noises was produced, which was useful, if anonymous. Only recently, in experiments with the latest 'sampling' techniques in the Greenwich Village studio of the rock music producer, Mike Thorne, have the potential variety and flexibility of the breathing effects come to fruition. I don't blame conductors for regarding the breathing noises as of low priority in rehearsals: there are enough notes in the piece to be got right without holding everything up while the various electronic machines are made to operate properly.

It is sometimes suggested that composers should try to follow Stravinsky's example and make definitive recordings of their own work. I don't really take that view: music, for me, is a performing art and I feel that compositions of substance will withstand all manner of interpretation by different artists. Once I have finished a work, it is

211

outside me, for others to make of it what they will. Some will show insight into my intentions and in some cases this will have the force of a blinding vision: an example would be David Atherton's conducting of the London Sinfonietta in *King Priam*. But then, Atherton is a conductor of genius. Others start from a basis of respect and ascend gradually towards impressive goals. The marvel is always of new minds and muscles being applied to the old pieces. Making records, as I have once more begun doing, may provide some guidelines in matters of tempo, phrasing, string-bowing, dynamics or whatever. But I don't have the real conductor's technical proficiency and I succeed best in relaxed conditions with those who love me (like the BBC Philharmonic Orchestra). Apart from my eyesight problems, which necessitate specially marked-up scores that I have to try almost to memorise, the main hazard I find is that I begin to listen to the playing as a composer and not as a conductor – which means I can lose my objective control of the performance: and I have to train myself not to go that way. I've also coached innumerable young singers and instrumentalists in my works, and that has paid great dividends: for these days I encounter students who play the quartets (for instance) with perfect understanding, because they've been trained by the Lindsay Quartet – who themselves learnt the pieces under my guidance.

In 1965 I was rung up by Malcolm Sargent and invited to conduct my Piano Concerto at the Proms that year, with John Ogdon as soloist. 'There will be a full house,' Sargent boasted, 'as in the second half I shall be there to conduct *The Planets*'; and indeed the hall was full. When I came off stage after the concerto, Sargent called me into his dressing-room and held up a piece of manuscript paper on which he had written out the National Anthem, using my favourite device of additive rhythm. I am spared that kind of parody nowadays. Conductors and performers still need to consult. Even in the 1970s, 1980s and 1990s, not all have heard of maracas, claves or roto-toms, or are happy to use the electric organ (instead of the pipe-organ), specified in *The Mask of Time* and *Byzantium*, or are intimate with the dub and reggae styles adapted in *New Year*. But now they not merely tolerate my unorthodoxy, they rejoice in it.

CHAPTER TEN

STAGE AND MARKET-PLACE

CABALS AND RIVALRIES

A long way back I read a volume (in Italian) of Verdi's letters, interspersed with an account of his life. One of his remarks has for ever remained in my mind: 'All composers want to live in their ivory tower, but they must go out into the market-place.'

It is now a cliché to observe that my own musical reputation burgeoned only during the sixties. In a way, I expected it to be so. When I first knew him in the 1940s, Ben Britten and I discussed our future ambitions. Ben said he would become first and foremost an opera composer. This, as everyone knows, he did; and although he wrote songs, chamber and orchestral music, it is on his stage-works, from *Peter Grimes* to *Death in Venice*, that his achievement is founded. I myself at that time was quite clear: yes, I would write operas, but I was equally keen to produce symphonies, quartets and concertos of stature. That, I guessed, might mean waiting some time before the music profession, let alone the general public, was able to make a full assessment: there would have to be an *oeuvre*, a range of works in all the genres, before my accomplishment was fully understood. I was happy to go along with this: I have often said that what sustained me was a mixture of patience and arrogance – the patience to wait until I had built up a sizeable corpus of diverse compositions; the arrogance to believe in the quality of what I was to write.

Other contemporaries of mine became agitated about Britten's meteoric rise to the forefront of British music in the mid-1940s. William Walton was one such: he admired Ben enormously, but the success of *Peter Grimes* and, later, of the Aldeburgh Festival, made him incredibly insecure. Before *Peter Grimes*, it was Walton who had been the great white hope, though I confess I never took to *Façade* or *Belshazzar's Feast*. I remember Ben staying with me at my Oxted cottage in the 1940s and we listened to a radio broadcast of Willie's

Violin Concerto. Ben, with his incredible ear, was able to sit down at the piano immediately afterwards and identify those melodic and harmonic mannerisms that recur in all the Walton scores.

. Rather unfortunately, I think, Walton associated himself at that time with a cabal of composers who were trying to debunk Ben or undermine his reputation: figures like Elisabeth Lutyens, Constant Lambert, Alan Rawsthorne, all of whom used to indulge in heavy drinkng bouts with the critic Cecil Gray, the writers Dylan Thomas, Louis MacNeice and the painter Michael Ayrton. They all had great chips on the shoulder and entertained absurd fantasies about a homosexual conspiracy in music, led by Britten and Pears.

I thought Walton's behaviour was ridiculous. One morning I arrived early for a rehearsal at one of the BBC's Winter Proms at the Royal Albert Hall. I saw Walton sitting alone and went up to him. Introducing myself, I said, 'You know, you can't be Ben, I can't be Ben, we none of us can be each other: so isn't it time you stopped all this nonsense about a conspiracy?' It seemed to bring him to his senses. At any rate, from this first meeting onwards we became firm friends and remained so until the end of his life. He was always very generous to me and I loved his sardonic humour. When he went to live in Ischia he kept in touch and sometimes came, with his colourful Argentinian wife, Susanna, to stay. I gather that he constantly demanded tapes of all my latest pieces and, though I doubt whether they were his cup of tea, he once joked (when I visited him in Ischia) that he had put two bars of my Second Symphony into his latest composition! On one of his last and sweetest postcards he informed me that he had recommended me to the Queen for the award of Order of Merit.

Willie never lost his sense of rivalry with Ben. Once I accompanied him to and from a concert he had conducted in Brighton. On the way back, sitting in the front of the car next to Susanna, who was driving, he let out a great cry, saying, 'Everyone is queer and I'm just normal, so my music will never succeed.' To me he seemed at times almost childlike about it all. Ben told me that when they met, on another occasion, Willie took out his chequebook and showed him the cheque-stubs. 'There,' he said, 'you can't pay out that kind of money'. I tried to help him over his difficulties and was once invited to lunch with him, Susanna and Sir John Anderson (later Lord Drogheda, Chairman of Covent Garden Opera). After the meal, we went into a sitting-room and Willie revealed the purpose of the meeting: 'I have heard,' he said, 'that Britten may be appointed music director of the opera house. There are enough buggers in the place already, it's time it is stopped.' Drogheda had to persuade this grown-up man not to be so silly. During the period when Walton was writing *Troilus and Cressida* for Covent Garden, I was invited to dine with him and Walter Legge. Imagine my amazement when Willie announced that he was going to include a musical representation of heterosexual copulation – there would be the greatest orgasm in music since Wagner's *Tristan* – and the two of them spent the greater part of the meal working out the rhythmic patterns of sexual intercourse!

SOHO THE DOG

When I wrote *The Midsummer Marriage* I had no idea that it would ever reach the stage. Over six years, it evolved from a masque with the title, *The Man with Seven Daughters*, through various intermediary stages: in an early sketch it was called *Octett*, and consisted of the eight main trigrams from the I Ching, linkng the seasons to the elements, to musical instruments etc. then it acquired the title *Aurora Consurgens* (a term from alchemy), *or The Laughing Children.*

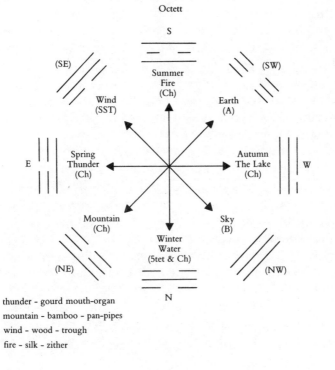

Octett

thunder - gourd mouth-organ
mountain - bamboo - pan-pipes
wind - wood - trough
fire - silk - zither

At that stage, I tried to collaborate on the text with Douglas Newton, but we were soon at cross purposes. In any case, the down-to-earth Max Steffens of Schotts (rightly!) thought that the title was a non-starter. In its final state as an opera, I spent six years or more writing text and libretto, from about 1946 to 1952. I had no commission – such things were rare then; the writing of it came only from inner necessity. Midway through, I began to despair of ever finishing it: the physical strain led me at one time to think I had cancer. I wrote to Willy Strecker at Schott Mainz to say so. His letter back was one of the best I've ever had from a publisher: 'You don't behave like that. Once you start on a work of that sort, you should complete it. As for what you suggested to me, regarding the nature of the piece, *Das ist die Welt zu erroben* [By that means is the world to be won].' He knew that it was going to be a kind of modern *Magic Flute* and to be upheld by this publisher in what might well be a commercially unremunerative venture seemed to me ideal, but it is rare. After receiving Strecker's reply, I never turned back.

It was a surprise to me that it should ever reach Covent Garden at all; I suppose Strecker must have sent along the vocal score prepared by Michael Tillett. Edward Sackville-West, who acted as unofficial dramaturg, urged Covent Garden to arrange a play-through. I did not attend this, but received a letter soon afterwards saying that they would like to stage the piece, but it would have to be cut, as it was three hours long. I responded by saying that if it were played at the right speed, it would last two and a half hours! In the event, I agreed to some cuts: the Ritual Dances in Act 2 were too long for the choreography; and the confrontation scene between King Fisher and the Ancients, which was thought to hold up the action of Act 3, was removed.

I soon discovered that dealing with opera-houses is far more complicated than getting an orchestra to take on a symphony or concerto: and all young composers will tend to have the same kind of experience. At first, I wanted the best international star singers available. As I now know, that is fantasy: most singers of that sort do not want to do new opera, they want to be heard in repertory pieces that can be a vehicle for their stardom. I was lucky to be given the young Joan Sutherland and Richard Lewis, both of whom sang beautifully, even if their acting was stiff. The role of King Fisher was entrusted to Otakar Kraus, who sang it like Caspar out of *Der Freischütz*, with peculiarly mangled English diction: I told him it was a Shavian character, but he had never seen a Shaw play. For Sosostris,

216

they managed to engage a Mexican contralto, Oralia Dominguez, who sang voluptuously even if she had no idea why she should be so completely wound up in veils.

The main difficulties arose over who should direct the production. David Webster, who had moved from the Liverpool Philharmonic to be the general administrator at Covent Garden, backed the opera but procrastinated over the engagement of a producer and designer. My real desire then – as now – was to find a producer with my own intellectual breadth. Webster had begun a policy of using well-known painters to design the Covent Garden productions and he tricked me now into accepting the idea of Graham Sutherland as designer. This was quite wrong: it should have been the producer who chose the designer. In the event, Sutherland could not participate (he was busy with his Churchill portrait), Ben Nicholson was approached, he also wasn't available, and so the task fell to Barbara Hepworth. One day Barbara telephoned me and asked if I would like to come to London, as she was now proposing to make the costumes and needed my assistance. I was nonplussed. I telephoned Evelyn Maude for advice and she suggested approaching my god-daughter, Stella Maude, who was Peter Brook's secretary. I asked her to accompany me to Covent Garden. She had been a dancer by profession and saw immediately that this was the wrong way to go about things: she made the obvious recommendation – get a producer.

It was Eastertime, 1954, and the opera première was scheduled for January the following year. I went along to try and bully Webster but still he wouldn't settle for any particular director. At one stage he suggested John Cranko, who had agreed to do the choreography, but luckily I disagreed: previously I had heard Cranko talk of his work for Ben Britten, in which he had told the composer, 'I'm only here to do exactly as you want'; that was not for me. Cranko anyway said he couldn't possibly direct the piece, only do the choreography. Ultimately, I enlisted Howard Hartog's assistance and we confronted Webster at a lunch meeting. Webster responded by saying he had considered the work very seriously and he now thought it to be more like a masque than an opera: why not use Freddy Ashton? 'Done,' I said. Some time in July I discovered, by telephoning around myself, that there was still no producer – for Ashton couldn't make the dates in question. By now Webster had to resort to using a house producer, Christopher West, who naturally wanted his own designer – Anthony Craxton, the designer of a *Daphnis and Chloe* ballet production I had found rather insipid. Lord Harewood was then working at the theatre and I solicited his support. We suggested that before Hepworth was cast aside, they should remember that she had at least discussed the piece with myself and had thus done some thinking about it. Christopher now arranged for us to travel immediately on the night train to St Ives for a meeting with Hepworth next morning. After breakfast, she straightaway put him on his mettle and settled down to work on the details of the production. She had formulated a number of technical solutions and Christopher had to cede to her wishes. It was too late to do otherwise: the costumes were already being made.

Webster then asked me the question that most composers have to be able to answer: how much rehearsal time will it take? I replied that it was not as difficult to play as *Wozzeck* (which they had recently presented under Erich Kleiber), but it would need as much rehearsal. The young John Pritchard was asked to conduct, but (rather like Sargent) relied on his fluency at score-reading. Webster warned him that unless he learnt the score fully, he would never conduct at Covent Garden again; and in the end, he did his stuff. What none of us calculated was the length of time it would take the chorus to learn their huge part, let alone the time needed to stage all three acts convincingly. In the event there was hardly any production in Act 3 at all: Hepworth never had time to light it properly – even though, before the première, West was given two whole days of technical rehearsals on the main stage. What Hepworth managed in Act 2, however, has never been equalled: she designed abstract trees – gauzes which could be lit in many ways from inside, their colours signifying the passage of the seasons. I attended the lighting rehearsals and was riveted.

At that time, I was fairly clear that the composer should come to rehearsals to help sort out the production. But I soon learnt the limits of intervention: moreover, the many explicit directions I had given in the libretto were absurd, because they were unrelated to any particular stage. It's always a delicate matter, how much freedom a composer should allow the producer and designer in matters of staging. My view now is that one must trust them, for they have a technical knowledge of lighting and other presentation techniques far beyond that of the average composer. My inclination, with all succeeding operas, has been to consult with them well in advance, and not appear at rehearsals until the last moment, and only then at their express invitation.

The Midsummer Marriage probably demanded more of Covent Garden, in matters of staging, than could be achieved at that time. I was asking them to move away from verismo into the world of symbolic dream theatre, in which the action took place beyond, beneath and above, as well as on the stage itself. Of those who saw the original production of *The Midsummer Marriage*, Edward J. Dent most appreciated its masque-like character (though, in his anti-clerical way, he disapproved of the 'Protestant' chorale that appeared in the orchestra part near the end). The press had a field day, some of them trying to stir up a scandal by reporting comments by baffled members of the cast. The worst of it reached publication on the day of the première, and when I went backstage with John Pritchard to wish everyone luck, some of them were in tears and denied having said any of the things attributed to them.

The bulk of the serious criticism was directed, in any case, at the libretto. I was at first delighted, because it meant that critics, instead of ignoring what was being sung (because it was in a foreign language) and simply talking about the quality of the singing and orchestral playing, now actually engaged with the drama. Gradually, I realised that the problem for the composer starts when the critics think they can do better! No matter how often I have said that my texts are for singing and not to be read as literature, this is how they tend to be assessed – right up to the present. All the other operas receiving premières at Covent Garden in the 1950s had libretti by well-known playwrights or writers. But this was no guarantee of the operatic viability of their texts. Arthur Bliss, for instance, had received a libretto from J. B. Priestley, for *The Olympians* – an opera whose plot had a lot in common with that of *The Midsummer Marriage* – which was conceived in terms of spoken theatre: and Bliss never asked him to cut or revise it for operatic purposes. The result was that the scene lengths and their relative proportions were seriously askew and the overall duration was far in excess of their expectations.

While I was writing the opera, various friends saw my draft text and tried to dissuade me from continuing with it. Jeff Mark thought it might lead me into folksy *Wandervogel* music. Desmond Shawe-Taylor, an arch-rationalist in most matters, thought it was rubbish; but then he had read Schikaneder's libretto for *The Magic Flute* and thought that rubbish too! To do Desmond justice, he later became a passionate admirer of the music of *The Midsummer Marriage* and of much else that I have written. Meanwhile, no one who saw the draft text indicated how any of it could be improved: they only recommended finding someone else to write it for me. The most helpful were David Ayerst and Eric Walter White. I had originally constructed the piece in two acts which were like two Aristophanic plays, with an *agon* (or contest) between the sexes (Act 1) and between age and youth (Act 2). Between the acts came a set of dances, and Eric suggested that these should be separated out into an act on its own: and once I started, the new Act 2 became a kind of extended *L'Après-midi d'un faune*.

Despite the hostility of much of the press (Ernest Newman, in *The Sunday Times*, admitting that he had written his review before hearing a note of the music, declared himself unable to make head or tail of it), there were many who saw in it something special. Walton himself, whose *Troilus and Cressida* was being held up as the true alternative to my confused effort, saw it and told me, I believe in all sincerity, that this was the real opera. The publicity for the piece had been good. The young Peter Heyworth, who had replaced Eric Blom as the *Observer*'s main music critic, was sent to do a profile of me as his first assignment: he proved a great ally. Meanwhile, Hepworth was profiled in *The Sunday Times*. Glock also came to it with his independent mind, and eight years later, as Controller of Music for the BBC, he mounted a radio performance which Norman Del Mar conducted, superlatively: this turned the tide in its favour. Colin Davis heard the broadcast on his car radio and determined that if he became music director at Sadler's Wells or Covent Garden, it would be high on his list for a new production. The rest is history: after conducting a new production at Covent Garden in 1968, Colin made a stunning recording of the work with the same forces, which became a bestseller. A number of international stage interpretations have followed since then. The most bizarre was one in Swedish, by a breakaway young people's opera group, the Stockholms Dramatiska Ensemble, managed by the ultra-eccentric Robert Carlsen: what was so vital about it was that rarity, a chorus of the right age group, speeding around the stage on roller-skates!

I still cherish Sargent's comment after he had seen the original production. Observing how I had extended the vowels of the text in the final Ritual Dance (so rapturously sung by Joan Sutherland and Richard Lewis) –

> . . . So the dog leaps to the bull
> Whose blood and sperm are all fertility.

– he enquired, 'And who is Soho the Dog?'

THEATRE GAMES

The 1960s and 1970s were an exciting period for opera in Britain, not least because of the rise of the regional companies in Wales and Scotland, Norman Platt's lively Kent Opera Company, and English National Opera, newly housed at the Coliseum. Covent Garden at that time nurtured young English singers, and production standards developed in a way hitherto unknown. When David Webster agreed to do my second opera, *King Priam*, I made no bones about who should direct. I asked for someone out of the theatre or cinema. The choice fell to Sam Wanamaker and he and I were able to consult from the outset. He couldn't deal with a musical score, so I arranged for a tape of the entire opera to be dubbed, with one person speaking all the roles, accompanied by a Covent Garden piano *répétiteur*! By this means, Sam was able to gauge accurately the lengths of each scene and each episode. This procedure has been adopted with my subsequent operas (though with Andrew Parrott singing all the roles!) as a service to the director.

Other decisions concerning the visual style of the presentation were made early on; and so that Sam could show me what was possible with contemporary lighting techniques and moving stages, he took me to some musicals, notably *Oliver!* Sean Kenny had created a wonderful moving stage for *Oliver!* which led myself and Sam to think him exactly the right designer for *King Priam*. Sam asked Webster for a revolving stage, but was told none existed at the Garden. Kenny solved the problem, producing a set incorporating two large saucers which comprised a revolve set upon the stage. With Webster's encouragement Sam and the lighting designer, William Bundy, introduced the Covent Garden technical staff to new lighting techniques and the lighting sequences were thus both imaginative and complex.

The première of *King Priam* in 1962 took place at the Coventry Festival – celebrating the opening of the new Coventry Cathedral – and in the same week was juxtaposed with première performances of Britten's *War Requiem*. The night before the first performance, Sam stayed up painting over the proscenium arch in the theatre. This time, although the singers were magnificent, there was still trouble from Pritchard, who wanted to make small cuts, and had reduced the impassioned rhetoric for all the violins in Hecuba's motif to a feeble single instrument; it took years to persuade conductors to have this played by a full section of violins the way I intended – Roger

221

Norrington, in fact, was the first to do so, in Nicholas Hytner's superb Kent Opera realisation of 1984. Whatever anyone thought of the work, the Royal Opera production, in its pristine original form, was something of a landmark for the company.

For my next opera, *The Knot Garden*, I was supremely lucky in having both Colin Davis as conductor and Peter Hall as director – a formidable partnership that gelled from the start. Once again, I was able in advance to talk at great length with Peter, explaining the nuances and interactions of the seven characters in the piece. Peter asked for singers who hadn't been 'Verdi-ized' – i.e. who would not simply rely on ham gestures. He and Colin picked a number of fine young singers, who have since become stars (e.g. Josephine Barstow) on account of their ability to act as well as sing.

Crucial to the presentation was Tim O'Brien's lighting: for the knot garden that assumes many forms – actual and symbolic – in the course of the work was conjured simply with miles of hanging rope, enveloped in lighting and film. Visually it was breathtaking. As *The Knot Garden* is an intimate opera, Peter obtained permission to take away the (sacred!) prompt-box and build out across the orchestra pit. Thus, at the 'climax of forgiveness' in Act 3, he was able to bring all the characters out to the front, turn off the film and stage-lighting so that one just saw the bare ropes, and bring up the house lights: when this scene ended, they retreated to the stage, the house lights faded and ropes were transformed into a knot garden again. Real theatre.

With my fourth opera, *The Ice Break*, there was almost a repetition of the problems I had encountered over *The Midsummer Marriage*. Peter Hall was due to direct, but in 1976, a year before its première, he became Director of the National Theatre, and would not be free. I was conducting in Los Angeles when this news came through. Not long afterwards I went to see the musical, *Pacific Overtures* in New York: and, as John Tooley (David Webster's successor) happened to be around there at the same time, I suggested he contact the director, Harold Prince. Tooley and I subsequently travelled to Vienna to meet him. He had been supplied with a tape and libretto, but by the time we arrived, he had already decided against doing the piece. In the event, Sam Wanamaker was brought in again: but since he had film commitments in Hollywood, his involvement in the production was somewhat belated.

Emulating cinema and television, *The Ice Break* risks the swiftest kind of stage-changes from indoor scenes to outdoor ones, and its surrealism also demands some degree of technical sophistication. Early in 1977 I went to an exhibition on holography, entitled *Light Fantastic*, and met one of its creators, Anton Furst. We saw eye to eye and I recommended him to Sam as someone who might assist in realising the opera's special effects (I believe Anton had worked with him previously); and Sam did indeed bring him in on the presentation. Unfortunately, there were workshop errors at Covent Garden which made the intended holographic images impossible, so the special effects were confined to laser beams. Musically, again, the opera was in Colin's safe hands and the cast and chorus ensured that it made quite an impact.

GALA OPERA

Covent Garden, in the mid- and late 1970s, was in any case moving in another direction – towards what I tend to call 'gala performance' opera, a result of inadequate state subsidy, which led to an over-reliance on private sponsorship and consequent need to hire ultra-expensive international star singers. This rather detached them from those works by living composers which didn't fit in with the 'gala' concept; also it meant the loss of those opera-loving audiences who couldn't afford high-priced seats. Recently, much has been done to repair the damage – specially sponsored opera Proms, film relays in the Covent Garden piazza and a more constructive attitude towards new work, within the so-called 'Garden Venture', reduced prices for major contemporary opera presentations, and so on. But there is still a long way to go.

For myself, in spite of continuing, sincere friendships with Colin and John Tooley, I began to think I didn't belong. Each year there would be promises of revivals or new productions, especially of *The Midsummer Marriage*, which were then postponed – mainly because singers like Jon Vickers and Kiri Te Kanawa could not be persuaded to sing Mark and Jenifer. I began to feel alienated from Covent Garden. Another side to it was that when Covent Garden and English National Opera met to do their joint planning of repertory, ENO were regularly blocked from presenting a Tippett opera because Covent Garden insisted they were planning for one. In the end, when a projected new *The Midsummer Marriage* for 1985 was yet again postponed 'due to casting difficulties', I called their bluff and insisted that they should no longer block ENO: and within forty-eight hours,

ENO's director, Lord Harewood, had rearranged the company's schedules to feature a new *The Midsummer Marriage* in 1985.

Opera in England unfortunately labours everywhere on shoe-string budgets. Luckily for me, regional companies, like Welsh National and Opera North, and independent groups like Opera Factory and Kent Opera, have seen the possibilities of touring (as not everything of mine needs a full orchestral line-up and *The Knot Garden* now exists in a reduced instrumentation using 22 players rather than about 78), and of co-production and video. What is exciting, more generally, is how new audiences for opera have been created by these small companies and nurtured through educational back-up projects. I was mightly angered in 1989 when the Arts Council of Great Britain, instead of safeguarding a valuable company like Kent Opera, chose to discontinue its funding from a year hence, thus ensuring that it would have to disband. Had I been of a different political persuasion, I dare say my published defence of this company would have carried more clout in the appropriate bureaucratic departments. We could do with more Kent Operas, and better long-term funding for the ENOs, the WNOs and Opera Norths, not the tantalising parsimony that so limits adventure and innovation. As everyone has been saying for years, the amount of subsidy needed to keep the arts in general flourishing is, relatively speaking, peanuts, in terms of our gross national finances.

The new world of internationally shared productions, which has been a sensible feature of the 1980s, benefited considerably my latest opera, *New Year*. Here, indeed, right from the start, I had no doubt that it would be better not to commit the piece in advance to Covent Garden – however grateful I was (and still am) for all the support and encouragement I had from this company, from the fifties onwards. I first of all talked to Peter Hall about the viability of creating the piece either for the National Theatre (where I had just seen *Guys and Dolls*) or in the commercial musical theatre. It became clear that there would be musical limitations in the National Theatre; also, Peter told me that the cost of a musical would, in London, require a three-month guaranteed sell-out and on Broadway, six months' sales: this would seriously have constricted what I could do musically, so I drew back.

After much investigation and negotiation, the outcome was a tripartite commission, involving Houston Grand Opera, Glyndebourne and the BBC. For all three it had been an expensive undertaking and a great risk. At the time of writing, the entire sequence of productions hasn't yet reached completion, though the final performance of the Glyndebourne Tour, in Plymouth, started with a bomb scare and ended with the orchestra sending up balloons and firecrackers and downing champagne!

Now, in my eighties, I could afford to employ assistants to keep everyone apprised of the requirements and preferred interpretations of this elaborate new work. But even with such constant back-up, for any company to mount a new opera implies an act of faith. So I particularly salute David Gockley at Houston Opera, who took the biggest risk of all in presenting the world première, and conductor John de Main: he was new to my music and had to cope with an array of physical problems in the small orchestra pit at Houston, but he triumphed. Gockley and de Main both identified with my effort to 'make it new' (in Ezra Pound's phrase) – which is rare, especially in the USA, where opera-houses hanker after star-studded galas even more than in England. There are still plenty of people around who are frightened by the 'newness' of content and style in my operas: but not the students who did *The Knot Garden* in Evanston, Illinois in 1974 or in Cincinnati in 1989 – for them it related entirely to their own psychological problems and the world they live in; though one Cincinnati business sponsor was reported to have said, 'It was so bad, I couldn't even sleep through it.'

For a composer to see a new opera through from conception to stage presentation requires courage and tenacity. Plenty of young ones have this, I'm sure: but they will continually face all those obstacles I have encountered myself. There is no need to despair: I never did, throughout all the disasters of the 1950s and the many agonies endured since; after all, I kept telling myself, Berlioz never lived to see *Les Troyens* performed complete. A few years ago I attended the première, at ENO, of Harrison Birtwistle's *The Mask of Orpheus*. I was totally shattered by this tremendous work. I was writing *New Year* at the time, and had to stop, take a breath and consider what lessons I might learn from it. As things turned out, I was not 'influenced', but I could only marvel at the way it (and everyone involved in it) so coura-geously, so tenaciously regenerated an art-form often regarded these days as dead.

CHAPTER ELEVEN

THE POST-WAR LIFE-STYLE

Although I accepted that as a composer I would be a loner, and some degree of isolation would always be necessary for me to work, I did not want a loveless existence. With Wilf long departed and Fresca recently dead, I felt at times very lonely. One evening in 1942 I returned to my cottage from London and was just preparing myself some late supper when a young man walked out of the bedroom. (The keys of my cottage were always left in the door, as I had little enthusiasm for locks.) His name was John Minchinton, and he had been recommended to contact me by Ben and Peter, for whom he had page-turned at a concert in Bristol; they thought him very gifted. He was attractive and obliging; we got on very well.

Although he never lived with me, we saw quite a lot of each other for the next ten years or so. He proof-read the full score of *The Midsummer Marriage* from the Mainz copper-plates and his meticulousness nearly drove the printers crazy. I introduced him to Walter Goehr and he worked as his assistant, becoming quite an accomplished conductor: he studied later with Karajan and was invited by Casals to the Prades Festival. John directed a number of enterprising concerts, including a lot of pre-classical and contemporary music. Particularly stimulating for me was his conducting of a late work of Stravinsky, *Agon*, in 1958, which was germane to my current compositional enterprise, *King Priam*. From Stravinsky's instrumentation I derived some clues as to how to deploy an operatic orchestra in an entirely new way – treating solo instruments as equals both within the ensemble and against the voices on stage, writing for heterogeneous mixtures of instruments.

John and I went on holidays together, hiking, immediately after the war, down to the Costa Brava. Early on, I had no idea that he had girlfriends as well – two in fact – and this ultimately complicated matters. One of our trips together was to Sicily, then still in a fairly primitive state with hardly any decent hotels or tourist facilities. The food was awful – no vegetables of any kind, nor potatoes or salad, just multicoloured fish, which I couldn't take: we lived almost entirely on eggs. One of John's girls joined us at Selinunte. Since by tradition no women appeared in the street or market or cafés, whenever we sat down for a drink in a piazza, people would ask me questions (since I was the only one who knew Italian) like, 'Who does the girl belong to?' The next question was always, 'Are you American?' and their faces fell when I said no, but lit up again when I told them we were British: evidently they wanted to leave their poverty behind and live elsewhere.

We travelled everywhere by train: and on the final part of the journey, round the south coast to Siracusa, the train was suddenly jam-packed. I enquired why this was: I was told, 'The Miracle.' Apparently a woman in difficulties had prayed to a picture of the Virgin and, to her astonishment, the virgin had wept tears: the picture has been sent to Rome for verification and returned with papal approval. We decided to go and see it. We had very little money but, keen to have some fun, we chose to go round Siracusa in a horse and carriage. We asked the driver to take us first to somewhere cheap for lunch, then off to the Greek amphitheatre and finally to the miracle. The crowds were huge and we had to walk the last part of the route to the piazza. The picture was on a pedestal in the centre guarded by a monk and barricaded, so that we had to take our turn in a long line of people to see it. On reaching the picture, the monk took a scarf or handkerchief from you, put it on the picture and sent you on your way. At the end was a market. John's girlfriend was outraged at this commercialisation of a religious ceremony.

Nevertheless, I took to Sicily in a big way and returned for holidays in later years – once with Norman Del Mar and his family; twice again, in my late seventies, with the Ayersts and Ian Kemp, respectively. Belatedly, I was able to visit Mount Etna and the superb Roman villa at Piazza Armerina; and one evening, in a Jolly Hotel, I was propositioned by a man who thought my demeanour younger than that of a septuagenarian!

Any intimacy I enjoyed with John didn't last very long, for he soon married. By that time I had renewed my acquaintance with Karl Hawker, the young painter I'd first met before the war when Aubrey Russ had brought him to my cottage at Oxted. On that occasion, Aubrey went back to London and Karl slept with me (which made

Aubrey a bit peeved), thereafter visiting a few more times. Karl and his brother had already decided that if there were a war, they would be conscientious objectors. At their tribunals, they were ordered to do alternative service, chose agriculture and went to work in Cambridge – where they met Larema Ayerst's brother, Bryan Fisher. During the war, Karl met a doctor's daughter and married her: Karl's brother and Bryan also married at the same time, and when Bryan moved to Corsham, in Wiltshire, Karl and his wife and the Ayersts went to spend Christmas there – which was where all their children were born.

Some years later, I heard through David Ayerst that Karl's marriage had broken apart and something inside me said, 'That's interesting.' I met him again, accidentally, in 1957. I had just finished some teaching in the Mary Ward Settlement in Holborn, and was about to board a bus: just then I saw Karl. He leapt on board and joined me for the journey to Victoria station. As I left to catch my train, I suggested that he came to see me in Oxted. When he did, and settled with me on a regular basis, the relationship with John broke quite violently. John turned nasty, hurling curses and abuse down the telephone. Karl, unfortunately, was listening in on another line and was particularly disturbed when John expressed the hope that our aeroplane would crash on a forthcoming journey to Stornoway!

Although I dedicated my Second Symphony to John, I lost touch with him and it was unfortunate that his career disintegrated (mainly for financial reasons). A few years ago, he made contact again. He had been seriously ill but, happily, Jessica, his wife, cared for him right until his death. Karl, meanwhile, continued to live with me until 1974 – something like seventeen years.

Writing *The Midsummer Marriage* in the late 1940s, combined with the strain of working for Morley College and other outside engagements, began to take a toll on my health. In 1948 I developed severe hepatitis and had to take time off to convalesce. Ben and Peter generously invited me to stay with them in Aldeburgh, where I would have a holiday. They were quite well-to-do by then. 'We'll look after you, you don't have to do anything,' Peter said, 'the place is thick with servants.' It was at that time when Ben was writing *Billy Budd*, and his librettist, E. M. Forster, was also staying in the house. While Ben composed during the day, Forster and I had long conversations about literature and the writing of opera.

When I left Morley in 1951, I decided it was time to move home, and with some financial assistance from my mother, bought a large dilapidated house, Tidebrook Manor, near Wadhurst in Sussex. My mother came to join Karl and myself there. For a while, we were looked after by the extended cockney family of the young conscientious objector I had helped at his tribunal some years earlier: John and Thelma and three little boys. These boys went to the local primary school and in the morning, before they left to catch the school bus, I was enchanted to see them all line up to be embraced by their parents –something I hadn't experienced in my childhood. In the end, I couldn't afford to pay them properly, and when the post-war austerities relented, they sensibly returned to London. Next came a German ex-prisoner-of-war, known as Zeppe, who had opted to stay in England, having got his wife out of occupied East Germany. They brought their little son called Horst. As they worked on the nearby Tidebrook Manor farm, this arrangement was more successful. In democratic fashion, we all ate together in the kitchen (apart from my mother who ate in her own room). The response of visitors to this varied: by far the most gentlemanly was Edward Sackville-West – he charmed them. Ultimately, Zeppe's wife left him and he went to live in a caravan. In later years, Horst and his girlfriend became champion ballroom dancers, appearing on BBC TV's *Come Dancing!*

It was a difficult business having my mother there. In her large room, she kept the windows open, night and day, in all seasons and heeded neither the cold nor the birds, hares, rabbits and other animals that came in. I had a large room to work in myself and built roaring fires in the winter. There was a large jungle of a garden, which was apportioned out, so that my mother took responsibility for half, and I looked after the rest – not very satisfactorily, to her great annoyance. The garden was surrounded by trees, and to earn some money I did some forestation, for which it was possible to obtain a grant. Once, a tree at the end of the drive, near the main road, was declared hazardous and Zeppe and I set about chopping it down. Contrary to my predictions it fell across the main road and I had to stand there directing the traffic up the drive to the house and out the other side, until the portion of tree blocking the road could be cut away. My mother, unaware of what had happened, was suddenly amazed to see cars streaming past the front of the house and out again. My mother's quirks (such as mixing laxatives into everyone's food, even when there were guests) and her readiness to flare up into moral argument often made life at Tidebrook quite taxing. Morever, she found it hard to countenance Karl's neurotic behaviour.

For a six-month period, Paul Dienes came to live at Tidebrook. He had just had two heart attacks and was lonely, as Sari had already left him. Paul said that if he had a third stroke, it would be the end. We gave him an upper room and told him that if anything happened, he should bump on the floor with his stick and we would ring for an ambulance. He was a lovely person to have around, particularly kind to the family from London. For a while, he tried to instruct me in symbolic logic.

What affected him deeply was knowing that I had started the last act of *The Midsummer Marriage*, which he could hear me composing in the room below. He said once that he didn't know how I could survive with such intense emotions inside myself all the time. He was very musical, but found it difficult to reconcile this with his other, more scientific side. He began to feel he couldn't continue waiting for the final stroke and deliberately provoked it by trying to help me in the garden; I think he also had a dream of making it look like one of those huge ordered gardens in palaces and aristocratic houses where there were lots of gardners and machines. Ill-advisedly he began to start hewing down wood, and it precipitated his death.

One day he knocked on the floor in his room: I called the doctor and went with him in the ambulance to hospital in Tunbridge Wells. I then rang through to Budapest and made contact with his eldest son, Gee, who was unable to come; but I reached his other son, Zed. He was free to come to stay with us in Tidebrook with his wife and children, and visited Paul in hospital every day. By this time, I didn't particularly want to have to traipse back and forth to the hospital, so I kissed Paul goodbye. I never returned and he died soon afterwards. Many years later – in 1978 – at the end of a world tour, I attended a performance of my *Ritual Dances*, given by the New York Philharmonic Orchestra under Andrew Davis, at the Lincoln Center. As I took a bow on stage afterwards, a woman rushed forward to me: I bent down and kissed her – for it was Sari Dienes.

Karl and I lived at Tidebrook for nine years, before deciding to move again. Bryan Fisher and his family were leaving their home in Corsham and after a decade in the country, I thought it might be nice to live in a little town, even though it was twice as far from London. I took over from Bryan the rental of his Georgian house, Parkside, in the High Street, which was owned by the Methuen family: they gave me very good terms, as a result of which we were able to do some repairs and renovations. The house had a lawn with a gazebo in one corner and I used this for composing, while repairs were under way. The lawn was highly irregular and bumpy and I spent a whole summer levelling it out with a plank. By the end it was reasonably even and thus suitable for croquet. Karl and I were quite accomplished at this game and inveigled various visitors into participating: I recall a splendid game with the young Harry Birtwistle and Sandy Goehr, watched by Peter Maxwell Davies, perched like a pixie on the wall. Beyond the garden was access to Corsham Park, designed by Capability Brown, and this was a boon: afternoon walks, when the morning's composition and lunch were over, had become part of my routine and nothing suited me better.

I only moved from there to my present house, outside Chippenham, in 1970, when plans to build a multi-storey car park at the back of Parkside were approved and I would have had to put up with the noise. My mother had gone to spend her declining years in Essex. When she died in 1969, she left me a sizeable sum. No mortgages were available at that time, but I had just enough to pay outright for this modern, American-style Colt house situated in an enclave in the middle of a farm. The previous owner of Nocketts (as it is called) had been a Naval Commander who had wanted to do some farming in his retirement: after only five years there, a heart attack ended his agricultural activities and he went to live in Spain. Amongst the facilities I inherited were a stunning view of the countryside, a heated indoor swimming pool and fields that I could rent out to a local farmer and roam in at leisure.

My relationship with Karl remained a turbulent one. Already after the first six months of living together, he was threatening to go back to London: he kept a tiny flat in Notting Hill Gate and it was a relief to me sometimes when he went there for short periods. Karl vacillated much of the time between wanting to paint and teaching. He continued part-time teaching (at which he was very accomplished) right on into Parkside days, but gave it up after that. Any physical relations between us never lasted for long. Tensions developed, Karl would remain aloof and even wonder whether he was truly gay. For two or

231

three sessions, he went to Layard for treatment. Even at Tidebrook we were moving apart. Karl had a large upper room, while I stayed in my big lower room. When his Welsh mother came to stay, he was especially difficult.

I was the only one with any money – not that I had very much – and I gave him a weekly allowance, partly to enable him to buy cigarettes etc. He could be very suspicious of guests or gay friends who became too familiar. His two daughters often came to stay and we got on extremely well. We all went on holidays together, especially to the Mediterranean. Once I went to Norwich with Karl to collect them from their mother: she was a lovely woman and we immediately became friends.

The turning-point came with the arrival of a newcomer on the scene. In October 1962 I received a letter from an ex-student at Birmingham University: I had been told about him by his tutor, Nigel Fortune, who had visited me that summer, but the letter was quite curious. Initially, he wrote to point out a wrong note in the score of my Second Piano Sonata (recently premièred in Edinburgh by Margaret Kitchin), but it was also a fan letter of a peculiar kind. Early the following year, Bill Bowen (known to his Welsh family and in professional music circles as Meirion Bowen) and I met briefly for the first time during the interval of the BBC's concert performance of *The Midsummer Marriage*. Then he came to visit, while Karl was away. By this time, having relished the training and excellent opportunities for music-making which he had had at Birmingham under Anthony Lewis's professorship, he was regretting having gone to do post-graduate studies at Cambridge under Thurston Dart. Gauche and vulnerable, he was by turns shy and garrulous. He was full of idealism. He shared my passion for Beethoven; he was a pacifist and CND member; by temperament anti-establishment and left-wing; isolated in every way at Cambridge, he had already decided to leave and try his luck in what he regarded as the real world, and had even considered abandoning music for work as a probation officer or in prison reform. We talked all weekend. It was the middle of an especially hard winter and the whole country was under snow: nevertheless, I took him for a drive up on to the Downs and we walked in the snow, which stood as high as the hedge-tops! Bill visited a few more times when Karl was present, and Karl was immediately suspicious.

A year or so later, after being kept apart by our respective work commitments, Bill came to Parkside again and a closer relationship developed. Subsequently, he visited regularly at weekends and during his vacations from Croydon Art College (where he taught music) – sometimes when Karl was there, sometimes not.

Parkside was close to the Bath Academy of Art: two members of staff, Helen Binyon (one of the grand-daughters of the poet, Lawrence Binyon) and Isabel Simmonds, and two young art students, Bob and Jenny, often came to dinner, or to play Mah-jong. Sometimes we went to the theatre – the Bristol Old Vic was not too far away and amongst the plays we attended were Anouilh's *Poor Bitos*, Albee's *Who's Afraid of Virginia Woolf?* and Priestley's stage adaptation of Iris Murdoch's novel, *A Severed Head*: all great stimulus at a time when the psychological charades of *The Knot Garden* were taking shape in my mind.

Karl, meanwhile, began to take the car out at night, returning in the early morning: this became so constant that I consulted his wife, who told me that exactly the same thing had happened during their thirteen years of marriage. Always claiming to be the one who knew about relationships, Karl had the greatest difficulties in coping with them in practice. I was by nature disinclined to ask Karl to leave, as I felt responsible for him: he had threatened suicide if I ever did that. When I realised he knew about what had developed between Bill and myself and was extremely jealous, I felt Bill should not be subjected to this. I wrote to him explaining the situation and for a while we did not meet. But it was not long before I sensed that the need to remain in touch with him went deeper – and so we made contact again.

For the next seven or eight years, we met in secret either at Bill's flat near Clapham Junction or at a prearranged rendezvous: and this entailed constant subterfuge and stealthy planning. But with Bill, I was increasingly able to discuss all aspects of my life – creative and professional, personal and social. He was a good source of technical information on musical matters, and when I took over direction of the Bath Festival, I often consulted him over the phone or by letter regarding the repertoire for particular programmes and up-and-coming artists.

[Letters to Meirion Bowen]
[7 October 1965]

Thurs.

I put a first draft libretto down of all 3 Acts [of *The Knot Garden*]; but am unsure whether Act 3 hasn't gone round a wrong corner, so am waiting on outside comments & advice, & Karl hasn't had time yet to deliver me clean typed copies, as he teaches the first half of the week. So I'm held up; & occupy the time proof-reading ([*Vision of*] *St Augustine*, min. score; *Child of our Time*, ditto; Pf. Concerto ditto.) & considering what kind of orchestra for the new opera. Hence the enquiry as to that tough effect Boulez (?) got with electric guitars. It seemed to me potentially excellent for certain music out of a theatre well. But I can't remember how he did it? Just a single line? And is that the normal use of it with beat groups? . . .

[23 May 1966]
Corsham, Mon.

Dear Bill,
Thanks for the letter & the singers' names etc. But I'm always a bit scared at a letter from you, because K. is in fact my secretary. I mostly see letters first, even when the typing etc. is being done at weekends & so forth. But not always. The thing to do please if you can is to avoid anything that pre-supposes a previous & continuing communication. And better maybe just to let me ring you every so often & see you when possible. I hate involving you in deception, but I practise it myself after due consideration because my partner is still suffering from deep-seated insecurity – wh is only now beginning to pass. I'll talk it out with you when I see you. I'll ring you some time this week . . .

[2 February 1966]
Corsham, Wed.

Dear Bill,
Sorry I seemed cagey last night on the phone. I was in fact (unknowing) alone in the house. I'll ring you when it's easy & mutually possible.

I'm still extremely exhausted. Partly the weather I suppose. But the chief trouble was the huge endeavour with the Leic[ester Schools] Orchestra in Belgium followed immediately by 'Augustine'. I had a nervous 'bad turn' the day I flew to Brussels, as a warning of how much it was all going to take. So I am v. slowly unwinding. I have started the music of the opera, but it's at present exceedingly slow. However – good news. Solti rang

me last week to say '*M[idsummer] M[arriage]*' is to return to Cov.
Gdn, season 67–68 (*Priam* is 66–67). And Webster confirmed
(Colin Davis). So that was a wonderful outcome of all the press
notices from 'Augustine', wh. is already what set Solti off.

I thought I was due to go to London this last Tues, but got a
week out! So I'm up next Tues. Might try to see you somehow.
I'll try & ring you anyhow. I cld fetch you from Egdon House
[BBC, where Bill was now working as a producer] the moment
you come free. My last train is really 7.45. Keep the time free just
in case it works, if it's alright for you.

Will ring.

Luv.

M.

In June 1966 I took part in a BBC radio *Any Questions* programme; a
dreadful affair, with an obviously reactionary audience and fellow
panel members. I was already feeling quite ill beforehand, unable,
specifically, to urinate: I don't know how I survived the programme.
In retrospect, I was amazed that Isobel Barnett, who was on the panel
and a doctor by training, didn't guess what was wrong. Immediately
afterwards I was rushed to hospital for a prostate operation.

[3 August 1966]

Dear Bill,

I rang last week out of impatience – not because I was alone in the
house – I wasn't. But recovery seemed so long delayed. One day
off, one day on – & the off days I felt deeply depressed. In fact
only Karl's endless kindness & gentleness really kept me on an
even keel. It's what happens sometimes after big ops. But now I
have turned the corner & am nearly myself again. And the scar
isn't so sensitive etc. etc. So I'll phone you again sometime soon.
In any case keep Thurs. evening 18th free – looking ahead. But if
gone already don't phone or write – I'll phone soon.

Fidelio Q[uartet] recorded No. 1 v. well finally. And they go on
to 3. Issue in November. Otherwise nothing to report beyond that
I'm back at work on the opera. All the more detailed news when we
meet.

Love,

M.

[22 September 1966]
Thurs.

Dear Bill,
I'd meant to ask you on the phone to write out for me a possible
12-bar blues bass sequence for L.H. (piano) using a boogie-
woogie formula. I think I cld do it myself, but wld v. much
welcome it from an 'expert'! I can get it from you next week. I
shan't be in fact putting it to final use till the New Year . . .

[This Bill supplied and I was able to adapt it for use in the final blues
ensemble of Act 1 of *The Knot Garden*.]

[from The Lorne Hotel, Glasgow: 8 November 1966]
Mon.

Dear Bill,
You're certainly more patient than I am, I think – luckily. I fancy
you said things can't settle down till I myself get settled down.
This Scotland jaunt is the last long 'away' assignment. We got
back Sun. Then there's the Palace in London on Tuesday [to
receive a knighthood from the Queen] & after that months of
jog-trot hard work at home – right thro indeed till next May.
Wonderful for me – boring for my partner, who is driven to
London every so often, if not every week. So I want to phone
you on the spur of the moment as I become alone on the chance,
or rather certainty that sooner or later it will coincide with your
being free to [meet]. This wld seem to be fool-proof. Tuesday
week, 15th, isn't quite that (my impatience again!) – because tho
it's planned that I come home by train on my own, it might not
operate – so forgive my sticking once more to an old method that
seems too fraught for comfort.
    I expect to finish the British Council thing in New Oxford St
about 4.30 or so & will come then to get you & we'll catch the
Pullman 5.45 (if I'm not with you by 5 then something has
intervened.)
    I would like maybe too sometime to fetch you for lunch in
London & then a leisurely afternoon – but that's more difficult.
It's always supposed to be known where I am in town.
    The on the sudden call to you from Corsham when I'm really
alone (there & then) is the best & then there is a time for a proper

236

evening together & night. I'll tell you how all this up here has gone when I see you at last at home.

Luv,
M.

[8 April, 1967]
Sat

Dear Bill,
Work seems to have gone so hard & so well this week that by last night I was exhausted – & doubt if I can do anything this morning. My head is too far gone – & is what it feels like. However, am virtually all set to start the blues, the final ensemble of the act. I desperately want to get finished before we go away for the 10 days break.

Go later today to drive to London to pick up K. & to drive to Essex so as to bring my ma here tomorrow, Sunday – for 3 weeks.

It was a nice stolen meeting in the sunny town [Bath] – we shall manage others as the luck comes & goes.

I'm writing in case I get 'cut off'. Tho usually K doesn't like being here much when my ma is staying.

The Fidelio Qtet in the Purcell Room (No. 3) were not v. good, so he said. Rough & out of tune. I guess they can only really make it under recording conditions. They can then make enough takes to get things right. But I'm sure the disc will help towards the proper players for no. 3 – wh haven't appeared yet.

I shall have to come to London to talk 'Midsummer Marriage' over with Colin Davis & Ande Anderson sometime after April 18. But it may not work to be of use to you & me. I'll let you know tho if it does. Otherwise May 2 isn't v. far away.

Luv,
M.

[16 April, 1967]
Thurs.

Dear Bill,
I've got the *two* 80 yr-old grandmas [ie Karl's mother and mine]

in bed & under the doctor now. So for the moment I'm fully engaged!

Meanwhile, I've talked to [the composer] Alan Ridout. He's v. sympathetic to you & me, & I'm hoping he can provide a simple alibi to help me on May 2. But I haven't told him in any detail, of course, what we are to each other, just that we like meeting. Tho if he guesses, or knows, or you even tell him I shan't mind. But Karl always flies to him when I get 'found out', & so he already knows we (you & I) see each other. But my general inclination is to keep mum & with Ingpen & Williams I gave the idea that I never see you off my own bat. The fewer that are in the secret (on my side) the better. And in any case it's so absolutely a personal matter to us both, a curious lucky dip, that has its own quality even from its secrecy. It always does me good to know that you're there when the chances conspire. I'll ring you, with luck, next week, if I'm on my own (barring the mamas!) wh is v. likely.

Luv,
M.

[8 August 1967]
Tues

The restlessness [Karl's] is v. evident, much as I expected, tho still don't know how far afield it will go. I think the London flat becomes free again next week & that's the week most likely, as I see it.

I shall send you a clean copy soon of the libretto [of *The Knot Garden*] to date (tho no hurry) as I've done the words for Dov's (Dov is to replace Piers: he's the musician; & Dov is David, who played the harp & loved Jonathan) 'ballad'. Then I can talk to you abt it some time.
Luv,
M.

[9 April, 1968]
Tues.

Dear Bill,
I think Bath Festival might v. much like the Renaissance carnival

idea – i.e. an outdoor 'do' wh wld be both musical & fringe, in the sense of games & fun etc. Then an indoor 'concert' of some sort. Can you get David (?) Munrow (?) (sorry I always forget names!) to write as soon as poss. to Jack Phipps c/o Bath Festival, Linley House, Pierrepoint Place, Bath, saying he had heard of our (Bath) interest & wld like to meet to discuss – or some such – & most important, the date & place of your own day's 'do' [a Renaissance masque performance at Kingston Polytechnic] – because I think someone will come to see how it goes. I'll try to phone you myself when I can (at the moment I'm alone but you're out) to get this date & place into my own head so that I can try to arrange here & now a visitation when everyone is around at this year's Festival of a local & a professional [sort] possible. (Tell him [Munrow] to keep yr name right out.) . . .

April 25, 1968
Thurs.
Dear Bill,
Got back from the States on Tuesday & went straight to film with the Leics. Schools lot in Chippenham! It's all been pretty mad – & v. exhausting. But also exhilarating. The St Louis concerts were a great success. One of the best performances of [Elgar's] Enigma [Variations] in the USA ever, I shld guess. The orchestra played with love & fire – & they were good as such. Concerto for Orchestra a trifle under-rehearsed, esp. the long cello line in slow movt, but good too. Marvellous clarinet, trumpet (a red Indian boy!), xylophone, tuba. A brash & brilliant perf. of Holst's *Perfect Fool* – & weird slow do of [Ives's] 'Unanswered Question'. I met my agent [Herbert Barrett] who came from N[ew] Y[ork] & is v. nice man indeed, & explained the strict limits of my availability. Because it was all in all a success, I shan't go back (for the English American programmes) till the fall of next year, when the opera is completed.

I'll ring you tomorrow morning to see how you are & hear yr news. K has just gone up to London for 'M[idsummer] M[arriage]' tonight, & I shall follow on Sat. That seems to have gone well. Schotts had to reprint librettos overnight. I'm still a bit overwhelmed by it all.

When we shall see each other next, I don't see. I am here all next week but probably not alone. Then the week following I have to be mostly in Bournemouth to rehearse, & on May 10 go for a 10 days holiday away, ending with 3 days (official) at the Bergen Festival. Get back May 24 & have to film with Leics Schools again on Sat May 25. After that life becomes normal!

I want to make some Monday dates in London to see Sir D[avid] W[ebster] & metronome new Act 2 at Cov. Gdn. I'd hope to dash Clapham way if you were there. It isn't really so long in fact since we were in Bath together – but it seems ages to me because of America in between. I worry for you abt the kind of loneliness you were describing on the train. I know it v. well. Not that *I* cld solve it for you even if I were 'single'. I had tho so many years of it earlier that I can only promise you it's never final.

Will ring first thing tomorrow

Luv,
M.

[22 May 1968]
Mon

Dear Bill,
Alone this aft. I've tried to phone but you were out I guess. So a letter just to say am back & will phone you when possible & that June 10 (afternoon with you) still stands – but in Cov Gdn area to give time together.

Israel was fascinating – & will tell you abt it when we meet. Norway was boring, in that I had to attend 4 official 'banquets' with the King on end – 2 lunches, 2 dinners (same salmon menu at each)! But 'Child' was as usual a moving opening concert for such a Festival (Bergen).

Now am back & have got thro a mountain of correspondence & hope to begin Act 3 again tomorrow.

If I get to a phone one way or another I'll hear your news – it seems ages since I went away, but it isn't long really – so not much will have happened.

Missed you at times *v*. much.

Luv,
M.

[November 1967]
Wed.

Dear Bill,
Monday was fine. Have been singing away since. Also yr
remarks abt Beethoven 3, 5 & Pastoral stimulated me a *great* deal
& by some means helped further classify the shapes of the new
Symphony [no.3] that I'll start in 2½ years or so. That is, things
you said, tho I didn't really get all the gist of yr own trains of
thought, set me considering & reconsidering, as tho there were
something significant buried away & about to be brought out to
view by an effort. And a tremendous sense that the constant
preoccupation with the immediate journalistic stylistic matters
of today wasn't finally my line – so that yr remarks worked as a
fresh release into my own proper more time-extended world.
    That all sounds a bit pretentious, but it's roughly how it was &
is . . .

Luv,
M.

[8 May 1969]
Thurs.

Dear Bill,
Was nice talking to you both before & after [Boulez's] 'Pli selon
Pli'. And it will be nicer still to see you in person. On the 21st, all
being well, I go early to London to see John Hopkins, the ABC
[Australia] man at 11 & some TV boys for working lunch – & so
to Charing X abt 2.30 or so. I have to get the 4.45 back as I have a
TV do that evening in Bristol!
    What a jamboree of music London is now & even elsewhere
around the country. Composition, in such a whirl of a world, gets
harder & harder. But of course the v. word 'composition' begs the
question. And to explain what I mean wld take pages & not be v.
interesting at the end. Suffice to say I long to be settled down, come
the autumn, at the new Symphony [No.3] which has been so long
in the cogitative process & is mighty ripe for making.
    See you,
Luv,
M.

For accountancy reasons, Karl was employed as my secretary and driver. He did what suited him. The longer he stayed, the deeper his identity crisis became. Most of the time we were two entirely separate individuals living in the same house. We never ate together. I would remain in my ground floor studio in the evenings and read or listen to the radio; Karl would watch television. He continued to go out at night, driving constantly through the tunnel of car lights into the dark – searching, I suppose, for his identity. While he was out, I was free to telephone without being overheard. Fewer friends came to stay than in the past. By the early 1970s my existence had become quite bleak. Those who stood by me through it all were the Ayersts, Ian Kemp, Eric Walter White [the Arts Council's Literature Director] and his wife, and especially, my housekeeper, Lily Speirs. I also had intimations of what a new life with younger people could be like through Michael Vyner (when he was at Schott and subsequently at the London Sinfonietta) and Paul Crossley: when I went on holiday with them to France, I sensed that they understood my predicament. I simply did not have the toughness to shake Karl out of his situation or (at that stage) to tell him he would have to leave. I certainly felt I could not live out my old age with such a figure around. Bitterly, I wrote to Bill:

11.10.71

Dear Bill,
There have been moments, during this 'bad' time, when I have wished K. totally not there. Not as surprising, I dare say, as my seemingly unshakeable loyalty. But what is to be done after 15 years of being together? Or even not together! For I keep hearing the inarticulate cry for help.
. . . being with you, on the other hand – that needs no expression beyond itself.

Love
M.
I'll phone when I can.

A few years later, one of Karl's sons-in-law, John (a qualified doctor), helped me make the break. Walking with me down the drive from the house one day, he said that in a real marriage, what was going on wouldn't be tolerated. He told me that if I didn't change my life, I would lose my self-respect. Up at the Edinburgh Festival, I put it to Katherine Wilkinson (public relations lady at Philips Records) that Karl might have difficulty surviving apart from me. She told me this was presumptuous: I was not his master, and of course he could manage to survive. As so often before, such advice, instead of being a negative matter for me, cleared the way for a positive aim: I wanted a new life.

Wondering in the end whether Karl had any sort of rights, I discussed the matter with various friends, including Peter Makings, the then Managing Director of Schott. I then made a quite generous financial settlement and that was that. A few times thereafter, Karl tried to suggest that he should return to live with me, but there was no going back. Now that Bill was openly part of my life, numerous changes were under way. Above all, as Lily Speirs observed, laughter returned to Nocketts.

Karl went to London and back to teaching for a while: Michael Vyner often saw him and helped him adjust to his new life. But he never really settled for long – he tried living in Cyprus and elsewhere. It was no good. In June 1984, he took his own life.

For some years I had suffered from indifferent eyesight and in 1970 macular dystrophy was diagnosed – an hereditary disease which comes from the mother's side of the family and which entails a degeneration of the retina. I lost my central vision: nothing could be done about it and I had to acclimatise myself to reading with large magnifying glasses. The children from the Leicestershire Schools Orchestra made me a special (and invaluable) desk that would fit on the front of the piano, so that when composing I could peer very closely at the manuscript. Naturally, my partial sight affected my driving, with obvious consequences. Once, returning alone from an evening television session in Exmouth, I had an accident in which the driver of the car was badly injured; I gave up driving from then on. On another occasion, returning late at night from an engagement in London, with Karl driving, we had another accident. This was due simply to fatigue, and I decided that from then on we would not take any more such risks. I (or we) would either have to be independently chauffeured, or stay in London. The whole matter of organising my life, my professional schedules etc. indeed became quite complex in the 1970s, such were the demands that were being made upon me. When Bill officially came into the foreground of my existence, from

1974 onwards, I relied on him increasingly to sort out all kinds of matters which otherwise would have distracted me from my music.

Bill also began to accompany me on professional tours, as my eyesight made it difficult for me to read signs in airports etc. and also he could 'protect' me from overbearing hosts or journalists. The first such trip was an expedition to Zambia in 1975 to hear a performance of *A Child of Our Time*, given by a mixture of expatriate British singers and combined Zambian choirs, under the direction of an ex-Guildhall School of Music student, John Cockin. The performance was moving, if in some respects bizarre, especially as regards the orchestra. A fine brass section was supplied by the Zambian Police Band, and the Government gave them special new white shirts for the occasion! As there were no viola-players, two clarinettists had to be allotted to the viola lines; the bass recitatives were accompanied by a tuba (instead of cellos). The singing, especially of the spirituals, was at times impressive. Regarding one particular error, however I sent a card to Colin Davis on my return:

Tues.
I've been meaning to tell you that, in Zambia, the alto solo at a rehearsal confused her consonants & sang: 'But the soul, watching the chaotic mirror knows that the *sods* return'. A marvellous emendation!

M.

Locally, the event aroused a lot of interest, and President Kenneth Kaunda attended one of the two performances. We had lunch with him at his state residence with the Education Minister amongst the guests. I asked Kaunda if he would allow a specially gifted young Zambian go to study abroad and he would not answer. The Education Minister answered for him: no, they wouldn't, as they doubted such a student would return. Also present was a figure prominent earlier in the Peace Pledge Union, John Papworth: he had known Kaunda in London at the time when he was in trouble with the colonial authorities and had subsequently persuaded him that he knew the way to deal with the regeneration of tribal village life – hence his position in the Zambian Government. It was Papworth who had secured our invitation to lunch with Kaunda, a rare honour for white visitors.

At a British Embassy dinner I was treated with a reverence that was

244

perhaps more than my due. Not long before, Sir Arthur Bliss had died and there had been press speculation about who should succeed him as Master of the Queen's Musick, which included a reference to myself as being willing to accept the role, 'in an impish mood'; all this reached the Embassy, so they were on their best behaviour! Afterwards Bill laughed immoderately about all the official etiquette at dinner.

Our itinerary included visits to schools in the bush; to a snake pit, where an enormous boa constrictor, brought out of its cage to be shown to us, got angry and bit one of the two young people accompanying us (not a serious bite, luckily); we went to watch a village drum-maker at work; and drove down to Lake Victoria, where we stayed the night. At a training college some distance from Lusaka, we sat late into the night talking to two Irish Jesuit fathers. I was at the earliest stage of turning over ideas for *The Mask of Time* and I embroiled the Jesuits in an argument over the origins of the Zodiac. The following morning I teased them that, from what they had heard from me, I was unlikely to go to Heaven. 'Ah, Sir Michael,' said one of them in his wonderful Irish accent, 'we'll be getting a crick in the neck looking up at you!'

Most romantic was being taken out after dinner one evening to a bush farm owned by a young expatriate hippie and his girlfriend. Performing before an enormous fire was a Zambian rock band, whose 'sets' were interspersed with traditional dances done by young children from a local village. None of the audience – local Zambian youths (no girls allowed out at night) – moved at first; then one began a solo dance to the group and the others soon joined in. I asked Bill what this meant: his view was that they wanted to be with others of their generation the world over. This scene, which could have been translated to a London or Los Angeles discotheque, showed rock music breaking through the frontiers.

By the late 1970s it was clear to Bill that far too many people were involved in sorting out my affairs, and he persuaded me that it would be better to centralise everything in an office of my own. I agreed to this. At that time there was some turmoil at Schott, because of the (unsuccessful) attempts by Peter Makings to separate the London branch off from Mainz. So, for the time being, office space was found near Covent Garden, and Bill 'stole' Christopher Senior from his publicity job at Welsh National Opera to undertake most of the administrative work under his direction. Chris was splendid, but after two years he defected to the newly opened Barbican Arts Centre to do the publicity and marketing there. Bill then brought in Nicholas Wright, an Egyptologist and antiquities dealer, with a keen interest in music and a shrewd business sense; Nick also has a passion for frogs (live and toy ones). He has run the Tippett Office (from Schott) ever since.

The Nocketts life-style of my later years remains focused on composition, which means isolation most of the week, apart from the mornings when two local ladies, Josey Sims and Heather Sweet, come in to do the housework. In general, the weekends are given up to visits from friends, especially younger ones, now in abundance, thanks to Bill. I have, of course, outlived a number of friends from early days. Not long after the war, Evelyn Maude's husband (who had assisted Aneurin Bevan in the creation of the National Health Service) died, and Evelyn herself eventually succumbed to memory loss. But before her death, I used to meet her, along with her daughter Stella, once a year at the Ritz Hotel in London for lunch or tea.

In the 1970s, my biographer Ian Kemp managed to track down Wilf Franks in Middlesbrough. Subsequently, in the course of a holiday with the Ayersts, I went to visit him. He and his wife, Daphne, talked mainly to David and Larema, while his daughter, who was studying a Tippett set-work for a school examination, consulted me about the piece in question. While on my way to lunch with the conductor, David Lloyd-Jones, just after the première of Opera North's production of The Midsummer Marriage in 1985, I visited them again with Bill. It was a fine Sunday morning and Wilf took me for a stroll in the park. We were late back, for we became deeply embroiled in political argument: Marxism had remained for Wilf a vivid reality. Seeing him again after forty years or so, I went emotionally into a flat spin, but Bill helped me out of it. When Wilf visited me at Nocketts in 1988, I was apprehensive, but as things turned out, it was sheer delight. Politics and personal relations never entered into our conversation: instead, I listened avidly to Wilf's stories of his past in Germany and elsewhere.

I have rarely wanted a 'local' social life, relying instead, when I am alone, on the telephone: though that can sometimes go wrong.

[To Bill Bowen, 8 June 1976]
Tuesday
The phones saga is splendid but annoying. A drunken tractor

driver first sprayed the lower field with something that killed all the grass – then demolished the 3 telephone poles – then took a gate off its hinges & let the cattle into the green corn! Then he got dismissed . . .

But no-one has come from the P.O. yet – & I doubt we get the phones back within the week. I'll phone you as soon as – if yes – go finally to a call box – if no. . . .

M.

Occasionally I go to London, where Bill can accompany me to the theatre (rather than concerts).

[22 October 1976]
Fri.

Dear Bill,
Tho I was tired suddenly at the interval, I wldn't have missed [Tom Stoppard's] 'Jumpers'. This really *is* our present world – but in the Yeats sense of 'grim & gay'. No tears of self-pity. So I'm mighty glad we went . . .

But increasingly I have relied on television, both for the serious programmes (which have included Jacob Bronowski's memorable *The Ascent of Man* and David Attenborough's many nature programmes) and for light entertainment – from soap operas like *Dallas, Dynasty* and *Fame* through to *Miss Marple, Bergerac* and *Some Mothers do 'Ave 'Em.*

The biggest invasion of my Nocketts sanctuary occurred in the summer of 1984, when Opera Factory and London Sinfonietta brought their production of *The Knot Garden* to the Bath Festival. Bill organised a buffet lunch for the entire cast, orchestra, staff and administration – about fifty in all. Overnight there had been heavy storms, but by the time everyone arrived, the sun was shining and they were able to eat and drink *al fresco*, swim in the pool, sunbathe and relax and take long walks in the fields. One of the Sinfonietta players was overheard to comment, as he surveyed the scene, 'I used to do some composing once. I wish I'd stuck at it: all this could have been mine!'

CHAPTER TWELVE

THE WORLD: MY COUNTRY

THE NEW-FOUND LAND

America didn't exert much of an appeal upon me until my mid-sixties. But then it became my dream country. I had, it is true, long ago read Walt Whitman: my mother was a great fan of his and I followed in her footsteps. I read a biography of him in the late 1920s and I remember telling one of my composer contemporaries, Elizabeth Maconchy, about it. She was recuperating from tuberculosis and lived outside in a summer house in Kent, and I visited her there. She was deeply torn between her desire to become involved in social and political work and her great natural gifts as a composer. I tried to comfort her, telling her how Whitman, during the Civil War, would spend the day in a hospital, helping to look after wounded soldiers, some on the brink of death. As he left in the evening, one would call out to him, 'Come again, Walt.' On reaching home, tired and worn out, he would wash and then begin the task of writing. The calls of public and creative duties were, for Whitman, not incompatible. Years later, Whitman still fascinates me: and I certainly identify with his habit of carrying everywhere a trunk full of notes and jottings, which he then proceeded to fuse together to create *Leaves of Grass*. My mind is rather like Whitman's trunk.

My early reading had extended to Herman Melville, Nathaniel Hawthorne and others, and from Fresca I obtained a sense of the exhilaration of New York and noted this as something I might one day want to experience for myself. I also heard stories from Ben and Peter about their time in America. But I only began to understand something of the character of that vast continent when doing the Schoenberg programmes for BBC Radio and took in what had happened through the extensive emigration to the West Coast in the first half of this century – and the change from Viennese café life to Hollywood.

In 1949 I had seen the first production in London of Gershwin's *Porgy and Bess* and was deeply moved by it. Here was a work similar in theme to Berg's *Wozzeck* yet staking out its own territory, independent of the musical traditions of Europe. I have since come to revere Gershwin: in an age of experimentation with rhythm, percussive and fragmented musical textures, Gershwin kept song alive. I sometimes wonder now what might have happened to that irrepressible creative spirit, had he lived on through the Second World War and into Vietnam. After all, he was born only seven years before I was.

Aaron Copland, when he first visited me in the 1960s, not only sang and played his American folk-song arrangements to me, but also told me about Charles Ives. This was a revelation: I began to be aware that America had a vibrant, diverse culture of its own. This impression was reinforced when I read Wilfred Mellers's *Music in a Newfound Land* – a superb book full of insights into relationships between the music and literature of America, between its vernacular and art-musics, and recognising altogether its sheer plurality. This triggered off a lot more reading: Fitzgerald, Faulkner, James Baldwin, Charles Wright, John Updike, Gore Vidal. . . the list continues to this day.

Up to that time I never really considered going to America. Unlike Auden, Britten and others I had little chance of surviving financially if I tried to establish myself there: I was not a performer and I didn't want to take on academic responsibilities. I had indeed set my sights on a reputation within Europe. The critic Peter Heyworth had told me early on that *The Midsummer Marriage* belonged in Europe: in fact it has yet to take a hold there. No one on the continent was much attuned to what I was doing. Ken Bartlett, who undertook promotion for Schott Mainz, explained that operas had to be accepted first by the big companies in Germany, then they would be done by the smaller ones. With myself, though, it has been the smaller companies who have been the first to show any interest. I dare say Willy Strecker, had he not died, would have exerted more influence on my behalf.

When I began to meet some of the continental Intendants, their somewhat patronising attitude was off-putting: it was partly to do with money – they were wealthy, I was poor; I didn't belong in their respectable bourgeois world. The one I disliked the most was Rolf Liebermann. Additionally dubious was the continental habit of putting composers in charge of opera-houses, radio music stations and other major institutions. It is one of the factors which has militated against the dissemination of British music generally in Europe. Another aspect of the problem is that I didn't belong to the serial school and had not considered the post-war Darmstadt courses – which brought Boulez, Stockhausen and others to prominence – as the Mecca of the avant-garde. Much of the time my music has come up against an implacable serialist dogma, resistant to alternative compositional approaches. The signs of change have come only lately, through the efforts of highly idiosyncratic figures like Harry Halbreich and Patrick Szernovicz, and through a few major successes like the 1988 production of *King Priam* at Nancy.

In this earlier context, I was ready, by the mid-1960s, to discover a new and sympathetic audience elsewhere. It came first through the recordings of my music, sponsored by the British Council and Vaughan Williams Trust: these found their way to U.S. campus radio stations, where they were played for free. Quite quickly, in the course of visiting the USA, I found that a lot of young people were already familiar not only with my music, but through discs and radio had an incredible knowledge of British contemporary music in general.

As luck would have it, the countertenor Alfred Deller had recently been touring the States: it was a country he disliked, and he made pejorative remarks about the food, the hotels etc. But it was he who persuaded Jim Cain, manager of the Aspen Summer School and Festival in Colorado, that he should present *A Child of Our Time* there and invite me out. Cain issued an invitation against the wishes of Aspen's composer-in-residence, Darius Milhaud, who appeared to regard me as a rival!

Thus in the summer of 1965, I set off on my own, flying to New York and (unaware of the huge distances involved) straight on to Denver. On arrival I went straight to a rehearsal of the Denver Chorale and then collapsed exhausted at the Brown Palace Hotel – a splendid architectural period piece built in the 1890s. On Jim's advice, I left the following day for Aspen, not by air, but in the huge transcontinental train that climbed up over the Rockies – a first spectacular journey. Although it was not New England, I felt I had arrived in my own private *Mayflower.*

To my delight, the Amadeus Quartet were in residence at the festival. At one of the sponsor's parties, we sat talking and joking together on a sofa, but were interrupted by our hostess, who remarked, 'Is this a Quaker meeting?' Concerts in Aspen are held in a large tent, with excellent acoustics. The only problem is the occasional thunderstorm. In the first half of a concert featuring some of my music, Milhaud himself conducted some of his music from a wheelchair. To my malicious delight, when a thunderstorm came and made a tremendous noise on the roof of the tent, it did so during the Milhaud, but not the Tippett.

When Karl joined me later (having been delayed by teaching commitments) there were inevitable difficulties. He felt left out when I conversed in French (which Karl didn't know) with the Milhauds: and he had to find ways to amuse himself while I was at rehearsals. Sensibly, however, we had planned to have a holiday after the festival and I wanted especially to visit the Indian reservations. One of the hostesses who supported the festival had an expert knowledge of Indian culture and worked out an itinerary for us according to the time we had available.

We hired a car and drove to all those places that have haunted me ever since, and which I have revisited several times: Mesa Verde, Monument Valley and the canyons – Grand Canyon, Bryce Canyon, Canyon de Chelly etc. Here was geographical terrain of a kind I could never have encountered in Europe: red rocks eroded over millions of years into natural cities; great cleavages in the land, with the climate of Canada at the top and the tropics below; vast expanses of desert. At the very least, it gave me living evidence of those new dimensions of space and time that have drastically altered our understanding of the cosmos in this century.

On the way down into Canyon de Chelly we encountered a man and a wife, with a child on her shoulder, who told us that the following day, if we came further westwards, we would see Indian dancing at First Mesa. We all went, staying the night in a railway wagon that had been converted into a motel. The next day we watched the dancing. It was terribly hot and after an hour of these stylised routines, we left. In any case, it wasn't all a romantic experience. The Indians in the three mesas (of which only the first was officially open to the public; thereafter no cars, no cameras) threw their detritus over the escarpment, so that the place was as filthy as a poor Southern Italian town.

Later on, we came to the assistance of this couple when the fan belt of their car broke. In incredible heat, we went to the nearest place to find someone who could rescue them – Tuba City! We took them to Grand Canyon: it was high season, everywhere was booked up and we had to stay à quatre in a primitive, cheap wooden chalet. The

251

following day we all walked two-thirds of the way down to the bottom of Grand Canyon, and had to struggle to get back in the heat. But the whole affair was visually spectacular and I was hooked. The trip continued with a long drive across the southern desert to Los Angeles, then up the coast to San Fransico (disappointingly under mist), before flying to New York for the last few days.

In New York, we were looked after by the Dallas music critic John Ardoin, who was then acting as a correspondent in America for *The Times*. He and the pianist, Ivan Davies, took us on the Circle Line riverboat tour and to other tourist attractions. Late one night we went up through the back door of a skyscraper, when no one was around. As I looked over the balcony at the top, I felt myself being hoisted up and heard one of them say, 'We've been asked to do this by Benjamin Britten!' John also took us to meet Samuel Barber, who was then relishing the prospect of writing *Antony and Cleopatra*, for the opening of the new Metropolitan Opera.

My appetite for exploring all of America now became insatiable. I was invited to Goucher College for Girls in Baltimore to conduct *A Child of Our Time*: the male singers were black Catholic ordinands from a local theological college – a very odd affair, aimed partly at supporting the unification of black and white communities. Since, this time, I was earning some money from the trip, I took along Karl and his daughters and we flew down to New Orleans, spent two or three days there seeing the river, and four or five more driving up along the ridge of the hills into Virginia. Visiting the tourist city of Williamsburg, we stood in line for a table in a coffee-house, where the servers were in eighteenth-century costume. The hostess knew from our voices we were English. She came over and said, 'Do you know that, by permission of the Queen, the Union Jack flies over Williamsburg? Welcome home, brother!' I realised parts of America could be more British than Britain: and there are indeed more English there than in England. Having seen something of Indian, Spanish and English America, and encountered the mixtures of races in the cities on the East and West Coast, I was now impelled to steep myself in American history.

Through Copland, I was introduced to a New York agent – Herbert Barrett – and quickly became close personal friends with him and his sculptress-wife, Betty. One evening at Parkside, in 1968, I received a call from Herbert: I told him I would call him back, as I was watching a Bette Davis movie on television. It appeared that Stravinsky was ill and had cancelled a conducting engagement with the St Louis Symphony. The orchestra did not want Stravinsky's assistant, Robert Craft, but another composer-conductor: here was my chance. I went and did an all-English programme: Elgar's *Enigma Variations*, Delius's *Brigg Fair* and my own Concerto for Orchestra. It was intriguing, partly because only one member of the orchestra had played any Elgar before – he had performed *Enigma* in Houston under Barbirolli – otherwise it was all new to them. For both this and the Delius, I obtained clean scores from the publishers and tried to intepret them afresh, without the accretions of past conductors; a revelation, for everyone, I think.

From that point onwards, the invitations blossomed. Karl didn't want to travel with me constantly, so I obtained a welcome relief from the bleak existence at Nocketts by conducting and appearing at perform-ances in many US cities. One of the more peculiar visits was to a festival at a university outside Philadelphia, which was also a kind of summer music school. They had invited Copland and myself but, as they had little money, they hired the cheapest orchestra available – the Zagreb Philharmonic Orchestra – and in advance I had to go to Zagreb to rehearse them. As I wanted to feature some American music, I included Charles Ives's *Three Places in New England* (a work I adore). But they found this, and my Concerto for Double String Orchestra, outside their musical experience and had a struggle learning them.

Jeff Anderson, a CBC producer I had met when he was working in London, invited me to Toronto and I was filmed conducting an English programme for television. Since the studio was too small for the orchestra required for Delius's *Brigg Fair*, the music and my conducting had to be filmed separately. When the players were sent away after the recording, I was filmed standing alone in my tails: I introduced the works to the (unseen) audience, and mimed my conducting to the recording played back in the studio. The TV people sat in the orchestra seats, convulsed with laughter: I did my best to ignore them! I have returned to Canada quite a few times since, most recently for a performance of *The Mask of Time*, in 1986, conducted by Andrew Davis, with the top-notch Toronto Mendelssohn Choir. Not long before this, Bill had given me some books by the Canadian writer, Timothy Findley, and I had greatly enjoyed them, especially *Not Wanted on the Voyage*. I was keen to meet him. It turned out he was a fan of my music: he attended the first performance of *The Mask of Time* and came to meet me for lunch the following day, while Bill was lecturing to the orchestra's Women's Committee.

In 1974, so many major performances suddenly came together – the US première of *The Knot Garden* at Evanston University, Illinois, the Third Symphony conducted by Colin Davis in Boston, and myself conducting the same work in Chicago – that Philips decided to take advantage of it all for media promotion. I was thus besieged by journalists and reporters most of the time. The whole enterprise stimulated interest in other American capitals: and in the next six years or so, I participated in Tippett festivals in Cleveland, Los Angeles, San Francisco and Washington, and Sarah Caldwell gave the US première of *The Ice Break* in Boston.

My travels to the USA took on a new dimension when Bill came to the States for the first time in 1977 (I was there at the outset to give the Doty Lectures at the University of Texas at Austin and later conducted a concert with the Los Angeles Chamber Orchestra). Bill already knew contemporary American music pretty well and his great ambition was to go and find the Harry Partch instruments down in San Diego. So after a holiday in the canyon and mesa country, and the concert in Los Angeles, we set off for La Jolla. We met up there with another of Bill's friends, the great exponent of the contemporary contrabass, Bertram Turetzky, who has a duo-partnership with his flautist wife, Nancy. Through Bert, we were able to meet Danlee Mitchell, who inherited Partch's 43-tone instruments and scores after he died, and he treated us to a studio demonstration, also showing us some films of the Partch dance-dramas. I had reservations about these microtonal plectra and percussion instruments, but found the films intriguing. Sadly, Danlee was doing little to promote further performances. When we took him for lunch, he produced from his pocket a letter written the previous year from the Berlin festival, offering a huge sum of money for fees and transportation costs for him to bring the Partch ensemble on tour. He hadn't even answered it.

After I had conducted the second (afternoon) performance of my Symphony No.3 in Chicago, four students came backstage – two young men and their girlfriends – and said, 'We have saved up to come from Dallas, Texas, to hear you conduct. It would be an honour if you would join us for a meal somewhere.' I was quite taken aback: for I found that they knew not only my music backwards, but all sorts of other music – all through records and radio broadcasts. They later appeared at a performance of *A Child of Our Time* in Houston wearing 'Turn on to Tippett' T-shirts, and brought one specially for the guest conductor, Sir Charles Groves! Steve Aechternacht and Victor

Marshall soon became great friends of mine. They were not trained musicians, just *aficionados*. Steve lived next door to the critic, John Ardoin, and had the most enormous record collection imaginable. He and Victor, after leaving university, took over a disused store in Dallas and turned it into a highly successful record supermarket. Steve went on to work for Phonogram and the Houston Symphony; before he joined the Dallas Symphony as artistic administator, Victor was for several years a classical disc jockey and helped manipulate opinion in favour of a Tippett celebration in Dallas. He wrote to Schott:

May 4, 1977 Wed.

Good news. The Dallas Symphony Orchestra has agreed to perform some music by Michael during the 77–78 season. This came about this past weekend when we broadcast a 56-hour marathon program to raise money for the symphony. One of the incentives given to donors to the Dallas Symphony Orch. was that whoever won the popularity contest among composers – the DSO would perform one of their works during the upcoming season. Mahler got off to an early lead followed by Beethoven, but it wasn't long until the active support given over the air by Stephen and myself brought Tippett into the lead to stay despite several close calls. You see if someone gave $35 to the DSO they could have 35 votes for their favourite composer. In the end Michael came out ahead, so now the DSO management has agreed to program some of his music.

I'll keep you informed on any further decisions concerning the playing of Michael's music by the DSO. It's very exciting for us here – at least for the Dallas Chapter of the Tippett Fan Club which has been growing for the past several years.

The plan as it turned out, was that I would conduct a concert that included Menuhin in the Elgar Violin Concerto and my own Second Symphony: a big task. On my way there, I stopped off in Boston to hear Colin Davis conduct *A Child of Our Time* (to great acclaim). But the intensity of interviews and public appearances, and other contingent factors (Boston was under deep snow and I was unwise enough to venture out in it) meant that when I arrived in Dallas, I collapsed. It was clear that I would be unable to conduct and the orchestra sent for David Atherton instead. Meanwhile, I was taken to hospital and placed in the only bed available – in the intensive care unit. It was not that serious, in fact: only a recurrence of the heart fibrillation which had been diagnosed some years earlier and which is controlled all the time by drugs. Nevertheless, every doctor imaginable came to examine me (and sent a large bill to Herbert Barrett) and I was wired up to all sorts of electronic equipment. Steve and Victor, visiting me, quipped, 'Ah, our bionic composer!'

Rumours reached London that I had had a stroke: Bill was rung by *The Guardian* and asked to update their existing obituary (which ended in 1959!). When he made contact with me I shrieked with laughter at the idea. Proper arrangements were then made for me to return home. I flew to New York but was confined to a hotel room in Kennedy Airport for 24 hours because of a great blizzard. Finally, I left on Concorde (my first time). Bill was due to meet me at Heathrow, but went down with violent gastric flu that day and couldn't appear. Back home I immediately felt better; gleefully I rang him the following morning and asked. 'Shall I write *your* obituary?' From then onwards, I never undertook professional engagements without Bill being there to look after all the arrangements and keep me from the excessive attentions of the media, or whoever.

WORLD ADVENTURES

All my extended professional trips in the States and elsewhere have since then included holidays – some of them ridiculous adventures for a man in his seventies and eighties. I had been told about great Mexican sites by the Swiss conductor, Paul Sacher and his wife. Reading Bernal Diaz's *True History of the Conquest of Mexico*, I became drawn into his account of the rape of Indian civilisations by the Christians from Europe, something I had previously encountered also in Claudel's *Christopher Colomb*. My father, who had long ago visited Paraguay intending to look for the wealth reputedly buried on some land he had bought there, had shared my sadness, not about the gold that had been melted down, but about the savage treatment of the people. We both had this feeling that we had come to the end of a world that was God-centred.

I went on two trips to Mexico, both of them full of ridiculous escapades, in retrospect, but unforgettable for their tropical jungles and ancient sites. A typical tour was that in the autumn of 1977. It began with the world première of Symphony No.4 in Chicago, under Solti – my first American commission; then a week at the University of Columbus, Ohio; another in Cleveland, where I shared the conducting of an all-Tippett concert with Lorin Maazel (Prince Charles was on tour in the States at the time and delayed his departure from Cleveland to attend *A Child of Our Time*; as a result I was constantly approached by Americans for advice on etiquette); then ten days' holiday in Mexico; and back to the New York première of Symphony No.4.

After Cleveland, we flew to New Orleans to pick up an architecture student-friend of Bill's, Graham Modlen, who was going to drive us in Mexico: then on to Merida, which we immediately found was flooded and tricky to negotiate. Finding hotel accommodation in Mexico is one hazard: even if you can obtain an advance booking, there is no guarantee that it will be honoured. We took pot luck and survived, just. Stupidly, we had brought no proper maps and when we went off the main road for fun, found ourselves driving miles and miles along the country roads, entirely deserted except for birds, iguanas and other animals. Occasionally we would stop in a village to find out where we were. But everyone spoke Mayan dialect and they rushed to find the only person who could speak Spanish. I would ask, 'Name of this place, please?', would be told some incomprehensible name, then we drove off to great cheers.

After visiting Chichen Itza and Uxmal we drove along the Gulf coast and eventually reached Palenque, one of the greatest, most individual Mayan ruins set in a high plateau surrounded by dense, lush mountains jungles, kept fresh and moist by the greatest amount of sun and rain in all Mexico. Lunching in a nearby hotel (including my favourite cocktail, margarita, which Bill has since learnt to make superbly), we continued our journey, again taking a country road. This time, though, it led up into the mountains, and as we climbed up and up, rain began to fall. Soon the road gave way to rough tracks. Graham drove with incredible skill, once crossing a wooden bridge at high speed with the back wheels off the edge of it. Darkness fell and on we drove through unknown territory. The inevitable then happened: we got stuck in the mud.

Graham could discern some people in a field nearby and went off to ask for assistance. He was away quite a long time and, growing impatient, I got out of the car to join him, straight away standing in a puddle and splashing myself all over with red mud. Even Bill blushed at my expletives. I climbed over into the field where Graham had gone, and of course the cowherds there only laughed at our predicament. Then along came a lorry and to our relief the driver had a chain and was able to pull us out. We had not driven much further, however, when another large car full of Mexicans overtook us and stalled in the mud ahead. Everyone in it was in a state of great agitation, as grandfather was dying in a distant town. In the collective effort to push the car out, Bill this time was splashed all over in mud. Having left Palenque at about 3.30 p.m., we arrived in San Cristobal after 11 p.m.; and looking like three desperate outlaws, booked into the nearest motel we could find.

Our lowest point was undoubtedly reached at Tehuantepec, where the hotel conditions were primitive and Bill was stricken with the local bug, known as Montezuma's Revenge (he didn't recover fully until we returned to England). More enjoyable were Oxaca and Mexico City itself, despite its traffic and pollution.

Our return flight to New York was delayed. Meanwhile, the luggage we had sent on from Cleveland to our New York hotel had not been delivered, so we had to attend a formal Central Office of Information party (prior to the Fourth Symphony at Carnegie Hall) in colourful Mexican jackets and holiday gear. But it was there that I met Peter Pears, for the first time since the death, in his arms, the previous November, of his beloved Ben.

My music itself seemed now to be spreading across the world. So, in 1978, for the first time ever. I took an extended break of nearly three months from composition. Initially, I had been invited to Australia for the first performance there of *The Midsummer Marriage,* at the Adelaide Festival. But Bill persuaded me that at my age I would find the direct flight too much of a strain, so we stopped off for about ten days *en route*, in Singapore, Jogjakarta and Bali (paradise for Bill), attending numerous dance-drama performances and climbing up the huge temple at Borobodur. The pervasive sounds of gamelan orchestras on Bali were directly relevant to the Triple Concerto, then taking shape in my mind; and the serenely flowing music of a gamelan (with singer) in the hotel lobby at Jogjakarta suggested at once the kind of melodic line I wanted all three instruments to play in the slow movement. I noted its general pattern on a piece of card (supplied by Bill) which had been used to stiffen a shirt back from the laundry! In the 1930s, Aubrey Russ had lent me his copies of the Curt Sachs recorded anthology of ethnic musics, and I had been most fascinated then by the Indonesian variety. In my ignorance, I had thought it was all music played in dry savannah: reaching Bali in person, I was amazed to find such a tropical green jungle landscape.

As with America, Australia had been far from my sensibilities and ambitions. Yet here was another surprise: a country with its own unique geography; and a small population of curious, cultured people, open, friendly, hospitable. Our first stop was the Perth Festival, where the performances were not of the highest standard: when I revisited Perth in 1990, the festival – still under David Blenkinsop – had developed into one of the best in the world. The Adelaide Festival, under David Steele, was the main focus of our visit, with the opera a great success in their new auditorium, and concerts of all sizes and descriptions. The then Prime Minister of South Australia, Don Dunstan, who attended the first night of the opera in his unpompous way, invited us to lunch, where I was particularly delighted to meet Naomi Mitchison: for many years earlier I had read her book, *The Corn King and The Spring Queen*, whose climax is a public copulation to fertilise the fields, and this had had a big influence on the final Ritual Dance in *The Midsummer Marriage*.

In the middle of the festival, we took a short break in Alice Springs (where Bill bought a didgeridoo and a pair of boomerangs from an Aborigine) and Ayers Rock. The flight to and from Ayers Rock was in a tiny propeller plane, landing not in an airport but by a palm tree in the desert! After lunch in a motel, we noticed that a coach was taking a party of tourists out to see the rock and decided to join them. Unfortunately they were mainly caricature American tourists, more concerned with discussing the price of hamburgers in Memphis than with the scenery. We drove round to the other side of the rock and then stopped for photographs etc. I said to Bill, 'Let's walk back, I know the way – it's only a mile and a half.' We waved goodbye to the bus and set off in the scorching afternoon heat along the path. Hordes of flies immediately descended and we had to wave handkerchiefs frantically to keep them at bay. We reached a fork in the path where there was a signpost. In one direction it said Kalgoorlie 685 miles; so we took the other fork and reached the wrong motel, whereupon we had to be escorted back to our own. Following dinner in the motel, we retired to the bar and were there much entertained by a young dentist from San Francisco who was following around a team of kick-boxers.

After a brief stop-over in Sydney to do a forum at the Opera House and take a cruise round the harbour, we flew now to Hawaii, to take another little break on the volcanic Hawaiian island of Hilo; and from there to San Francisco, where we met up with Graham Modlen, and proceeded to Los Angeles where I was due to conduct *A Child of Our Time* with the Philharmonic. All of us became close friends with the young conductor Calvin Simmons, who was Zubin Mehta's assistant at the Philharmonic. Calvin was an incomparable talent. When he later came to stay with me at Nocketts, he sang and played the piano from morning to midnight. I recall him taking a volume of Purcell's *The Fairy Queen* from my shelves and putting it on the piano, to sing and play through it: 'This is my music,' said this black, quarter-Cherokee Indian. His death in a boating accident on Lake Placid in 1981 was a tragedy of the first order.

During the period I have been travelling to America, wine-drinking began to supplant cocktails in the bigger cities; though you have only to stay in the smaller towns and find it less of a custom. Previously, I had no idea Californian wine was so superb and was delighted to be driven into Napa Valley by Deborah Borda, during a visit to San Francisco for the US première of the Triple Concerto in 1980. Likewise, I was staggered at the quality of Australian wine on my first visit. I am not a really knowledgeable wine connoisseur: I like variety – but Californian and Australian wines now figure prominently in my wine closet.

My second world trip, in 1984, provided a remarkable chance to get to know the Far East a bit better. (I have wanted most of all to go to India but I'm uncertain whether I could manage it now.) The different styles of living, the cuisine and customs of Hong Kong, China, Japan and the Philippines were an unexpected joy. Artistically the high point of my Far Eastern visit was a performance of *A Child of Our Time* in Tokyo, with Japanese soloists, the Tokyo Symphony and a student choir who sang the work (for the second time) *in English from memory*. When the conductor, Takashi Yamaguchi, brought me on to the stage afterwards to take a bow, he was in tears. I later found out that he was born in Hiroshima: an aunt had taken him away a few days before the atomic explosion occurred, and he had thus narrowly missed being wiped out. At the end of the trip, after working in Australia and taking a week's holiday in Tahiti, we reached Boston for the world première of *The Mask of Time*, and its *Hiroshima, Mon Amour* movement took on a special significance.

It is probably every composer's dream that something he or she has written will reach an audience in the world at large. In my case, *A Child of Our Time* really does seem to have spoken its message in most parts of the globe. It was a long time before it could be performed in Israel as, for a short time, the word 'Jesus' in the text was disallowed. When it did get performed in Tel Aviv in 1962, Grynspan's father was in the audience, manifestly touched by the work his son's precipitate action twenty-four years earlier had inspired.

But the work was not about the Nazis' persecution of the Jews and, as I have found, people constantly relate it to their own concerns and difficulties. When I conducted it in Atlanta, Georgia in 1981, the predominantly black members of the choir regarded the piece as about their struggles against persecution; and the audiences (also mainly black) joined in the singing of the Negro spirituals. In Brazil in 1985, it seemed chillingly relevant to the acute situation of unwanted, abandoned children there. It has yet to be performed in South Africa and Russia.

In 1986, André Previn conducted a performance of the oratorio at the Festival Hall in London; in the audience, by chance, was a German doctor who had been attending a conference on AIDS. He wrote to me afterwards to say that he could not help but relate the piece to the plight of the many AIDS sufferers who were now victims of discrimination and ostracisation in many countries. I could only share his view. When he published a medical study of AIDS he used lines from the oratorio as his motto.

CHAPTER THIRTEEN

THOSE TWENTIETH-CENTURY
BLUES

THE SINGING WILL NEVER BE DONE

In 1984, as part of a second world tour Bill and I spent six weeks in the Far East, prior to going to Australia and the USA. For one week, we were guests at the Music Conservatory in Shanghai. It was winter and the city was under snow. Since there was a government restriction on the central heating of public buildings (with the exception of hotels) south of the Yangtse, everyone at the Conservatory wore coats, hats and scarves and shivered in front of electric fires. I had previously caught a cold in Hong Kong and this developed into severe bronchitis. Despite my condition I managed to conduct a short piece in the final concert of British music (Holst, Britten, Vaughan Williams and Tippett, with Elgar's *Pomp and Circumstance No. 1* as an encore!), played by the Shanghai Symphony Orchestra; and I particpated in one or two seminars with Chinese composers and music students.

One of the questions they asked was, 'What do you most need to be a successful composer in the present-day world?' I responded immediately, 'You need to be born in the right place at the right time. In other words, you need luck.' This was a direct reference to their 'luck' in being born in China around the time of the Cultural Revolution. Near the end of our visit, the young man in his twenties, who had been our main interpreter, said he would like to tell us a bit about his own life. His father had been in trouble during the Cultural Revolution and was now dead. His mother advised him when he was due to go to college not to choose music, as this was too dangerous: instead he should undergo some industrial training, which would be safer; he could then see how things went afterwards. While at college, he taught himself English. As he had no easy access to books in English, he had to make his own 'dictionary' from films and rare encounters with British visitors. By this means he obtained the

262

interpreter's job at the Conservatory. He expected to get married soon but saw no prospect of ever travelling. He accepted his luck without tears.

I couldn't help recalling how the Japanese conductor, Takashi Yamaguchi had recently told me of his narrow escape from the bombing of Hiroshima. Bill and I had just been there to lay a bunch of flowers on the simple memorial stone directly under where the bomb exploded. On that fateful day, Yamaguchi had had luck. Not so the woman, it is thought, who was sitting on a concrete bench at the epicentre of the explosion. She was incinerated instantly. But in that instant, her body obscured the flash of the explosion: you can see the result in the Hiroshima Memorial Museum – a human being reduced to a shadow on a stone.

What was my luck then? I had already lived in relative safety through two world wars with the freedom to create music so far as I knew how. I had not been 'a child of our time' in the terrible sense that millions of others had been. It seemed to me, as I reached old age, that the oratorio of my thirties needed to be supplemented by another, wider, richer, deeper work for voices and instruments.

At the première of *The Ice Break* at Covent Garden, a critic asked me if I intended to write a fifth opera. I said no. I meant simply that, given the age I was, and the years of intense work which a theatrical project would entail, I didn't expect (at 80) to have the physical strength, after I had completed the four works I had planned for the concert hall – a fourth symphony and string quartet, a triple concerto, and *The Mask of Time*. The last of these pieces – which had its première in Boston in March 1984, a month or so after the Tokyo *A Child of Our Time*, under Colin Davis's masterly direction – was in any case of the greatest scope: a summatory piece concerned, on the one hand, with the transcendental and on the other, with the survival of individuals.

I knew that however far away in infinite time and space the work began, through the text sung by the chorus, it had to be answered immediately by a solo voice crying out from the here and now of the concert hall, where this singer was situated. If that voice were a tenor, then towards the end, a woman's voice, a high soprano, should sing the threnody for all those who, through some throw of the divine dice, were broken by life. My original intention was to set something out of the poetry of Wilfred Owen. But Bill counselled that Owen was too much associated with the First World War and (apart from the fact

that Ben Britten had set Owen so memorably in his *War Requiem*)
something wider in scope was needed. He suggested I consider the
Russian poet, Anna Akhmatova, and lent me Amanda Haight's
excellent biography. Almost inevitably, I was drawn to Akhmatova's
Requiem and *Poem without a Hero*: they were exactly what I needed. I
named this threnody *Hiroshima, Mon Amour*, after a film script by
Marguerite Duras for the actor Alain Resnais: a heart-rending
portrayal of love across the political barriers of wartime.

In *The Mask of Time* the threnody was the gateway through which
the work had to go, to reach some epiphany of survival at the end. The
clue to this affirmation came from one of Rilke's *Sonnets to Orpheus*,
which I had planned to set within the penultimate movement of the
work:

> 'Who alone already lifted
> the lyre among the dead
> dare, diving, sound
> the infinite praise.'

Just so, an English poet, Siegfried Sassoon, lifted his lyre amongst the
dead on Flanders battlefields of the First World War:

> Everyone suddenly burst out singing;
> And I was filled with such delight
> As prisoned birds must find in freedom,
> Winging wildly across the white
> Orchards and dark-green fields; on – on –
>   and out of sight.
>
> Everyone's voice was suddenly lifted;
> And beauty came like the setting sun:
> My heart was shaken with tears; and horror
> Drifted away. . .O, but Everyone
> Was a bird; and the song was wordless; the
>   singing will never be done.

I took this ending to the poem as the title for my final movement of
The Mask of Time where the wordless voices and the 'instruments of
joy' may, for the duration of the song at least, 'sound the infinite
praise'. In that sense only, unconnected with any specific creed or
liturgy, the end can be regarded as a religious affirmation.

I have always been troubled by endings, as I dislike empty bombast
of the kind too easily relied upon by composers in the wake of Mahler
and Strauss. Willy Strecker, when he first saw *The Midsummer*

Marriage, felt that the opera should have ended with the big, orgasmic climax of the fourth Ritual Dance. But I knew that I had to bring my audience out of the theatre:

> Was it a vision?
> Was it a dream?
> . . .Here in this magic wood on midsummer day,
> 'All things fall and are built again
> And those that build them again are gay.'

So in *The Mask of Time* the final surge of affirmatory singing is suddenly cut off, like a door closing on the performance (an effect only fully experienced live in the concert hall). As Colin Davis once wrote, 'the magic lasts no longer than the length of the song . . .'; afterwards, we go out into the street.

THE UNIVERSAL DREAM

Some time in the 1920s, I saw a London production of J. M. Barrie's *Dear Brutus*. I don't remember the plot in detail, but two scenes etched themselves into the memory. First the thrilling *coup de théâtre* at the end of Act 1: the curtains had been drawn at evening, across the line of french windows occupying the whole of the back wall of the stage drawing-room – then, suddenly, they were drawn apart to disclose that the distant wood had moved over the garden right up to the house wall. Into this wood, Lob, the enigmatic, gnome-like figure, gently pushed all his guests. Curtain.

In Act 2, the wood had moved downstage, filling the entire space, where the whole act was played out. What I recall most clearly of the story here was the scene where a middle-aged man, the nice guy, sitting before an easel as the artist he had never had the courage to be, played an enchanted scene with a 'real-life' daughter he never had.

In the daylight of Act 3, next morning, back in the house, I don't think many of the characters had been much changed by their adventure in the magic wood of dream. That seldom happens in Barrie's plays. But I have remained haunted all my life by the implied questions of Lob's wood. Does the dream have power, or is it just ephemeral fantasy? If it has power, do we know how to use it to lift us up; and do we know, or do we refuse to recognise its power to put us down – to cause personal depression or communal violence?

Not long after finishing *The Mask of Time* sometime in 1983, I saw on BBC television a film called *The Flip Side of Dominick Hyde*. I was intrigued straight away by the theme music, its simplicity and directness; even more so by the accompanying lyric sung by an invisible voice:

Are there somewhere islands over the horizon
Hidden in the morning mist for ever out of reach?
Are there somewhere islands where the cocoa ripens
Wild canaries in the trees, a footprint on the beach?
Are there somewhere mountains talked about in whispers
Himalayas mountain-men have never dared to climb?
Are there somewhere mountains where the tiger dances
Hill-sides sweet with temple-bells
Half as old as time?

[Refrain]
You'd better believe it, babe,
You'd better believe it, babe,
For in this mad man's universe
At least the dreams are cheap,
You'd better believe it babe.
[Refrain repeated]

For if you don't it makes things worse –
Who wants a dreamless sleep?

In the film-story the young man, Dominick, is sent on a mission three generations back to research the transport problems of the present time. He lands his flying-saucer somewhere in the west of London and wanders, contrary to his instruction, in search of his own origins. He meets up with Jane, as young as himself, who runs a small boutique. They make love. Jane becomes pregnant: so Dominick will, in fact, have fathered his own grandfather.

The literary and operatic tradition of the dream-lover from the unknown is very old. To father your own grandfather is possibly an unusual twist, and in the context of space-time travel by, say, the Tardis, is clearly of our day. When I began the arduous struggle to hammer out a scenario for *New Year* in 1985, I invented six characters: two women and one man from Somewhere and Today, and two men and one woman from Nowhere Tomorrow. But the almost banal story of a young woman who obtains from her dream-lover the strength to go out through the self-locked door of her room into the

Terror Town, to help the deprived children there, was deepened and enriched by many layers of allusion and meaning.

In a first (and rejected) draft scenario, I wrote some propositions. For instance, the famous postcard (on which the theatre director Gunther Rennert maintained the essence of any good opera could be written) might read: What is the nature and use of dreams (awake and asleep) in our present life-style? Are they only an escape from an ever harsher reality? Must they always be projected and acted outwards, generally bringing confusion and conflict? Can they sometimes be interiorised as a source of balance and renewal? That was the intellectual or didactic route to go.

In searching for possible titles, I first thought of *The White Herons:*

> God has not died for the white herons.
> God has not appeared to the birds.

That was the poetic road. I'm sorry the white herons had to be discarded, like so much else – even, sadly, a scene involving a giant panda! As Charles Stanford used to say to his composition students: 'Now you have to murder your darlings' – i.e. abandon all those subjective, fanciful notions that can't really be justified within the presentation. Also, Bill pointed out to me that what I had drafted out was far too close, in many respects, to the *Dominick Hyde* film.

Gradually, I moved towards the central focus of the piece: the rites of passage at the winter solstice, New Year — like those at the summer solstice, Midsummer Day – which are amongst the oldest and most widespread communal celebrations of all. New Year is a time to turn our backs on the failures of the Old Year and attend to the projects and promises of the new one ahead; alas, these are seldom accomplished or fulfilled. This public celebration, it seemed to me, could provide the fast-moving theatricality that the central act of the opera would need. But when the spaceship unexpectedly arrives, bringing Nowhere to Somewhere, the collective dream, as so often, goes sour. The ordinary people aren't permitted the experience of flying in a saucer: and it departs, leaving them in furious frustration and disarray.

Balancing the collective activities of Act 2, the final act could have its private dream-time, where the lovers sing their version of the eternal love-duet –

> Moments out of time and space
> Flame and flower
> Face to face

– as a lyric without named singers, till they name themselves, beginning –

JO ANN:	I love you, Pelegrin
	I love you
PELEGRIN:	I love you, too, Jo Ann
	Within the dream
	Come the bad moments
	Hold to that
JO ANN:	Bad moments?
PELEGRIN:	Stay radiant while you may
	Now you shall dance.

As it emerged in its final form, *New Year* linked together operatically communal and personal dreams and fantasies; and as such, it took me down new avenues, quite different from those of *The Mask of Time*, with its ever-present polarities – the cosmic and eternal set against the individual, here and now. Nevertheless, quite late in its composition, I couldn't resist interpolating something representative of my own stance and commitment. One evening in 1988 I watched for some time the 70th birthday concert for Nelson Mandela, which took place at Wembley Stadium and was televised worldwide. At the end of each rock group's contribution, the lead singer or performers usually made a statement of some sort. A number were silly or just scatological. But one – Mark Knopfler of Dire Straits – declared quite simply:

> One Humanity,
> One Justice.

For me, that said everything.

Near the end of *New Year*, the cacophony of Terror Town stops momentarily, and the Presenter steps forward to sing those very words; as the surtitle in the first production rightly commented – 'My Dream'.

What then of my public dreams, and of those of my own generation – people like my cousin Phyl, Alan Bush or David Ayerst?

After a decade or more in which she had not communicated, Phyl had telephoned me from London in 1948. I think the party line from Moscow must have changed and pacifists were possibly regarded as useful in relation to the Peace Conferences the Soviets had planned for Warsaw and New York, and which were frowned upon by Western hardliners as a political ploy. My call from Phyl was followed in 1949 by an official invitation from the Russian Embassy to the conference in New York, where Shostakovich would be present. I refused, for I knew that if I had gone, I would have had to ask Shostakovich questions which showed I knew the meaning of Siberia. Many of my left-wing friends thought this strange on my part, as the period of disillusionment with communism had not yet begun. But I had long been aware that Hitler and Stalin were both monsters, even though one was the 'enemy', and the other an 'ally'. Shostakovich himself, as I guessed, would have to follow the official line. Much the same occurred in 1968 when, after the invasion of Czechoslovakia, I was rung by the Russian Embassy and invited to be guest of honour at the Moscow Congress of Soviet Composers. Once again I refused: and at the opening plenum of the Congress, Shostakovich, in the presence of Kosygin and Brezhnev, read a special resolution of thanks to the Red Army for their heroic deeds. I never met Shostakovich, but knowing what he had to endure, I always felt him to be looking over my shoulder as I composed.

Oddly, in the early 1980s the Soviet composer Alfred Schnittke visited me at Nocketts, accompanied by David Stevens from Schott (we all three spoke German). It was a beautiful, sunny Sunday in June, and David drove us out to see the prehistoric site at Avebury. Young people, families with children, were having fun all around and I couldn't help observing that Schnittke was very touched by the sight of these people enjoying a degree of freedom and well-being he had not known. After he had left, I dreamt that night that Shostakovich had come to see me. As I opened the front door to greet him, a large piece of masonry crashed down between us, then I woke up.

When I met Phyl and Aschraf, her husband, in London, I told them about my recent experiences at the Bartók festival in Budapest. Aschraf was very disturbed. Neither of them would shift from their Stalinist convictions. Eventually they both went to live and teach in India, before settling finally in East Berlin, where they taught at Humboldt University. As an expert in Slavonic languages, Phyl was able to go and lecture in Moscow. But her main enterprise was producing a book of English political literature (working-class poetry etc.) and every year in the long summer vacations, she returned to England to continue her research for this. I saw her each time and once took her to a performance of *A Child of Our Time*, but she could not relate to such a work. She became more and more denunciatory about the state of England, and after the death of her husband, she didn't come any more. I visited her in East Berlin instead. She claimed it was a marvellous society to to live in, but found it odd that when she went to a factory, she couldn't communicate with the workers themselves –they were so many blank faces. She refused to acknowledge the actualities of life in a communist bloc country. She was convinced that the news promulgated there was the truth and that all her material needs were satisfied.

In the early 1980s, near the end of her life, I visited her a couple of times – once with Ian Kemp and lastly with David. Ian (who was finishing his book on me) asked her about Fresca. Angrily, she retorted, 'That's over. She is not to be spoken about.' She told David that when she couldn't have children by me, she wasn't able to have children at all. I knew this to be nonsense, because when I stayed with her in Belgrade in the 1920s, she revealed that she had already given birth to a child 'like a peasant' – i.e. out in a field!

Gradually, she lost her will and the strength to live. I felt I could no longer pitch into her about politics, but one final remark she made seemed to me prescient: 'They can't control the disco.' To some extent now, I wish she had survived to see the Berlin Wall come down and the fortress societies of Eastern Europe opened up. For her, as for Alan Bush – who in his late years is probably unaware of what has happened – it might have been quite disconcerting. For me it is the fulfilment of a dream. In the seventies, when I wrote my fourth opera, *The Ice Break*, I had furtively suggested that the conflicts between the ideologically self-righteous, either within stereotyped groups (blacks versus whites, etc.) or individuals of different generations (Yuri versus his parents, Lev and Nadia) could be resolved. In Act 3, the young people whirling through the hospital, after the operation to remove the injured Yuri from his plaster cast has been successfully accomplished, could well be the same young people who later danced on the Berlin Wall as it was pulled down. What they sing in the opera is Shakespeare's timeless invocation of rebirth and renewal:

> 'Spring, spring,
> Spring come to you at the farthest,
> In the very end of harvest.'

My timid hopes, at that time, were not just pie-in-the-sky. Lev, finally reconciled with Yuri, recalls a nor dissimilar situation in Goethe's *Wilhelm Meister*: Wilhelm's son has been operated upon after

270

falling from his horse into a river, and his father looks at his naked, sleeping body and comments:

> 'Yet you will always be brought forth again,
> glorious image of God,
> and likewise be maimed, wounded afresh,
> from within or without.'

That was about as far as I could go in 1977. Barely weeks after the final rhetoric of *New Year* ('One humanity, one justice') had been proclaimed from the stage of Houston Grand Opera, the Wall came down and the frontiers were opened in Eastern Europe; a few months later, Nelson Mandela was released from nearly three decades of imprisonment. Not quite an example of Jungian synchronicity, but close.

The dedication of *New Year* to David and Larema Ayerst was, in this context, apt. They have always shared in my public dreams, and remain the dearest friends of my own generation: the only regular visitors of their age group to Nocketts and companions on an annual vacation for a decade or more. Over the years, the left-wing fervour of David's youth has mellowed into what I regard as a donnish liberalism, allied to a deeply personal faith in Christianity. Still, however, our arguments over politics and religion remain animated, even explosive, and Larema has to put on a Marx Brothers video to clear the air!

My own socialist convictions have never waned but, more often than not, have tended to find apolitical expression, partly because of the vagaries of official Labour Party policy. For instance, I was never so dismayed as when (of all people) Michael Foot meekly lent the support of his party to the British military action in the Falklands. While allowing my own views to colour and sometimes burst into the foreground of a composition, as they did at the end of *New Year*, I continue to feel that there are other things for an artist to do: hence compositions such as *The Vision of St Augustine* or, most recently, *Byzantium*.

ARTEFACTS

About the time I was working on the scenario for *The Midsummer Marriage*, I said to Eliot: 'I've read all your poetry and prose and know it well. Who should I read next?' He replied, 'Yeats: begin with *The Tower*.' This I did. I read everything of Yeats and eventually knew it

271

all nearly as well as I had known Eliot. I came to feel, for myself, that both of these poets had a political dream, but that when the disillusion came, they reacted differently.

Eliot's dream was that England might be redeemed by the Anglican church. After *Murder in the Cathedral* for Canterbury Cathedral, he became active in church affairs, also writing prose monographs on religious issues (e.g. *Thoughts after Lambeth* and *The Idea of a Christian Society*). It already then seemed to me that his prose was losing the sharpness and clarity of his earlier literary essays, chiefly because of the continual use of traditional Christian concepts and phraseology, understood and accepted only by those within the faith. A good majority of his compatriots were left out. Meanwhile, in the verse-plays, he turned his back on the dramatic and poetic intensity of *The Family Reunion*, publicly criticising it, for the unpoetic, almost undramatic, theatre-pieces of his final years.

I used to go for my own professional purposes nearly every year to the Edinburgh Festival and I saw these late plays as they were premièred there. When the last one, *The Elder Statesman*, was produced, I happened to be dining with Karl Hawker in the restaurant of the hotel where Eliot was staying. He had recently married Valerie, his second wife, and we saw then enter, hand in hand, as was their custom, and go to their table. I went to greet them, as I rarely saw Eliot at that time. The next night I attended *The Elder Statesman* alone, and found myself sitting right next to Eliot, who was also on his own. I gently chided him over his retreat from the tone and technique of *The Family Reunion*, which is indeed the most Greek and least Christian of his plays. I asked him if he would return, as I hoped, in that direction, eschewing the almost over-cool language of the late plays? He said he might, though not in a very convinced tone of voice; as we know, he didn't.

Yeats' dream was of a free Ireland, united by a cultural Renaissance of Gaelic mythologies mixed with more general European literary influences. He worked with Lady Gregory when she collected, translated and published the Cuchulain stories in *Gods and Fighting Men*. They founded the Abbey Theatre in Dublin together and Yeats persuaded Synge, whom he had met as a virtual vagabond in Paris, to return to Ireland and live for a while on the Arran Islands off the coast of Galway, to learn Gaelic fluently.

When the 1916 Dublin rebellion went off at half-cock, Yeats was in

London. He had no prior knowledge of it and was a bit miffed. The subsequent, systematic daily shooting of prisoners from the rebellion – all of whom became Irish patriotic martyrs – and even more the brutal regiment of Black and Tans let loose over Ireland by the British, showed him that his own dream for Ireland was shattered, and that even his own poetry might have driven the younger generation towards their revolutionary violence and bloodshed. When the Irish Free State was set up at the 1920 partition, Yeats was given a seat in the first Senate, a position he took seriously. But as he realised what the stranglehold of the Catholic church really meant – illegality of divorce and of modern methods of contraception and abortion – his disillusion deepened; and when literary censorship was imposed, it became total. Yeats made a dignified speech of resignation from the Senate, saying he had not fought all his life for an Ireland of that illiberal nature and retired to the West of Ireland to nurse his wounds.

Yeats had bought a ruined Norman tower from Lady Gregory, had recently married (at 57) a much younger woman, and had begun to restore the tower, storey by storey, till he could climb through the winding stone tower to the roof:

> I, the poet William Yeats,
> With old mill boards and sea-green slates,
> And smithy work from the Gort forge,
> Restored this tower for my wife George;
> And may these characters remain
> When all is ruin once again.

At first Yeats tried to find again the vein of lyric love-poetry of his youth. It wouldn't, of course, work. With great inner strength he renewed his creativity by a new kind of poetry, a true hybrid, a mixture of the European cultural history he was steeped in and the esoteric strains he had absorbed long ago through Madame Blavatsky and others. He wrote in a letter: 'in my late poems I have called it *Byzantium*'. And by 'it' he meant any 'example of magnificence: and style, whether in literature or life' which 'comes I think from excess, from that something over and above utility, which wrings the heart'.

While at the tower, Yeats wrote two poems, *Sailing to Byzantium* and *Byzantium*. The first has more obvious poetic metaphors, from the point of view of a composer wanting to make a musical setting; but the second has been closer to me. Southampton University once sent me an offprint of a lecture by Helen Gardner

273

about the nature and use of original manuscripts. Gardner dealt with an excerpt from Byron, from Eliot's *Four Quartets*, and Yeats' 'Byzantium'. I became more and more fascinated with this last poem and how it had been hammered into its final crystalline shape. The result is the most unpromising text for anyone to set to music – a real challenge – but that is what engaged me, creatively. The poem is what I would call an artefact. In Yeat's jargon, an artefact is a work of art that is entirely separated from its creator – where the personal emotion has disappeared into the magnificence of the craft. My setting, which extends the fairly short poem into a big song lasting about 27 minutes, had to be just such an artefact – if not with a magnificence of craft, at least a sufficiency.

I first met the notion of artefacts in Eliot's essays (especially 'Tradition and the Individual Talent'), and I thus saw early on that I had ultimately to divorce myself as a person from what had been created. Working in amateur opera at Oxted, I met the unmarried daughter of Lewis Fry, a cousin of Roger Fry, who lived in a grand house near Limpsfield. They sometimes invited me to supper with them to discuss artistic matters: and at Lewis's death, his daughter gave me his complete edition of Goethe as a memento. In one studio at the house, there stood an easel with a canvas on it – invariably unfinished. Lewis told me that he always found it problematic to detach himself from what he put on the canvas in such a way that he could return to it as an outside viewer. I understood completely, but guessed that I had that ability and could nurture it. In my maturity, that detachment is complete. The work, once written, belongs to the outside world.

SINGING THE BLUES

While exploring how best to formulate the final ensemble of Act 1 of *The Knot Garden*, I came across Leroi Jones's book, *Blues People*. That taught me two things: firstly that just as the fugue was fundamental to the Baroque period, and sonata to the Enlightenment, so the blues is the most fundamental musical form of our time (not so Schoenberg's twelve-note method, which seems to me alphabetic); secondly, when you sing the blues, you do so not just because you are 'blue', but to relieve the blue emotions. When I heard Noel Coward sing, 'Those twentieth-century blues are getting me down' he sang because the blues were doing exactly that and the singing of them is his means of discharging their effect: simultaneous involvement and detachment, in other words – which is how artefacts are made.

I myself saw the young Coward act in an early stage-play of his about drugs. Whereas I couldn't follow him into a world of decadence, I had to recognise its existence. If blues belong in a decadent world, then I have to remake the blues within my own terms. In conceiving of a blues ensemble to end Act 1 of *The Knot Garden*, I never sought to imitate a Negro style or genre at all. I had a set of people on stage singing explicitly of their emotional dilemmas and I had to work out how best to put their situations across. The blues was an obvious vehicle. Mel, the black writer, became the natural leader of each section in turn: and it is he who expresses alleviation from the blues –

> So I sing the blues for me, baby,
> Maybe sing the blues for you?
> The black man sing the blues for Mr Charlie.'

Some critics thought I was attempting to write blues as a jazz form. I was not. The blues for me was a metaphor; an archetype, even.

Yeats was asked once how he knew when he had finished a poem. He said: It's like playing with the pieces of a jigsaw that has ultimately to fit into a box. All the time you are refitting the pieces together in different ways, until suddenly, inexplicably, they are inside and then the box snaps shut.

CHAPTER FOURTEEN

THE FINAL DREAM

In 1987 I took what seems likely to be my last adventure holiday. I wanted to go to Lake Van, on the eastern borders of Turkey, close to the frontiers with Soviet Georgia. A few years earlier, on an Italian holiday with the Ayersts, I met up with Freya Stark, by that time very old and blind and living in Asolo. She had written memorably of her own adventures in Turkey before the First World War and was intrigued to hear of my plans. She advised me to take a large, strong car as the roads were often poor. In the event, Bill (who wouldn't come – he can't stomach long driving holidays) planned the trip so that I had two good drivers, Graham Modlen and a young composer, David Haines. To hire a car east of Ankara was difficult and the hire firm had to send one down to Adana, which is on the Mediterranean coast and on one of the oldest roads in European history. The Persians used the road to conquer the Greek cities on the Aegean coast; Alexander the Great used it to march his troops down to Egypt, where he founded Alexandria; Mark Antony brought his armies down along it to Alexandria and succumbed to the charms of Cleopatra; the Ottomans used it to defeat the Roman Empire with the capture of Constantinople, which never went back into European hands until the time of Byzantium; and Napoleon brought his beleaguered army in Egypt back along it to Paris. Now it was Tippett's turn.

A branch road north-east went along the line of the present-day frontier dividing Turkey from Syria, Iraq and Iran; and near the Iranian border the road crossed to Lake Van by means of boats. In the late nineteenth century, a railway was built alongside the road from Adana, ending somewhere in Iran. We drove north-east over a period of three days, but unfortunately David had already been unwell before leaving England and almost immediately reacted against the local food: he never fully recovered until we reached a first-class inter-national hotel in Istanbul! I too fell foul of the food, but to a much lesser degree; as Graham was unaffected, the two of us were able to go up to the top of the high mountain pinnacle of Diyarbakir, David remaining behind in the hotel. The views from the mountain road into the fertile valley below were marvellous, but then the driving ended suddenly at a road-house, after which we had to walk. It was bitterly cold, due to the height. We were both in summer gear but, just as I had borrowed Wilf's under-shorts up in the Spanish mountains in the 1930s, I now quickly appropriated Graham's spare pair of gaudy Hawaiian shorts. We ascended into still colder heights. My heart began to pound, so I rested until Graham returned to haul me up around the final corner, step by step over the scree. At last we reached a strange temple built in Greek style in AD 1 and there were the gigantic heads I wanted to see, as large as those on Easter Island, many of them fallen from their pedestals and lying on the ground. I sheltered from the cold wind behind one of them while Graham photographed the overall scene and details: even he, in due course, was affected by the temperature, and rushed back, howling, 'My balls are frozen!' We descended as fast as we possibly could.

The next day, we continued on the last part of the journey to Lake Van itself, right up in the Caucasus mountains – a huge lake, white-coloured from floating sediment – where we stayed three nights. Most tourists visit the first-century Christian churches – which didn't interest any of us very much – and hope to see the albino cats with different-coloured eyes that swim in the lake and catch fish, but they are now almost extinct and the few remaining ones are kept alive in private. The lake affected me deeply, simply on account of its colour, setting and above all its history, at the edge of the Roman Empire.

On the last morning there, I woke to the sound of dawn muezzin – three signals coming from different locations in the town and reaching me at different times: another sound-memory stored up and later recalled for the main ensemble in Act 2 of *New Year*.

Enchanted, I drifted off into sleep again and dreamt I was in a new house, which Bill had built especially for me. I was being led around its many rooms, which changed according to what was needed of them. The rooms were full of young, happy people moving about freely. I tried to find Bill to thank him and someone offered to take me to him. But I said no – just let him know what an ideal house this is. 'You needn't worry,' came the reply, 'he knows you know that'. Then I woke up.

'*Kennst du das Land?*' *Land*, I had said to myself long ago, represented not just the warm South; but it must also be the land of the imagination. The second stanza of Mignon's song had never engaged my attention to quite the same extent:

> *Kennst du das Haus? Auf Säulen ruht sein Dach,*
> *Es glänzt der Saal, es schimmert das Gemach,*
> *Und Marmorbilder stehn und sehn mich an:*
> *Was hat man dir, du armes Kind, getan?*
> *Kennst du es wohl?*
> *Dahin! dahin*
> *Möcht ich mit dir, o mein Beschützer, ziehn.*

> [Do you know the house? Its roof rests on pillars,
> the hall gleams, the room glistens,
> and marble statues stand and look at me:
> 'What have they done to you, poor child?'
> Do you know it?
> There, there
> I long to go with you my protector.]

The house evoked in the poem is the one in Italy from which Mignon has been abducted. But I feel now that the house is also the unconscious. In my dream, the childhood nightmare of the fortress house, into which the Biting Lady was trying to intrude, has been replaced by the older man's vision, near the end of his life, of a house that is free and open.

INDEX